CRIME AND JUSTICE IN HONG KONG

90 0556806 7

CRIME AND JUSTICE IN HONG KONG

Editors
Harold Traver Jon Vagg

Contributors
Chan Wai-to Albert H.Y. Chen Stephen Chiu
Mark S. Gaylord Patricia Gray David A. Levin
Lo Man-chiu Harold Traver Jon Vagg

HONG KONG
OXFORD UNIVERSITY PRESS
OXFORD NEW YORK

Oxford University Press

Oxford New York Toronto
Kuala Lumpur Singapore Hong Kong Tokyo
Delhi Bombay Calcutta Madras Karachi
Nairobi Dar es Salaam Cape Town
Melbourne Auckland Madrid

and associated companies in
Berlin Ibadan

Oxford is a trade mark of Oxford University Press

First published 1991
Second impression 1993

Published in the United States
by Oxford University Press, New York

British Library Cataloguing in Publication Data

Crime and justice in Hong Kong.
1. Traver, Harold II. Vagg, Jon
364.09125
ISBN 0-19-585285-0
ISBN 0-19-585286-9 pbk

Library of Congress Cataloging in Publication Data
available

ISBN 0-19-585285-0
ISBN 0-19-585286-9 pbk

Printed in Hong Kong
Published by Oxford University Press (Hong Kong) Ltd
18/F Warwick House, Taikoo Place, 979 King's Road, Quarry Bay, Hong Kong

Contents

Tables

Contributors

CHAN WAI-TO has lectured in social work and social and correctional studies at Hong Kong Polytechnic since 1985. He graduated from the Chinese University of Hong Kong in 1977, and worked for eight years in the Hong Kong Social Welfare Department, with a variety of posts including probation and after-care work. He obtained his Masters degree in Socio-Legal Studies from the University of Birmingham in 1989. He has published articles on law and order in Hong Kong, services for offenders, victims, and community care.

ALBERT H. Y. CHEN joined the University of Hong Kong in 1984 and is a Senior Lecturer in the Department of Law. He is the author of *Hong Kong's Legal System and the Basic Law* (Hong Kong, Wide Angle Press, 1986); *Human Rights and the Rule of Law* (Hong Kong, Wide Angle Press, 1987); *Law and Politics in Hong Kong* (Hong Kong, Wide Angle Press, 1990); *The Workers' Compensation System in Hong Kong* (Hong Kong, Centre of Asian Studies, University of Hong Kong, 1987); and co-editor of *The Basic Law and Hong Kong's Future* (Singapore, Butterworths, 1988).

STEPHEN CHIU is a Ph.D. candidate in the Department of Sociology at Princeton University. He taught in the Department of Sociology at the University of Hong Kong from 1989–91, when he joined the Department of Sociology at the Chinese University of Hong Kong. His research interests focus on the development of East Asian societies and the labour movement in Hong Kong. He is co-editor of *Dimensions of Chinese and Hong Kong Movement* (Hong Kong, Hong Kong Christian Industrial Committee, 1986).

MARK S. GAYLORD is Senior Lecturer in the Department of Applied Social Studies, City Polytechnic of Hong Kong, where he has taught since 1987. His publications include *The Criminology of Edwin Sutherland*, co-authored with John F. Galliher (New Brunswick, Transaction Press, 1988). He is currently researching police powers in Hong Kong, and the death penalty in Hong Kong and China.

PATRICIA GRAY has lectured in social work at Hong Kong Baptist College since 1981. She was previously a social worker in the UK, specializing in work with juvenile and young offenders. She has published several papers in this field, and her doctoral study on juvenile justice in Hong Kong will be published in late 1991.

DAVID A. LEVIN is Senior Lecturer, Department of Sociology, University of Hong Kong. His main fields of interest are industrial sociology and industrial relations. He is co-editor of *Contemporary Issues in Hong Kong Labour Relations* (Hong Kong, Centre of Asian Studies, University of Hong Kong, 1983) and *Labour Movement in a Changing Society: The Case of Hong Kong* (Hong Kong, Centre of Asian Studies, University of Hong Kong, 1988).

LO MAN-CHIU studied law in Hong Kong and read socio-legal studies and philosophy at University College, Cardiff. He is a lecturer in the Department of Government and Public Administration at the Chinese University of Hong Kong.

HAROLD TRAVER has lectured in sociology at the University of Hong Kong since 1971. He was one of the founders of the Department of Sociology's postgraduate criminology programme in 1986. His research interests include organized crime and drugs.

JON VAGG has lectured in sociology and criminology at the University of Hong Kong since 1989. His previous publications include *Accountability and Prisons* (co-edited with M. Maguire and R. Morgan, London, Routledge, 1985), and *Policing by the Public* (with J. Shapland, London, Routledge, 1988). He is currently researching and writing on the Hong Kong criminal justice system and on prisons accountability in Europe.

1 Introduction: Crime and Punishment in Hong Kong

JON VAGG AND HAROLD TRAVER

CRIME and justice issues are often discussed in Hong Kong. However, most of the discussions appear in the newspapers, where pressures of space, deadlines, and attention-snatching headlines leave little room for measured reflection or systematic data collection. A less capricious, more academic, and usually more objective literature on Hong Kong crime and criminal justice does exist, but it is scattered. There are, of course, official statistics. There have been several books on the police, one on the Independent Commission Against Corruption (ICAC), and a few more generally on corruption. Some topics, such as vice and prostitution, have received passing attention in articles on wider social issues such as the place of women in society, and in small-circulation reports by interest groups. A legal literature exists in which occasional comments can be found on the relationship between law and law enforcement. Meanwhile, some academics have concerned themselves with historical rather than current events, including the history of Hong Kong's drug trade with China. Piecing together a reasoned and comprehensive account of crime patterns and criminal justice is a difficult and lengthy task.[1]

Our main aim is therefore to present a contemporary survey of crime and justice in Hong Kong. We try to answer three questions. First, what are the crime problems? Second, what is the criminal justice system doing? And third, how is it likely to develop in the future?

Chapter 2 presents an interpretation of crime trends in the territory over the last 40 years, as an initial step in getting to grips with the facts. The following five chapters each deal with a specific problem or set of problems of contemporary significance: juvenile crime, drug abuse, vice, financial crime, and the 'criminal consequences' of having a border with the People's Republic of China. In Chapter 9, the focus moves from offenders to victims. Chan Wai-to argues that the current levels of provision for victims are too low, and are based on an outmoded view of the proper place of the victim in the criminal justice system.

The police, the courts, and the Correctional Services are also described, discussed, and sometimes criticized. These three agencies are, of course, not the whole of the criminal justice system. In Hong Kong, a complete listing of criminal justice agencies would have to include the ICAC, Customs and Excise, the Immigration Department, the Social Welfare Department, the Security Branch, and a range of other agencies, such as the Securities and Futures Commission, which deal not with criminal activities as such, but with matters such as 'insider dealing' on the Stock Exchange. It is not possible for a single book to deal adequately with all these agencies, though most receive passing mention and there are pointers in the text to documentary sources about them. We have, however, selected what might appear to be an unconventional topic for Chapter 12, which looks at the role of the Factories Inspectorate in maintaining workplace safety. Our reason for so doing is that, in common with other jurisdictions, the criminal justice system in Hong Kong is increasingly used to regulate behaviour far removed from traditional conceptions of crime. Many new laws concerning issues as diverse as factory safety, pollution, and immigration contain criminal sanctions.

The third question can only be answered in the fullness of time, but nonetheless one contributor has asked it. What will happen to the criminal justice system in the run-up to 1997 and after the resumption of Chinese sovereignty? Albert H.Y. Chen, in Chapter 13, makes some suggestive comments on the development of Hong Kong's legal system, transplanted from England, and argues that any legal system is ultimately only as good as the people committed to making it work.

This short statement of our aims is by no means uncontroversial. The most obvious question is why, as the Hong Kong legal system and criminal justice agencies are about to pass through the watershed of 1997, it should be necessary to describe and criticize the way the system operates. There are two answers. The first is simply that such description and commentary is worthwhile at any time. Historically, far too few people have concerned themselves with such matters in Hong Kong. The agencies have been able to operate almost independently of any outside interest. What we have tried to do is something that should have been done, regularly and routinely, for many years. Second, our task is necessary precisely because of 1997. The criminal justice system is already changing at a rate almost too fast to keep track of. The Bill of Rights will have a massive effect on the system, and only a small proportion of its possible effects have yet been identified. Those that have so far been forecast go to the very core of the way that criminal justice is conducted in the territory (Wacks 1990).

For example, we often assume that Hong Kong obeys one of the basic tenets of 'common law' systems, that accused persons are presumed innocent until proven guilty. Yet the courts are allowed, in instances ranging from drug trafficking to loitering, to presume a person's guilt in the absence of evidence to the contrary. Such presumptions are in contravention of the International Covenant on Civil and Political Rights, which the UK signed on Hong Kong's behalf in 1976. The Legislative Council has nonetheless seen fit on many occasions since that date to pass laws containing such presumptions. The Bill of Rights, however, implements the majority of the provisions contained in the International Covenant, among them a clause asserting that accused persons have a right to be considered innocent until proven guilty. Moreover, when the Basic Law holds sway, this and other provisions of the International Covenant will continue in force. In short, it seems likely that the Bill of Rights and the Basic Law will implement far-reaching reforms. These, coupled with the probability of gradual though unpredictable shifts in the ways that administrators and legislators think and behave after 1997, will result in the criminal justice system looking very different six years after 1997 to the way it looks six years before that date. This book is a record of what happened, how we viewed it, and what we had identified as the problems. We hope it will be of increasing rather than decreasing utility as the years pass.

Failures and Omissions

Every edited collection is, to some extent, a hostage to fortune. It is worth enumerating the gaps in this volume because they constitute one agenda for future research. There is nothing of substance on the ICAC, despite its key role in Hong Kong criminal justice. Lethbridge (1985) is an excellent account of its beginnings. Its current position would be an excellent research topic, but for the moment readers will have to continue to rely on other sources for information.[2] Nor is there more than passing reference to recent developments in Triad activities and organization. Recent press reports suggest that they are being hard pressed, for example in relation to drug monies and vice, but still able to profit from investment in legitimate businesses. Information about such matters will probably only come to light as and when it ceases to be of operational relevance to the police, or as and when Triad members choose to reveal it.[3]

Turning again to the chapters, it will be readily apparent that some have been able to benefit from previous research while others have not. There is a degree of sociological knowledge about the police. However, previous work on the courts, and on the Correctional Services Department, is slight. And in almost every substantive area of criminal activity, the previous work on Hong Kong can hardly be portrayed as comprehensive or systematic. Much of it arises out of the deliberations of committees, or from small-scale and unfunded research. The baseline of sociological knowledge about these problems is correspondingly low.

Culture, Crime, and Criminology

We have not sought to impose any theoretical framework on our contributors, and a range of criminological approaches is evident. Chapters 2 and 3 utilize the concept of the 'moral panic', first described by Cohen (1973). Chapter 2 discusses the applicability of economic development models to Hong Kong. Lo, in Chapter 10, uses an approach to the description of the courts which is reminiscent of Goffman (1971). Chapter 5, by Vagg, reflects some of the ambiguities present in much of the sociological work on vice. The underlying point is that contemporary criminology, despite a recent growth of interest in comparative studies, springs from occidental concepts and preoccupations even where it is applied to oriental situations. This is also true of China, where much criminological theory can be traced to Soviet or Marxist models of crime causation.[4] There is not, or at least not yet, a criminology based explicitly on an Asian cultural viewpoint. It is, however, worth discussing the problem of working in Asia with a predominantly Western criminology.

The relationship between culture and crime has long been of interest to criminologists. Sellin's (1938) cultural conflict approach to crime[5] is an early example of how criminologists have tended to approach the relationship between cultural norms and criminal behaviour. In this view, criminal behaviour may occur whenever there are groups whose cultural norms enjoin acts that are prohibited by law; crime is the product of conflicting cultural norms. In the years since, the notion of cultural deviance has focused on the evolution and perpetuation of subcultures in heterogeneous Western societies. The result has been a series of studies and theories dealing with conflicting cultural norms in such subcultural groups as juvenile gangs, drug subcultures, and ethnic minority groups.

Despite this early attention to concepts of culture, criminologists have by and large applied it only within individual Western societies. They have rarely displayed any tendency to take an international comparative approach in applying them to the study of crime. The great bulk of criminological theory and research continues to be done in Western societies where universities, research funding, and research personnel are concentrated. And as Clifford (1978: 63) observes, 'nearly all the publishing has been done in the West where not only the writers and the students but the markets are'. The result has been a situation in which the average Western criminologist is woefully ill-informed about crime or crime prevention in Asia, Latin America, or Africa. By contrast, criminologists and criminal justice workers in these same areas are well-informed about the latest Western developments while often facing a lack of resources to undertake local research. Criminology has developed a cultural hegemony in which Western theories of crime and conceptions of justice, however bound to particular cultures or histories, almost by default appear to speak for the whole range of societies and cultures.

This is not to say that 'Western criminology' is a logically coherent, unified discipline. It is not. Nonetheless, the body of concepts and debates around which Western criminology is organized, is dominant. For example, in virtually all societies the most common form of crime consists of relatively petty property offences, and Western criminology offers a variety of explanations — not necessarily consistent with each other — based on factors such as relative deprivation, disorganization, youth subcultures, peer association, and the like.[6] Such perspectives are routinely applied in other contexts, such as Hong Kong, without considering how, say, patterns of peer association might differ between Hong Kong and other cultures. It is true that many parts of Asia experience types of crime now largely defunct in the West: the selling of women and children in China and other countries; piracy; roving bands of beggars in Sri Lanka (Ratnapala 1985). Even so, many such activities are intelligible through Western models whose easy availability discourages any engagement with the specifics of the Asian situation. Again, it is fair to say that Asia itself can hardly be treated as a single theoretical unit; the differences among, say, Hong Kong, Tokyo, Manila, Bangkok, and within rural areas of most Asian countries, are immense. Research on Hong Kong is unlikely to describe criminal activities that could not be interpreted through Western models. But none of this makes the search for specific cultural factors in crime less interesting or less valid.

It is possible to adopt any of several perspectives on this issue. One is a relativist position, which stresses the diversity, complexity, and uniqueness of each culture and thereby denies any possibility of comparison or generalization. Carried to its extreme, one would be reduced to developing culturally-specific theories and concepts — a criminology for each specific cultural group. Any possibility of a general science of human behaviour, criminal or otherwise, would cease to exist. A diametrically opposed and reductionist perspective would assert that certain types of behaviour are universally regarded as criminal, and that forms of response to them are equally common across cultures. A general theory of crime can thus apply globally; all that remains is to show, perhaps through the interpretation of 'underlying' factors, how any individual pattern of crime or criminal justice system conforms to a universal norm.

But we do not have to choose between these extreme positions. There are wide variations in the definition of crime and the operation of criminal justice systems across different societies. However, these differences do not preclude the application of Western criminology to non-Western settings. Quite simply, most of the tools that criminologists now have to work with were developed in the West for use in a Western setting. This is all we have to work with, whether we like it or not. The researcher who uses these conceptual tools should be aware of their limitations and the possibility that the application of local concepts may yield different results. Ideally, one should be receptive to modifications of concepts through non-Western sources. But in order for this to become more common, criminological research has to be conducted in non-Western settings and the results shared internationally so that there can be cross-fertilization of ideas and explanations. This book represents a small step down that road.

Culture, Criminology, and Hong Kong

We and our contributors have tried to consider such issues. It is possible to identify a couple of areas in which some adjustments have to be made to Western models when discussing Hong Kong.

First, we should remember the history of colonialism. Colonialism exported Western conceptions of crime and criminal justice to much of the world without regard for structural or cultural differences. However, the particular form of criminal justice often differed between the colony and the 'mother country'. This is so in Hong Kong, for example, in relation to agencies such as the police, which inherited and can still deploy a substantial paramilitary capability. Perhaps ironically, some writers (for example Brogden 1987) have argued that the rise of paramilitarism in countries such as Britain can be traced to colonial experience in managing such forces, coupled with domestic economic policies which effectively make much of the UK an 'internal colony'. Yet in Hong Kong (where colonialism is not at an end) and in other countries which have long since become independent, Western conceptions of crime and justice have persisted.

In contrast to many Western societies, Hong Kong has been able to maintain a relatively low rate of crime despite extreme disparities in wealth and high levels of urbanization. Hong Kong's comparatively low rate of crime cannot be attributed to the efficiency of its criminal justice system since similar systems elsewhere have proven unable to stem the tide of crime. The answer is not to be found in the criminal justice system itself, but in the way it is perceived and used by members of society. This brings us to the question of culture and how it affects crime and criminal justice.

Much Western criminology cites the importance of such social institutions as the family in crime causation and crime prevention. However, it has largely been left to authors from outside Europe and America, in countries where strong extended families still exist, to consider more seriously what social control influences families may exert (see for example Findlay and Zvekic 1988). Questions such as the role of the family, and possible cultural differences such as conceptions of shame and degrees of punitiveness, must be taken seriously in areas such as Southeast Asia in ways that they have not been for many years in the West (with a few noted exceptions, such as Braithwaite 1989). A further important variable may be the degree of individualism present in the society. Strong informal group controls are usually found in societies with little crime. In contrast, societies with higher levels of crime are often found to have the most laws and the most highly developed systems of criminal justice. In general, societies that have been able to maintain low volumes of crime or to reduce it are those that have also been able to mobilize public support for law and to maintain some form of group social control. That Hong Kong has been able to maintain comparatively low levels of crime in the face of considerable social and economic change probably has much to do with the continuing importance of the family in Chinese culture and the stress that the society places on group relations.

Agendas

Every book contains within it the seeds of another, more enticing book. A number of unresolved questions and intriguing details emerge in the following chapters that ought to figure in our agenda for future research.

It would be interesting to know why the legal manoeuvre of the *voir dire*, discussed by Chen in Chapter 13, has become so widely used in Hong Kong when it has all but died out in other common law jurisdictions. It appears to be widely used here as a means of challenging confessions, and this implies that it has become a *de facto* means of police accountability, which suggests that this too is due for detailed scrutiny. Meanwhile, the courts in the territory persist in their use of English, offering a ready-made environment for studying the ways in which legal concepts can be translated across linguistic boundaries. It is surprising that no one has thought of doing such work. And given Hong Kong's position on the edge of China, the territory seems ready-made for a full-scale study of the criminal consequences of having two so different, yet interlinked, economies so close to each other. On the subject of economic factors, it is also clearly time for a closer look at the extent of economic crime in the territory, and for a sober appraisal of the linkages between Hong Kong's popularity as a financial centre, based on the comparative lack of regulation in the past, and the ease with which monies can pass untraced through its financial system. Ironically, this lack of regulation may count against the territory's future interests.

It would also be interesting to look more closely at the phenomenon of 'net-widening'. This term refers to a situation where measures such as cautioning are implemented in order to divert offenders — usually juveniles — from the courts, but are instead used to process delinquents who would previously never have been dealt with officially by the criminal justice system. Gray argues in Chapter 3 that this has very likely occurred in Hong Kong, and it clearly warrants closer scrutiny because its occurrence has often been taken in the West to imply a corresponding decline in informal social control mechanisms. Its presence in Hong Kong, in view of our earlier comments on the role of the family as a social control institution, would not bode well for the future. Likewise, a more detailed study of recidivism rates is long overdue, since the rates currently claimed suggest that there are either radical differences between Hong Kong and the West in terms of correctional practices, or radical differences in cultural factors which make rehabilitation more possible. And in this connection, it would also be interesting to investigate broader cultural issues such as concepts of shame and guilt. Finally, it is worth noting that Hong Kong provides almost ideal conditions for studying the effects on crime levels of rapid social and economic development.

Such are the issues that we would have addressed, had we the time and facilities. We may yet have the chance; but for now, we are simply pleased to have started what we hope will be a continuing process of scrutinizing crime and justice in Hong Kong.

Notes

1. For works on the police, see for example Crisswell and Watson (1982) and Sinclair (1983). Lethbridge (1985) is a study of the origins and first years of the Independent Commission Against Corruption. Comments on corruption may be found in Hong Kong Observers (1981), and more detailed studies in Lee (1981). On vice, there are two readily available sources: Lethbridge (1978b) and Pearson (1989), the latter actually including prostitution within a more general discussion of the situation of women in Hong Kong. An example of the legal literature on law enforcement is Tsang (1982). Much general historical work includes accounts of the traffic in opium in the last century: Rodzinski (1984) is but one example.

2. For example, the ICAC produces annual reports and brief comments on developments which appear in the Hong Kong Annuals. For a view on the extent of corruption in Hong Kong, the best source is still Lee (1981). Comments on the scope of ICAC powers are in Litton (1989) and Vagg (forthcoming), and passing comments on the impact of the Bill of Rights on the ICAC may be found in Jayawickrama (1989).

3. Accounts of the history, structure, and activities of Triads may be found in Chesneaux (1971) and Morgan (1960). However, much of this material is outdated, and the newer material (Booth 1990, Bresler 1980, Posner 1988) is often regarded as impressionistic since it is usually based on earlier accounts and secondary sources. A recent exception to this observation is Chin (1990), which is based on fieldwork with Triads.

4. For a short account of Marxist criminology in Eastern Europe, see Connor (1972), Lekschas and Kosewhär (1988). On crime and criminal justice in China, see for example Leng and Chiu (1985), and Wilson (1984). Zhou (1990) is a brief account of current Chinese theories of crime causation. Shelley (1981) is a broader comparative account of the impact of industrialization on crime levels with special reference to Eastern Europe.

5. Theories based on these concepts are discussed, with varying degrees of criticism, in most standard criminology textbooks: see for example Downes and Rock (1988), Hagan (1987), Taylor, Walton, and Young (1973).

2 Crime Trends

HAROLD TRAVER

IT IS safe to say that if one asks the thoughtful citizen how a society could best set about curtailing crime, the response is likely to be that it could best be achieved by reducing poverty, increasing educational attainment, expanding opportunities for achievement, eliminating substandard housing, and generally increasing social services for people in need. After all, crime gives every indication of being more prevalent among the poor than among the middle class, and the former are distinguished from the latter by income, schooling, achievement, housing, and the need for social services. Crime levels, however, do not always perform in the way that common sense predicts. In fact, there is an important sociological paradox in regard to crime: it is frequently observed to increase when the conditions which are supposed to cause it are improving rather than worsening.

Hong Kong is a case in point. In the late 1960s, Hong Kong was just starting out on a period of almost unbroken prosperity and social advancement that has persisted to the present day. For instance, since 1960 the proportion of young people enrolled in secondary school has increased by 425 per cent, and per capita constant dollar GDP increased by 615 per cent while the annual income of industrial workers increased more than 20-fold. During the same period, about half the population moved into government subsidized housing and the unemployment rate remained a more or less constant 3 per cent. In fact, virtually any indicator of well-being that one might choose to look at points to significant progress since 1960. What did crime do? It increased; in fact, it soared. Crimes of violence like serious assault and robbery increased by 722 per cent and 3,116 per cent respectively, while nonviolent property offences like burglary and theft increased 311 per cent and 68 per cent. Meanwhile, the number of juvenile delinquents arrested increased by more than 500 per cent and Hong Kong's prison population grew faster than the population as a whole.

This chapter sets out to measure crime trends in Hong Kong and to consider what social and economic forces might have contributed to them. In so doing, attention is shifted away from the offender to the offence. Individual motivation obviously plays a role in crime but it cannot adequately explain why the incidence of crime changes over time, or why it is apparently higher in one community than another. Instead of being merely a reflection of personal problems, crime takes on wider significance. The extent of crime and the direction in which it is moving can serve as an important means for better understanding the society we live in and what is happening to it.

Data and Procedures

The examination of crime trends is limited to the period 1956/7 to 1988/9. This period encompasses most of the significant shifts in post-war crime as well as changes in the social structure and economy of Hong Kong. All data relating to crime are derived from statistics of crime reported to the police, as opposed to people arrested or prosecuted for criminal offences. The following discussion is limited to trends occurring in two broad categories of crime: property crime and violent crime. Between 1956/7 and 1988/9, these two categories accounted for nearly 70 per cent of all crime committed in Hong Kong.[1]

There is no question that official statistics underestimate the true amount of crime. The actual volume of crime is probably several times higher than that of crime which is actually reported and which appears in the official statistics. Moreover, on occasion the authorities may decide to devote more attention to certain types of offences than others, or public attitudes toward crime may change in such a way as to affect reporting. Police procedures and classification schemes are periodically altered in ways that affect the volume of reported crime. Consequently, there is no reason to suppose that the proportion of reported to unreported crime remains constant. Nevertheless, official statistics may be able to tell us something about the direction in which major categories of crime are moving, especially when compared with victim surveys. Though victim surveys are not without their limitations, they do provide a basis for estimating the volume of unreported crime.

Since 1978, Hong Kong has conducted four such surveys (Census and Statistics Department 1979, 1982, 1987, 1990a). The most recent found that in 1989, 34 per cent of all crimes were reported to the police, as compared with 32 per cent in 1986, 29 per cent in 1981, and 18 per cent in 1978. There is, therefore, good reason to believe that there has been a steady increase in the tendency to report crime since 1978. Public confidence in the police, reporting procedures, and public attitudes regarding crime contribute to the tendency to report; one consistent finding that emerges from victim studies, however, is that seriousness of the offence is the strongest determinant of whether an offence is reported to the police. For instance, in 1989, 56.5 per cent and 52.4 per cent of all serious assaults and robberies respectively were reported to the police. By way of comparison, only 2.8 per cent of all minor household thefts and 24.6 per cent of 'other personal thefts' were reported. The role of seriousness in determining reporting can be seen most clearly in the case of thefts of vehicles which are, in most cases, financially serious offences against which most car owners are insured. Here the reporting rate climbs to 79.5 per cent; in 1978 it was 100 per cent. It is safe to say that the observed crime rate trends are generated not only by the volume of crime but also by police practices, the seriousness of the crime, and the general willingness of citizens to report crime.

Trends in Crime

Viewed over time, crime rate statistics arrange themselves into consistent patterns. Crime rates tend to change relatively slowly, and any change that does occur is normally gradual and continues on in a given direction for some time. In other words, the crime rate acts as if it had a memory.

Violent Crime

The threat of physical harm means that violent crime is typically the object of considerable public and official concern. Fortunately, even at the worst of times, violent crime has been a relatively rare offence. In the period 1956/7 to 1988/9, there were a total of 792,425 offences against property but only 283,827 violent offences. Despite dramatic increases in the 1970s, violent crime continues to account for a relatively small proportion of reported crime. Between 1956/7 and 1968/9, violent crime represented only 8 per cent (17,390 out of 231,936) of all reported crime, and even though it increased rapidly between 1969/70 and 1978/9, it still only accounted for 25 per cent (112,289 out of 457,377) of all reported crime. In the years since, violent crime has constituted 19 per cent (154,148 out of 804,421) of the overall volume of reported crime in Hong Kong.

Homicide is almost always reported and is thereby less subject to any illusory changes due to reporting. A comparison of trends

Table 2.1 Crime Rates per 100,000 Population for Violent Crimes, 1956/57 to 1989/90[1]

Year	Murder/ Manslaughter	Rape/ Indecent Assault[2]	Robbery	Armed Robbery	Serious Assault	Total
1956/57	1.4	2.9	4.7	0.1	15.7	24.8
1957/58	0.7	3.6	4.3	0.3	13.3	22.1
1958/59	1.0	5.4	3.0	0.4	15.2	24.9
1959/60	0.8	4.4	2.2	0.3	14.8	22.4
1960/61	1.0	4.8	3.1	0.0	17.9	26.8
1961/62	0.7	6.5	3.3	0.1	20.8	31.4
1962/63	0.7	4.9	4.4	0.0[3]	19.7	29.8
1963/64	0.7	4.1	4.2	0.0	19.0	28.0
1964/65	1.4	5.0	8.8	0.0[3]	26.3	41.5
1965/66	0.7	6.6	10.4	0.0	25.3	38.1
1966/67	1.2	7.8	15.1	0.0	28.4	52.5
1967/68	2.1	6.3	44.2	0.0	28.5	81.1
1968/69	1.1	7.8	40.7	0.0[3]	26.6	76.2
1969/70	1.4	10.6	62.3	0.2	32.9	107.4
1970/71	2.1	9.9	87.7	0.1	35.0	134.9
1971/72	2.3	9.4	132.8	0.4	39.1	184.1
1972/73	2.9	14.3	200.5	0.5	44.2	262.5
1973/74	2.5	13.1	231.6	0.6	60.2	307.9
1974/75	2.8	15.5	301.0	1.1	98.5	418.9
1975/76	2.2	18.5	231.1	1.1	108.2	361.2
1976/77	1.4	20.3	182.1	1.1	102.2	307.3
1977/78	1.4	19.6	141.7	0.5	110.0	271.1
1978/79	1.2	17.7	118.7	0.3	113.5	249.8
1979/80	1.4	16.0	172.7	0.2	121.9	311.2
1980/81	1.9	16.7	176.6	0.3	121.6	316.6
1981/82	2.1	15.0	153.6	0.6	118.3	288.7
1982/83	1.6	16.3	158.0	0.5	139.3	314.7
1983/84	1.8	15.9	153.6	0.5	142.0	313.3
1984/85	1.4	16.0	124.0	0.4	141.6	282.5
1985/86	1.6	16.4	116.1	0.3	142.3	276.6
1986/87	1.3	16.6	97.2	0.3	143.9	259.3
1987/88	1.3	18.9	96.5	0.1	144.1	260.9
1988/89	1.2	17.8	100.1	0.3	147.2	266.6
1989/90	1.9	19.6	121.1	0.7	164.4	307.7

Notes: 1. Offences reported to the police, presented on the basis of the financial year (April–March). See note 1 to this chapter for further details.
2. See note 3 to this chapter for further details on the reporting of rape/indecent assault.
3. In 1962/3, 1964/5, and 1968/9 there was one reported case of armed robbery. Due to rounding the rate appears as 0.0.

Sources: Commissioner of Police, *Annual Reports*, 1956/7–1974/5 and Census and Statistics Department, *Monthly Digest of Statistics*, 1976–90.

(Table 2.1) confirms that murder and manslaughter have in fact increased much more slowly than other forms of violent crime. Still, the general direction of homicide trends resembles those associated with other violent crimes in that the rate started out relatively low but began to increase rapidly in the late 1950s. The rather sharp jump in the murder/manslaughter rate in 1967/8 can probably be traced to a series of riots in 1967 in which 51 people were killed.

In contrast to homicide, the social stigma associated with sex offences provides every reason for believing that they are subject to serious under-reporting. Certainly serious under-reporting must be suspected when it is noted that there was only one reported case of rape in Hong Kong during three of the years under study. Indecent assault may involve minimum physical harm but it still has sufficient social stigma associated with it to ensure under-reporting. The 1989 victim survey placed the combined rate of victim reports for rape and indecent assault at 80 per 100,000 females over the age of 12, or 60.8 per 100,000 total population. The latter figure is over three times the rate based on police statistics.[2] Despite serious under-reporting, the trend for rape and indecent assault parallels that of other forms of violent crime.

Serious assault, unlawful personal violence involving force, threats, and obstructions only really began to increase rapidly after 1972/3. Serious assault is the only violent offence that increased steadily throughout the 1970s and 1980s. Victim surveys in 1978 and 1981 indicated that 68.6 per cent and 61.5 per cent of all serious assaults were reported to the police. By 1989 this figure had declined to 56.5 per cent. In other words, current observed increases are occurring in the face of a possible increased likelihood not to report the offence. In fact, one of the reasons given for the decline in reporting is the increase in the number of attempted cases of serious assault. Moreover, in many cases the victim may have been acting illegally himself, or alternatively, be too frightened of retaliation to report the offence.

Robbery has remained the most common form of violent crime since it first exceeded serious assault in 1967/8. There were very dramatic increases in the 1970s and it has remained at relatively high levels since. In fact, the increase was such that 88 per cent (132,566 out of 149,401) of all robberies for the 34-year period 1956–89 occurred in the 16 years between 1972/3 and 1988/9. It is likely that some of the observed increase derives from greater reporting, in particular of robberies that involve a minimum amount of violence, relatively small financial loss, and little chance of recovering the stolen property. According to the victim surveys in Hong Kong, the percentage of robberies reported to the police has steadily increased from 25.5 per cent in 1978 to 52.4 per cent in 1989. Surprisingly, despite the possibility of increased reporting there has been a distinct decline in robberies since the early 1980s.

One type of robbery that should be relatively less subject to underreporting is that which involves the use of firearms. Such offences are usually sufficiently visible and serious to ensure that they will come to the attention of the police. Despite the relatively small number of cases, trends in armed robbery have until recently generally paralleled trends in ordinary forms of robbery. This suggests that observed changes in reported cases of ordinary robbery are not entirely illusory. In the last couple of years, of course, the number of armed robberies has dramatically increased for the reasons outlined in Chapter 7.

Property Crime

In Hong Kong, a slow and sometimes uneven rate of growth plus a lack of physical confrontation has meant that property crime has generally attracted less attention than violent crime even though it is much more common. Between 1956/7 and 1969/70, property crime accounted for 65 per cent (168,725 out of 258,915) of all reported crime, and even in the peak years of violent crime, between 1970/1 and 1979/80, property crime continued to account for 44 per cent (220,510 out of 497,256) of all reported crime. In contrast to violent crime, property crime continued to increase significantly throughout the first half of the 1980s (see Table 2.2). As a result, the contribution that property crime made to the overall amount of crime in Hong Kong increased to 55 per cent (430,190 out of 737,563) for the years 1980/1 to 1988/9.

The statistical category of 'theft from the person' consists of two offences: snatching and pickpocketing. Reported crime rates for these offences are misleading, however, since the proportion of such offences reported to the police has increased substantially. According to the 1978 victim survey, only 6.4 per cent of pickpocketing cases and 15.5 per cent of snatching cases were reported. However, the 1986 survey showed that the percentage of pickpocketing and snatching cases reported had increased to 47 per cent and 41.7 per cent respectively. Although not shown in Table 2.2, in contrast to the erratic trends associated with snatching, pickpocketing rates have remained relatively stable. Like other forms of property crime, pickpocketing started out high, in this instance at what was then an all time high of 26.9 per 100,000 population, and then slowly declined to a low of 9.9

Table 2.2 Crime Rates per 100,000 Population for Property Crimes, 1956/57 to 1989/90

Year	Burglary	Theft from the Person	Miscellaneous Theft	Total
1956/57	77.2	55.8	489.5	617.5
1957/58	48.3	42.7	363.7	454.7
1958/59	39.8	35.2	306.3	381.3
1959/60	40.6	28.4	266.6	335.6
1960/61	43.0	25.2	274.4	342.6
1961/62	49.4	26.1	268.2	343.7
1962/63	46.9	25.6	233.7	306.2
1963/64	49.1	25.6	211.9	286.6
1964/65	55.0	30.7	227.6	313.3
1965/66	61.6	35.6	268.5	365.7
1966/67	52.9	28.1	283.0	364.0
1967/68	60.7	54.4	237.5	352.6
1968/69	59.0	35.6	212.6	307.2
1969/70	59.1	40.4	242.4	341.9
1970/71	71.0	37.6	258.6	367.2
1971/72	90.4	46.2	254.8	391.4
1972/73	93.9	32.4	223.8	350.1
1973/74	125.6	29.3	325.7	480.6
1974/75	150.5	39.3	350.4	540.2
1975/76	141.6	39.3	325.4	506.3
1976/77	124.1	35.2	371.3	530.6
1977/78	121.2	33.9	375.1	530.2
1978/79	121.7	42.2	485.2	622.1
1979/80	164.2	62.1	470.0	696.3
1980/81	178.4	82.9	550.8	812.0
1981/82	209.9	78.3	554.8	841.4
1982/83	210.3	95.2	591.8	897.3
1983/84	217.7	105.0	574.6	897.2
1984/85	234.9	96.9	514.4	846.2
1985/86	250.3	97.2	545.4	892.9
1986/87	209.1	97.5	513.4	819.9
1987/88	203.5	76.3	516.9	796.7
1988/89	182.7	44.4	474.4	701.5
1989/90	197.3	44.9	494.9	737.1

Sources: Commissioner of Police, *Annual Reports,* 1956/7–1974/5 and Census and Statistics Department, *Monthly Digest of Statistics*, 1976–90.

in 1967/8—just when snatching was at one of its highest points. The volume of pickpocketing subsequently increased until 1986/7, when the rate peaked at 63.4. In the years since, it has experienced a significant decline, as has snatching.

Miscellaneous theft, as the name implies, is composed of a variety of property offences. The diverse kinds of crime covered by this label account for 68 per cent (537,287 out of 792,425) of all property offences during the period under study. Like many other forms of property crime, miscellaneous theft started out high, in this case an all time high in 1956/7, but then slowly declined to reach an all time low in 1963/4.[3] Though not shown separately in Table 2.2, theft from vehicles forms a somewhat different pattern from other types of property crime insofar as it experienced a relatively steady increase throughout much of the period under examination. This increase is probably related to the increased number of registered vehicles.

Changes in burglary — entering a building or vessel as a trespasser for the purposes of stealing or doing unlawful damage — closely resemble those associated with other types of property crime. During the period under study, rates of burglary started out high, then declined only to increase again in the 1960s. As with other property crimes, burglary has tended to increase more or less steadily until it peaked in the mid-1980s. According to the 1989 victim survey, 41.1 per cent of all burglaries is reported to the police. The victimization rate for burglary in 1989 was 538.1 per 100,000 persons. Assuming only one in three of all burglaries is reported, this more or less agrees with the official reported rate of 297.3 per 100,000.[4]

To summarize, despite under-reporting, there are good reasons for believing that the shape and direction of the trends are relatively accurate. First, crime in Hong Kong does arrange itself into consistent long-term patterns rather than a series of random fluctuations. Second, there is a degree of consistency between trends in different types of crime that probably would not be observed if crime were largely subject to the vagaries of public opinion and police procedures. In general, trends in violent crime in Hong Kong can be characterized as rising rapidly until the early 1970s and then declining, though somewhat erratically. Trends in property crime generally organize themselves into U-shaped curves—high in earlier and later periods, but lower in the middle of the time series. Finally, the trends for offences for which one would logically expect to find comparatively less under-reporting resemble those for which under-reporting is likely to be more common. Trends in burglary and theft from the person resemble those of miscellaneous theft, while trends in murder parallel those found in robbery, serious assault, and indecent assault/rape. Thus, even though reported crime may not accurately reflect the true volume of crime, it does provide a reasonably accurate indication of crime trends. For present purposes, this is all that is required.

Crime and Socio-economic Change

Viewed over time, crime rates display seasonal changes, periodic cyclical fluctuations, and as this chapter has indicated, trends involving longer term periods of growth and decline. These changes raise questions about why, for example, most forms of crime increased in the 1970s; about why property crime was at a relatively high level in the 1950s when violent crime was at its lowest point; and about why property crime declined throughout much of the 1980s while violent crime tended to level out. Two tentative explanations come to mind. The first involves changes in the police force, which could have influenced either the tendency to report crime or the ability of the police to maintain public order. The second relies on broader arguments concerning the shifts in the prevailing social and economic climate.

Crime Waves or Reporting Waves?

There is a good chance that certain events in the early 1970s resulted in the authorities inadvertently contributing to an increase in reported crime. The first of these events was a government crackdown on Triads and on syndicated corruption within the police force. Entrenched syndicated corruption had been a feature of the police since at least the 1950s (Sinclair 1983). The 1967 riots, which diverted the police away from normal crime prevention activities for much of the year, allowed organized crime to extend its operations even further (Lethbridge 1985). By the beginning of the 1970s, enormous amounts of graft were being distributed through the ranks of the police. One ironic effect of this was that the police used their illegal profits and links with organized crime to maintain peace in the streets (Sinclair 1983). This was not a matter of altruism. To the extent that the business of organized crime is business, it was in the interests of both organized crime and the police that order be maintained. Peace breeds profits. On the other hand, organized crime was becoming sufficiently powerful to challenge the power of the police. In any case, extensive police corruption was hardly compatible with Hong Kong's image as an emerging industrial and financial centre in the Far East. It has also been suggested that during this period the climate for organized crime was so favourable that vice establishments and the narcotics trade were expanding at such a rate that the ability of the police to maintain public order was beginning to weaken.

In 1973, the police started to take steps to put their affairs in order by moving against the chief organizers of police corruption. Ultimately, these efforts failed to satisfy the government or the public that the police were willing or able to stamp out corruption within their own ranks. As a result, in early 1974, the ICAC was set up to deal with corruption in all branches of Hong Kong society, including the police. Lethbridge (1985) points out that as the police and later the ICAC began to move against police corruption, Triads lost most of the protection that had been afforded to them by some members of the police force. Instead of receiving protection, there was now an all-out effort to suppress Triad activities. Reported violations of the Societies Ordinance, which makes it illegal to be a member of or participate in the activities of a Triad society, jumped from 110 cases in 1967/8 to 4,089 in 1976. Blackmail, which in Hong Kong essentially means 'demanding with menace' or extortion, is another offence commonly associated with Triads. Here reported cases increased from 344 cases in 1967/8 to 4,775 in 1976. There were also increases for other Triad-related offences such as criminal intimidation. All this is an indication that the previous informal arrangements between the police and organized crime, which entailed both a substantial level of non-reporting and a degree of 'informal policing' by the Triads, was in the process of breaking down.

The second significant event during this period was the government-sponsored 'Fight Violent Crime Campaign', which sought to make the public more aware of its duty 'to assist the police in dealing with criminals' (Government Information Services 1974: 8). Launched in June 1973 and lasting until 1975, the campaign actively encouraged increased reporting by streamlining reporting procedures, setting up neighbourhood reporting centres, and establishing new police stations. The campaign also resulted in the establishment of Mutual Aid Committees so as to better adapt the 'clan spirit [of mutual aid] to the new urban neighbourhood' (GIS 1974: 8; see also Keung 1986, So 1975). By the end of 1973, 1,214 of these community organizations had been set up as a means of organizing collective action against crime. In 1974, in an effort to establish greater rapport with the public, Neighbourhood Police Units were created to place police officers in specific neighbourhoods for at least one year. To the extent that these units were successful, the result would have been a greater willingness to report crime and an increased flow of criminal intelligence back to headquarters. By the close of 1977, there were 87 reporting centres, with 30 of them operating as Neighbourhood Police Units, and 46 police stations. There were also 17,597 police officers, compared with 12,800 officers in 1969/70. From the standpoint of reported crime, probably the most important consequence of the Fight Violent Crime Campaign and all that went with it was the attempt to promote public confidence in the ability of the police to protect the community from crime and criminals.

Crime and Economic Conditions

Economic or material conditions provide one of the oldest and most widely used explanations of crime. As early as the 1920s, serious crime was observed to fall in periods of prosperity and to rise during periods of economic depression (Thomas 1925, Ogburn 1923, Phelps 1929). Short (1952) has observed that property crimes involving violence show a definite tendency to increase during an economic depression. More recently, Zehr (1976) has successfully traced a direct relationship between annual fluctuations in the business cycle and the rate of property crime.

In Hong Kong, economic deprivation as a cause of crime also figured prominently in official explanations of property crime during the 1950s. For instance, in 1956/7 when simple larceny (now referred to as miscellaneous theft) accounted for the largest proportion of Hong Kong's crime and was at a level not surpassed until 1980/1, the comment was made that:

> Many of the offences reported were petty thefts involving property of only minor value and were committed in many instances because of extreme poverty. This particular offence indicates most sharply the present severe economic hardship pressing on many of the people in the Colony, who steal not because they are thieves, but because they are hungry (Commissioner of Police 1957).

Presumably the above observations could apply to other forms of property crime. It is, however, questionable if economic conditions improved sufficiently quickly to account for the subsequent decline in property crime. Moreover it would also seem logical to suppose that impoverished living conditions in the 1950s should have generated a considerable amount of frustration and aggression, yet all forms of violent crime were at their lowest levels during this period.

In the short run, material hardship may help to explain the relation between depressed economic conditions and crime. In the long run, there is little evidence that an improved standard of living contributes to a reduction in crime; if anything it would appear to have the reverse effect. Zehr (1976) found that a steady upward trend in theft rates was associated with a general improvement in living standards. Clinard and Abbott (1973), Clifford (1974), Vold (1958), Lopez-Rey (1970), Morris and Hawkins (1970: 48–9) have all persuasively argued that expanded crime and a good standard of living are closely related.

Precisely how affluence generates pressures that produce criminal behaviour is not clear. Affluence may simply mean increased criminal opportunities in that there simply are more things to steal and more spare time to engage in mischief (Lopez-Rey 1970: 189). Affluence may also produce some fundamental shifts in social values by encouraging a rising level of material aspiration. If this is true, and if certain segments of the population are typically precluded from achieving success through socially acceptable channels, delinquency and crime may result from the frustration produced by a differential distribution of opportunities. Even if opportunities were evenly distributed, modern society may still generate considerable frustration if it encourages unrealistic levels of material aspiration in its citizens. According to this view, crime as well as other forms of aggression occur because people feel deprived relative to what they have come to expect from past experiences or have been led to expect in the future. For instance, Toby (1969: 142), after presenting considerable cross-national evidence that affluence contributes to crime, concludes that 'the sting of socio-economic deprivation can be greater for the poor in rich societies than for the poor in poor societies' (see also Henry and Short 1954, Zehr 1976: 134).[5]

There are two opposing ways of explaining the apparent association between economic growth and the expansion of crime in Hong Kong. One view, based on traditional development theory, holds that any observed increases in crime are largely a result of increased opportunities, criminal or otherwise, combined with a lessening of social constraints. Development theory, however, also predicts an eventual decline, or at least a levelling-off, of crime as the effects of rapid social and economic change begin to lessen and the fruits of economic development start to spread throughout the society (Clinard and Abbott 1973, Clifford 1973, 1974). Historical patterns associated with crime rate trends in Western industrial societies are frequently used to support the idea that crime in developing countries will be a delayed replay of the Western experience.

Another approach to the problem focuses on the presumed retrogressive effects of contemporary capitalist expansion into the developing world (Fitzpatrick 1981, Onselen 1976, Sumner 1982). According to this view, to the extent that contemporary economic development is designed to benefit multinational capital, rather than spreading prosperity and opportunities throughout society, it does just the opposite. Sumner (1982: 24) contends that even 'success stories' such as Hong Kong may only really tell the tale of investment from advanced capitalist countries; the record of Hong Kong crime and justice does not provide much support for 'development' or the hope that crime will eventually decline as the society becomes more prosperous.

In Hong Kong, traditional social structures may have declined over the years and it may have been the recipient of a great deal of foreign investment. However, this has not resulted in the clear and consistent increases in crime that Sumner seems to predict. Quite simply, this chapter provides no support for the notion that Hong Kong is going to be subject to a continuing spiral of crime and disorder. Conversely, there is some support for the supposed beneficial effects of economic development. Most forms of violent crime have shown a tendency to level off or decline since the highs of the 1970s, which is what one would expect if violent crime really is the product of rapidly rising expectations. Moreover, property crime has also shown a tendency to decline or level out in the 1980s. The fact that property crime is still at comparatively high levels may well represent the fact that there are now simply more things to steal and fewer social constraints to keep people from doing so.

Conclusions

Two broad conclusions are possible on the basis of the data presented in this chapter. It seems that increased public confidence in the police, changes in police policies, and a subsequent increased willingness to report crime all contributed to an increase in reported crime starting in the 1970s. At the same time, there is also good reason to believe that the volume of crime reflects, at least to some extent, prevailing social and economic forces. And although it is difficult to sort out the relative contribution of 'real' changes and changes in crime reporting behaviour, several propositions about 'real' changes based on social and economic factors seem plausible.

It seems likely that the high property crime rates in the 1950s had something to do with the extensive poverty and social deprivation during this period. Conversely, dramatic increases in crime in the 1970s were quite likely fuelled by the rapid economic growth in the early part of that decade. And the fact that crime levelled off in the 1980s probably has something to do with the fact that as Hong Kong's economy matured, the benefits of economic growth started to spread to larger segments of Hong Kong society. A severe economic recession or another period of economic growth could produce shifts in the crime rate similar to those observed in the 1970s.

It should also be noted that this chapter has been entirely devoted to trends in what are essentially working class and street crime. These crimes are obviously important and the subject of considerable public concern. However, corruption and other kinds of crime, often described as the 'crimes of the powerful', arguably have a greater long-term effects on the quality of the society we live in. They are discussed at greater length in Chapter 6.

Finally, it is worth reminding ourselves that in the final analysis crime is a normal feature of society. Though we are reluctant to admit it, a great deal of crime appears to be an unintended by-product of such things as economic growth, the elimination of social barriers to achievement, and the expansion of individual liberties — in short, many of the things that we frequently hold up as important achievements of a modern, open society.

Notes

1. Between 1956/7 and 1974/5 the police reported annual crime figures on a financial year basis. Starting in 1976 the police changed their system of reporting to the calendar year. For the purposes of comparability the financial year system has been retained here by deriving relevant crime figures from the quarterly statistics appearing in selected issues of the Monthly Digest of Statistics published by the Census and Statistics Department.

2. The 1989 victimization survey estimated there were between 2,200 and 4,900 rapes and indecent assaults on females, with a mid-range figure of 3,500. The rates quoted in the text are based on the figure of 3,500. The figures quoted in Table 2.1 for rape and indecent assault are based on the total population, rather than females, in order to maintain consistency with the other offences listed there. Since females comprise roughtly 48.5 per cent of the Hong Kong population, the rate of reported rapes and indecent assaults per 100,000 females would be approximately 2.05 times larger than the figure shown in Table 2.1, or 40.2 per 100,000 females in 1989/90.

3. The most common form of miscellaneous theft to appear in the official statistics is in itself a catch-all category; originally referred to as 'simple larceny', it is now described as 'other theft'.

4. The 1989 victim survey estimated the absolute number of burglaries as somewhere between 26,900 and 35,000, with a mid-range figure of 31,000. It quotes the rate in terms of households rather than persons, thus giving a figure of 797.2 burglaries per 100,000 households. The rate reported in this chapter is based on the mid-range figure of 31,000 and the total population for that year.

5. Work by Davies (1962) and Gurr (1968) indicates that collective violence is especially likely to occur whenever there is a rapidly widening gap between social expectations and achievement. This observation applies to periods of rapid economic decline as well as fast economic growth. With respect to this, Zehr (1976: 24–5) has suggested that crime may serve as a safety valve for releasing frustration before it can accumulate and become directed into widespread collective violence.

3 Juvenile Crime and Disciplinary Welfare

PATRICIA GRAY

SINCE the late 1970s, there has been much publicity about the apparently dramatic upward trend in juvenile crime. Many public figures and committees have claimed to see the roots of this increase in the amount of time spent by juveniles in the streets, video centres, and billiard rooms; in dubious peer associations; in the decaying moral standards of youth increasingly faced with materialist values, Western culture, and pornography; and more widely in the deterioration of Chinese family traditions.

Such theories about juvenile crime have universal popular appeal. But Pearson (1983) warns us to be careful. He charts, in the UK for over a century, a series of 'moral panics' about youth crime. Every generation remembers a mythical crime-free golden age contrasting to a crime-ridden present, and the themes which constantly recur are precisely those of 'parental irresponsibility, deterioration of the family, temptations of affluence, erosion of social discipline and the corruption of national character'.

These delusions, if such they are, may be harmless. The danger is that they may influence decisions which affect the lives of young people. With this consideration in mind, it is worth examining what changes have in fact taken place in juvenile offending in recent years and the subsequent response of criminal justice agencies.

An Upsurge in Juvenile Crime: Myth, Reality, or Moral Panic?

The offender rate undoubtedly suggests a dramatic upsurge in juvenile crime since the late 1970s (juveniles are persons aged 7–15). Between 1977 and 1988, the juvenile crime rate increased from 250 to 925 per 100,000, a rise of 270 per cent. Over the same period, the offender rate for young adults (persons aged 16–20) merely doubled, from 823 to 1,613 per 100,000. The increase in adult crime was insignificant in comparison. The turning point for juvenile crime occurred between 1978 and 1980, when the offender rate more than doubled within two years, from 276 to 561 per 100,000. Since then it has risen more or less steadily to a peak of 955 per 100,000 in 1989. Young adult offenders followed a similar pattern, becoming the most 'offender prone' group in the early 1980s and reaching a figure of 1,889 arrests per 100,000 in 1989.[1]

A glance at prosecution rates is only slightly less depressing. Prosecution figures are seen as being more indicative of changes in the seriousness of juvenile crime, because the use of cautioning by the police has supposedly diverted less serious offences from the courts. Between 1977 and 1988, the total number of juveniles prosecuted more than doubled while there was a decline in the juvenile population. Over the same time period, a number of specific crimes of particular public concern committed by juveniles showed an even greater percentage increase: crimes against the person rose by 300 per cent, serious assaults by 356 per cent and robberies by 336 per cent.[2]

The official crime statistics therefore appear to confirm the widely-held community view that there has been a dramatic upsurge in both the amount and seriousness of juvenile crime. The question is whether such statistics reflect the real nature of juvenile crime. For several reasons, such statistics can give an unrealistic impression; as 'social products', they are heavily influenced by the response of juvenile justice professionals to community fears.

First, it is possible to see these figures in a slightly less dramatic light. Despite the increase in absolute figures, juvenile crime as a proportion of all crime prosecuted by the police showed only a modest increase from 7.7 to 9.8 per cent between 1977 and 1988. Over 70 per cent of juvenile prosecutions in 1988 comprised offences against property, often of a petty nature, such as minor shoplifting and theft.[3] Moreover, statistical groupings of offences are a poor guide to the seriousness of the offences themselves. For example, a large proportion of robbery cases appearing before the juvenile court involve bullying where one group of boys demands money from another group of usually younger boys.[4] The sums of money involved are often in the range of $10–$100. While such bullying is not to be condoned, it is misleading to consider it in the same light as more serious robberies carried out by adults and included in the same statistical grouping in the official statistics.

Second, juveniles commit the types of crime which are most easily detected and this distorts their representation in overall crime statistics.

In the overcrowded and congested conditions of Hong Kong, where juveniles spend a lot of time in the streets, their criminal activities are often open to public scrutiny. Juveniles do not make sophisticated criminals. The kind of burglaries, robberies, and assaults in which they get involved are often spontaneous and ill-conceived, committed in the company of peers for excitement and status. Such crimes are easily detected by the police. Moreover, for some offences involving a disproportionately high number of juveniles, the detection of the offender is simultaneous with the discovery of the offence. This is usually the case with shoptheft, where the offender is generally caught red-handed. The same is true of offences against public order, possession of an offensive weapon, going equipped for stealing, and loitering.[5]

Third, it is known from victim surveys that there has been a greater propensity for victimization to be reported to the police, and it seems likely that less serious offences as well as more serious ones are being reported more often.[6] Many of the kinds of offences committed by juveniles are comparatively trivial and, in the past, may well not have been reported. If victims knew that 'their offenders' were juvenile, they may well have resorted to informal measures within the neighbourhood rather than make crime reports. It is possible that media and public concern about juvenile crime in recent years has led to a decreased willingness to tolerate juvenile crime and to write it off as 'youthful high spirits', with a correspondingly greater likelihood of crime reports being made. It is also possible that broader social factors, such as the shifting of Hong Kong's population into new towns in the New Territories, has resulted in increased anonymity, so that people do not know the local juveniles and are less prepared to tolerate wrongdoing by them.

A fourth set of factors revolve around the nature of public concern and policing. Numerous crime campaigns were launched in the 1980s by District and Central Fight Crime Committees, drawing both public and police attention to certain categories of crime and specific age groups. Juvenile crime, particularly in relation to shoptheft, loitering, robbery, and assault, has been a focal point for many of these initiatives. For example, the 1985 Central Fight Crime Committee Report stated:

> The Kwun Tong, Tuen Mun, Sha Tin, and North District Fight Crime Committees were concerned about youngsters and students involved in shoplifting and snatching offences. The police were closely monitoring such crime and more police officers were deployed to patrol the blackspots (Report No. 5: 46).

It is possible that heightened public awareness resulted in greater likelihood of crimes being reported. Whether or not this occurred, the effect of such increased police deployment may well have been to increase the juvenile crime detection rates, and therefore the arrest rates.

Why has there been such heightened community interest in juvenile crime in recent years? Fears about juvenile crime are a recurrent theme in many countries, leading several writers in the UK (Box 1985, Hall et al. 1978, Pearson 1983; and see also Chapter 2) to argue that such panics often represent a means by which wider social anxieties and uncertainties are articulated and expressed. Concern over juvenile crime can divert attention away from prevailing political and economic problems and provide ample justification to exercise greater control over young people who are seen as a potential threat to social order during such periods. Over the past 20 years, Hong Kong has also had its social, political, and economic problems. At all times, the overriding concern has been to maintain the stability and prosperity of the territory. It may be pure speculation to link these events to panics about juvenile crime, but certainly each surge of concern over juvenile crime has resulted in a tightening of control over the lives of young people, as is reflected in a number of welfare and educational policies developed and expanded since the 1970s and in the attitudes of the justice system towards juvenile offenders.

The Juvenile Justice System[7]

A key question is whether the 'moral panics' about juvenile crime have influenced the decisions of juvenile justice agencies. Once arrested, two options are generally available for dealing with a juvenile; he is either cautioned by the police or he appears before the court.[8] There are two questions of particular interest here; has cautioning led to what Cohen (1985) describes as 'net widening', and have the courts become harsher or more lenient in dealing with juvenile offenders? The evidence is not conclusive on either count, but there are strong indications that both 'net widening' and harsher penalties have occurred.

Let us begin by examining the use of cautioning. In many jurisdictions, the 1970s saw a move to replace the formality of the juvenile court with measures to deal with young offenders informally. Cautions given by the police were part of this trend. In the UK, cautioning rates rose by 55 per cent between 1970 and 1979 (Morris and Giller 1987). However, this more liberal approach, which underlay the 1969 Children and Young Persons Act in the UK, backfired to some extent.

Ditchfield (1976) found that there was nevertheless an increase in the numbers of juveniles prosecuted, which could not be explained by increases in the quantity or seriousness of juvenile crime but was instead a direct consequence of changes in police cautioning practice. The police were using cautioning for minor or trivial delinquent acts which previously would have been dealt with by an informal warning. Meanwhile, slightly more serious offenders, the intended target group of cautioning, were still being channelled into court. Thus the caution became an alternative to an informal warning and not to prosecution. This phenomenon has come to be known as 'net widening'.

Has 'net widening' occurred in Hong Kong? Certainly there has been a massive rise in the rate of juvenile cautioning, from 89 to 574 per 100,000 between 1978 and 1987, though there has since been a sharp decline.[9] Over the same period, however, there has been a decrease in the number of convictions of juveniles from 555 to 370 per 100,000.[10] The combined effect is an increase of 47 per cent in the number of juveniles officially processed. Given the very large increase in the number of arrests over roughly the same period, these figures give little support to a contention that 'net widening' has occurred. However, anecdotal evidence paints a different picture.[11] One would expect that if cautioning was working as intended there would be an increase in the seriousness of cases appearing before the courts, and that a good proportion of such juveniles would have been cautioned for earlier offences. This is not the case. Many juveniles continue to appear in court for quite minor offences with no previous caution. The large increase in cautioning may therefore indeed be attributable to bringing more juveniles into the system rather than diversion of less serious offences from the court. Certainly this is an area that warrants further and more detailed research.

Turning to those juveniles convicted by the courts, any attempt to examine sentencing trends in Hong Kong is beset with major difficulties. Until 1986, the police, Correctional Services Department, and Social Welfare Department each had its own statistical systems, often using different classifications, counting rules, and time periods. In 1986, they adopted the 'Standardized Law and Order Statistical System', thus providing a greater degree of comparability.[12] Analyses using years on either side of the 1986 divide run the risk of comparing non-comparable figures. Table 3.1 shows sentencing figures for juveniles in 1978 and 1987. These two years, spanning a decade, are used as they best represent the 1970s and 1980s. Figures for each year were collected from a range of juvenile justice agencies as shown in the *Annual Digests* of the Hong Kong Census and Statistics Department.

In general, juveniles not subject to Social Welfare or Correctional Services programmes are dealt with by fines, discharges, or bind-overs.[13] In 1978, these methods comprised 82 per cent of sentencing disposals, but by 1987 they accounted for only 48 per cent. Conversely, probation and residential and custodial sentences increased and became the major sentencing disposals. Thus the chance of a juvenile who appeared in court being put on probation doubled over the period, and the chance of a custodial or residential sentence increased by 73 per cent, with particular emphasis on detention centre and training centre orders, which increased six-fold. As community service orders only came into operation in 1987 and are not available in all magistracies, it is too early to comment on them.[14]

This grim picture is rather simplistic, however, since it ignores three significant complications. First, it can be seen that in 1978 convictions exceeded prosecutions. This apparent illogicality arises because many minor offences, such as hawking and littering, are not recorded in police prosecution statistics. Usually the defendant receives a summons to appear before the court and receives a fine, bind-over, or discharge. The appearance of such offences in conviction, though not prosecution, rates makes it difficult to disentangle precisely what kinds of sanctions were being used for which kinds of juvenile crimes (as opposed to minor offences). Second, although by 1987 the numbers convicted had declined by more than 33 per cent while the number of prosecutions had increased and overtaken convictions, it was quite clear that cautioning had assumed a much larger role in the criminal justice process, distorting comparisons over the period. Third, the sentencing details in Table 3.1 are for all juveniles admitted into Social Welfare and Correctional Services programmes; the conviction rates are only for the juvenile and adult magistrates' courts. The number of juveniles dealt with in the district and high courts, which could influence comparisons, is not known (see Chapter 10 for the distinctions between types of courts).

One way of firming up the analysis is to look more closely at sentencing trends within the juvenile court, based on figures provided by the judiciary.[15] Table 3.2 refers to juveniles convicted by the juvenile court of what are now called 'standard list offences', thus excluding most minor offences categorized as 'offences against local laws', such as hawking and littering. It therefore gives a clearer picture of sentencing trends for more serious offences, even though what the law regards in this light may not be 'events that most of us would regard as particularly serious' (Bottomley and Pease 1986: 2).

Table 3.1 Comparison of Juveniles Admitted into Social Welfare and Correctional Services[1] Programmes in 1978 and 1987[2]

	1978		1987	
Programmes	Admissions per 100,000	Percentage of Convictions	Admissions per 100,000	Percentage of Convictions
Non-residential				
Probation	60.5	10.9	121.5	32.9
Community Service	—	—	3.2	0.9
Residential/ custodial				
Probation home	24.4	4.4	34.4	9.3
Reformatory	12.7	2.3	16.5	4.5
Detention centre[3]	1.5	0.3	10.7	2.9
Training centre[3]	0.9	0.2	5.7	1.5
Prison	0.1	—	1.2	0.3
Drug centre	0.1	—	2.6	0.1
Total residential and custodial	39.7	7.2	68.8	18.6
Conviction rate (per 100,000)	555.4		369.8	
Prosecution rate (per 100,000)	186.7		421.4	
Cautioning rate (per 100,000)	89.0		573.7	

Notes: 1. Figures for females below 16 years admitted into Correctional Services programmes are excluded, but both males and females are included in all other statistics.
2. Compiled from Social Welfare, Correctional Services, and Judicial Statistics published in the 1988 Annual Digest of Statistics. Population statistics provided by the Census and Statistics Department, 1990.
3. Figures for 1978 are not representative. Figures for 1977 are more typical — for example detention centre = 5 per 100,000 (0.9%) and training centre = 2.3 per 100,000 (0.4%).

Table 3.2 shows no significant rise in the use of probation, but confirms the large increase in the use of reformatory school and custodial sentences. Comparing Tables 3.1 and 3.2 is unwise because they are derived from different sources. Yet two possible but opposing arguments could be drawn from them. First, if one accepts that cautioning has 'creamed off' many lesser offences and that the juveniles appearing

Table 3.2 Comparison of Sentencing Disposals for Juveniles Convicted of Standard List Offences in 1978[1] and 1987[2] in Juvenile Court

	1978		1987	
Disposals	Numbers per 100,000	Percentage of Convictions	Numbers per100,000	Percentage of Convictions
Residential/ non-residential				
Probation[3]	118.7	60.2	110.6	66.2
Community service	—	—	1.2	0.7
Reformatory	4.3	2.2	10.7	6.4
Total residential/ non-residential	123.0	62.4	122.5	73.3
Custodial				
Detention centre	1.3	0.7	9.0	5.4
Training centre	3.2	1.6	4.8	2.9
Prison	0.1	0.1	0.6	0.4
Drug centre	—	—	—	—
Total custodial	4.6	2.3	14.5	8.7
Fine	6.2	3.1	5.8	3.5
Compensation order	—	—	1.0	0.6
Bind-over[4]	62.1	31.5	22.9	13.6
Suspended imprisonment	—	—	0.3	0.2
Hospital order	—	—	0.1	0.1
Caning	1.2	0.6	—	—
Conviction rate (per 100,000)	197.1		167.0	

Notes: 1. The 1978 data refer to 1 April 1978 to 31 March 1979. Compiled from Annual Judicial Statistics 1977–1980. Disposals and convictions for offences against local laws excluded to allow for compatibility with 1987 data.

2. The 1987 data refer to 1 January to 31 December 1987. Compiled from unpublished data provided by the judiciary. Refers to sentencing disposals and convictions for standard list offences only. Population statistics provided by the Census and Statistics Department, 1990.

3. Includes probation home.

4. Includes absolute discharge, conditional discharge, and discharge with caution or bind-over.

before the court were on the whole more serious offenders, then it might reasonably be expected that court sentences would on the whole be harsher in 1987 than in 1978. Conversely, if one considers that as a result of 'net widening' those offenders appearing before the court in 1987 are not that different from those of 1978, then it could be argued that the dramatic rise in the use of residential care and custody and the subsequent use of probation for less serious offences has been the result of a hardening in attitudes by juvenile justice professionals, possibly in response to community fears about the breakdown in social discipline amongst young people.

Inside the Juvenile Court

Analysis of sentencing statistics gives a somewhat sterile image of the experiences of juvenile offenders within the justice system. A clearer picture emerges from an examination of the decision-making process in action within the juvenile court. Asquith (1983) argues that juvenile justice professionals have different 'frames of relevance', that is, sets of values, attitudes, and beliefs which they use to interpret delinquent behaviour and decide how to tackle the problem. These are absorbed from a set of 'available ideologies' about the causes and prevention of crime, gained through professional training, education, the media, and general life experiences.

Official policy documents in the 1970s in the UK promoted a welfare orientation within the juvenile justice system. However, research evidence on decision-making processes within the juvenile court clearly shows that the combination of the often conflicting personal and professional attitudes of juvenile justice personnel distorted the extent to which this objective was actually realized. Justice, welfare, and punishment principles merged to create a 'punitive treatment' approach to juvenile crime (Parker et al. 1981). The juvenile was punished not only for the offence but also for his social background. Morris and McIsaac (1978) argue that a 'tariff based on needs' was grafted onto a 'tariff based on deeds'.

The legislation and court proceedings in Hong Kong similarly indicate a mixture of justice, welfare, and punishment ideologies. The Juvenile Offenders Ordinance begins by focusing attention on the offence, stating that the purpose of the juvenile court is to hear 'any charge against a child or young person'.[16] The initial proceedings in juvenile cases are adversarial and similar to that of the adult court. Pleas are taken and, if the juvenile denies the charge, a trial ensues to establish guilt or innocence. Throughout the legislation and proceedings, a strong undercurrent of justice ideals are in evidence. The legislation lays down clear guidelines for the protection of the juvenile's legal rights. In addition, the services of the Law Society Legal Advice and Duty Lawyers Scheme are available in court. The separation of adult and juvenile courts (though they are generally in the same building) and the exclusion of the press and general public from hearings, are intended to safeguard juveniles from adverse criminal influences and publicity.

The legislation is less clear, however, as to the aims of sentencing once guilt has been established. Paragraph 8 provides some clues:

> Before deciding how to deal with the child or young person, the court shall obtain such information as may be readily available as to his general conduct, home surroundings, school record, and medical history, in order to enable it to deal with the case in the best interests of the child or young person . . . (Juvenile Offenders Ordinance: 8)

The phrase 'in the best interests of the child' is open to a number of interpretations. Juvenile justice professionals usually seem to interpret it to mean that the welfare needs of the juvenile should be taken into account before sentencing. Indeed, in the majority of cases, magistrates will call for social enquiry reports before passing sentence, and if probation appears an unsuitable option they may also call for reformatory school, community service, detention centre, or training centre suitability reports or a Young Offenders Assessment Panel report.[17] These reports concentrate heavily on the writer's analysis of the juvenile's social background, gleaned from the individual, parents, teachers, and employers. Generally only one paragraph discusses the offence.

For the past 18 months, the writer has been engaged in a research study of the operation of the juvenile court in Hong Kong.[18] Data was collected through a content analysis of court reports, unstructured questionnaires, and interviews, in order to collate the values and attitudes of juvenile justice personnel towards sentencing. Whilst there are obviously differences in individual views, the following is a brief analysis of the main operational ideology which the research findings reveal is strongly embedded in the decision-making processes within the Hong Kong juvenile court.

Offence factors do not receive a high priority in weighing information to make a recommendation or pass sentence. This may be, as Parker et al. (1989) argue, because justice professionals take these for granted or see them as being too obvious to mention. There are exceptions, for example, where the offence is seen as particularly serious, perhaps involving assaults or woundings and substantial injury to the victim. But the key point is that for the mundane cases of theft, minor robberies, and assaults—the main substance of the court's work—welfare rather than offence considerations are of paramount importance. Moreover, it is a particular aspect of the juvenile's welfare which is of interest to the court, that is, his disciplinary needs. The chief concern of court personnel is the degree to which the juvenile is out of the control of various social systems, from the home to the workplace.

These social systems are seen as moral thermometers, deviation from which indicates the need for intervention by the juvenile court. In the case of the family, great emphasis is placed on its inability to discipline and control the young person, the offence itself being viewed as symbolic of the family's failure in this direction. At school, poor academic performance is noted in passing, but incidents of unruly behaviour, such as fighting, truancy, and breaches of school rules, are seen as much more significant. If the juvenile has left school, attitude to work and regularity of employment are used as further indications of the juvenile's willingness to conform. Leisure and peer networks are often mentioned, with attendance at billiard rooms and video game centres and staying out late or overnight being offered as evidence of a hedonistic lifestyle. A thorough investigation is made of peer associates to identify the degree of Triad affiliation. Reference is often made to the juvenile's personality and his inherent level of self-discipline. The stereotyping of individuals is common, with description ranging from the playful, immature, and easily-led adolescent to the impulsive, aggressive, hardened delinquent who has no regard for authority.

In short, the decision-making process seems to centre around a concern about the juvenile's willingness to 'conform', while the emphasis on discipline and control leads to a situation in which negative rather than positive factors are stressed—a process also noted in the UK, where it has been described as not unlike 'character assassination' (Morris and McIsaac 1978). In this context, it is not difficult to understand the dramatic rise in the use of residential care and custody outlined in the previous section, particularly in an atmosphere where community fears place further pressure on the juvenile justice system to offer more effective guidance and control over young people.

There are a number of scenarios which commonly surround a juvenile being sent into residential care and custody. A boy being considered for a reformatory school sentence may already have had experience of probation or have resided in a probation home, usually following his first appearance in court and often for a quite minor offence. He may have breached his probation order either by committing a fresh offence or simply by failing to comply with its conditions by not attending school, not finding a regular job, staying out late, or failing to keep appointments with his probation officer. A breach of probation is often treated as a type of crime in itself, indicative of the juvenile's unwillingness to respond to control in the community or rejection of authority. Generally, it is a combination of disciplinary and offence factors which accelerates the juvenile's progress into residential care. By this stage, the juvenile would be seen as totally beyond the control of the family, which is powerless to guide and discipline him. Descriptions of the juvenile's personality would have deteriorated—'stubborn', 'lazy', 'carefree', 'wilful', 'rebellious', and 'irresponsible'. The usual problems appear at work and at school, but the disorganized pattern of living has become more serious. Late night activities have become more frequent and Triad affiliations stronger. By the end of the story we have a picture of a fairly wayward young person in need of long-term character training and discipline in a structured setting, where he will learn to develop a constructive, regulated, and industrious lifestyle.

Detention or training centre sentences were rare events in the writer's research. Usually young delinquents had already been placed in a reformatory school until approaching their sixteenth birthday, thus giving them few opportunities to experience these programmes. Although the nature of the offence and age seem to be crucial factors when considering subjects for custodial sentences, it seems that here too, behavioural problems, breach of probation, or approaching over-age for reformatory school, might lead a juvenile into custody. The juvenile would be portrayed as unrepentant, with an indifferent, defensive, or evasive approach to report writers. Community rehabilitative programmes would either have been tried and failed or seen as unlikely to curb the juvenile's delinquent tendencies. On the home front, we again see permissive parental discipline or even a total lack of parental control. School and work have long since been rejected by the juvenile. Violent or aggressive tendencies may also be cited, giving the overall impression of a deep-rooted, hard-core delinquent with no regard for authority and a strong identification with Triad culture. Such characters are seen to require either the deterrent effect of the 'short, sharp, shock' or intensive long-term character training to instil a regulated pattern of life and respect for authority.

Unintended Consequences and New Directions

Let us gather up the strands of the previous discussion, indicate current problems with the juvenile system, and advocate some reforms.

Whilst the evidence is far from clear, it is possible that there has been an increase in juvenile criminality. If so, it may well be linked, albeit indirectly, to some of the features identified by public figures and Fight Crime Committees. But it is much more certain that there has been a massive expansion in the scope of juvenile justice agencies; a decreasing tolerance for juvenile misbehaviour; policing strategies targeted at youth; and a probable 'net widening', resulting in the official processing of juveniles who previously would have been dealt with informally by the community or by the police. Much of the apparent increase in recorded juvenile crime is due to these factors rather than greater wrongdoing by the young.

In the courts an ethos of 'disciplinary welfare' holds sway, no doubt strengthened in recent years by panics about juvenile crime. Justice professionals use probation, residential care, and custody as a means to tackle the young offender's family, school, or peer group problems. However, they tend to see the solution to these welfare problems as being increased discipline and control, leading to a result which Parker et al. (1981) describe as 'punitive treatment'. Recommendations for and sentences of probation, residential care, and custody are made very early in the juvenile's offending career, often for minor offences and for juveniles who have not previously even received cautions.

Social Welfare Department research found that first offenders made up 79 per cent of admissions to probation homes and 61 per cent of admissions to reformatory schools in the period 1979–81 (informal sources suggest that these rates have reduced somewhat in the 1980s). Most of the remainder had only one previous conviction.[19] Even in 1988, Correctional Services statistics indicate that 68 per cent and 76 per cent of males under 20 committed to training centres and detention centres respectively had no more than one previous conviction.[20] There is no doubt that the use of residential care and custody in Hong Kong features far earlier in a juvenile's criminal career than is usual in other countries.

It could be argued that the early use of such measures can be justified by the seriousness of juvenile crime. Yet the majority of young offenders in residential care and custody in the 1980s had committed crimes against property. Offences against the person constituted only 9.5 per cent of crimes committed by juveniles in probation home and reformatory schools in 1985 and 12 per cent by males below 20 in detention and training centres in 1988.[21] Whilst detailed knowledge of these offences is not known, a high incidence of danger to the public is unlikely. There seems little doubt that many young people are in residential care and custody not for the serious nature of their crimes, but because of problematic behaviour at home, at school, at work, or at leisure, or because of failure to comply with a probation order.

What, then, is to be done? Research evidence from the UK seems to confirm that the indiscriminate adoption of both welfare and punishment considerations in the juvenile justice system has a negative effect on the careers of young offenders. Legislation and policy changes in the 1980s attempted to redress the mistakes of the past and led to greater awareness of the consequences of unchecked discretion in the juvenile court (Hudson 1987, Pitts 1988). Hong Kong may have something to learn from these developments.

A new frame of relevance now underlies UK juvenile justice policy, often referred to as the 'just welfare' approach (Harris 1985). There are three main components to this new approach. First, despite the trivial nature of much juvenile crime, it cannot be ignored because it is upsetting both to the community and its victims. Young offenders must be made aware of this through an element of punitive sanctioning. At the same time, overreaction might intensify the problem and promote further delinquency (Jones 1980). Therefore, the 'justice' principles of 'proportionality' and 'least restrictive measures' or minimum intervention should provide the basis for punishment. The full range of non-custodial options should be tried before resorting to residential care or custody. This includes the expansion of cautioning schemes, with stringent monitoring to safeguard against 'net widening'. Second, the juvenile justice system cannot ignore welfare, though it may be necessary to place restrictions on its abuse. There is an association between persistent delinquency and socioeconomic background, even if it has not proven to be causal (Rutter and Giller 1983). The juvenile justice system should offer welfare oriented services to delinquent youth, which will offset deprivations in their social background (Jones 1981). This could involve elements of control and discipline or help of a more practical nature, such as resolving family conflicts, settling in at school, or finding a job. However, welfare and punishment measures must be provided separately, so as not to escalate the sentencing tariff. Third, a preference for residential care and custody has been replaced by developments in community treatment. In the UK, high recidivism rates have demonstrated that residential care and custody have failed to prevent juvenile crime. Community treatment on a wide scale is relatively untested, but is almost certainly less damaging to youth.

In Hong Kong, the development of such a new frame of relevance would require major changes in the attitudes of juvenile justice personnel. It would mean acknowledging the often minor nature of juvenile crime; and that today's young offender is unlikely to be tomorrow's hardened criminal, and ensuring that intervention measures are proportional and relevant to today's crime. It would mean recognizing that overemphasis on social problems is an infringement of the juvenile's civil rights, pointing to the need for legal representatives to pay more attention to the content and abuse of social background information in court reports. It would mean balancing disciplinary needs with the other needs of the juvenile by providing more adequate services to tackle problems at home, school, work, and leisure. Many social workers in Hong Kong already attempt this, but high case loads and lack of resources make it a difficult task. Finally, it would mean replacing a faith in institutionalization with one favouring community-based programmes. Young people learn how to commit crime in the community; therefore, their behaviour must be challenged in that same community.

It could be argued that such a new frame of relevance is not culturally relevant to juvenile justice in Hong Kong. However, existing cultural attitudes and values have already been tainted by outdated Western concepts of juvenile justice and have not yet recognized their negative consequences. Moreover, the opportunity to make improvements to juvenile justice is at hand, since the very idea of a Bill of Rights ought to encompass a complete review and rethinking of the rights of juveniles in relation to justice, as it will have to do in every other area of Hong Kong life. 'Cultural relevance' is no longer a concept that justice professionals and legislators can hide behind, since the concept itself is fast losing its relevance.

Notes

1. The offender rate is the combined rate for prosecution and discharge under the Superintendents' Discretion Scheme. Offender rates (per 100,000) for 1974–89 were kindly provided by the Royal Hong Kong Police Statistician.
2. Data from Census and Statistics Department (1978, 1989).
3. Ibid.
4. This comment is based on the writer's current research on the juvenile court in Hong Kong (Gray, forthcoming).
5. See for example the table 'Number of Cases Reported, Detected, and Detection Rate, 1987 and 1988' in Commissioner of Police (1989).
6. Census and Statistics Department (1987).

7. This term is used to describe the policy and practice of police, courts, social workers, and correctional services in dealing with juvenile offenders.

8. The majority of juveniles from 7 to 15 years old are dealt with by the juvenile court. However, juveniles may also be tried and sentenced in the adult, District, and High Courts, for example where the crime is committed with an adult.

9. In 1989, the Superintendent's Discretion rate had dropped to 340 per 100,000 (figure provided by the Royal Hong Kong Police Statistician).

10. Census and Statistics Department (1988).

11. The following section is based on the writer's research.

12. Central Fight Crime Committee Report No. 7, p. 37, November 1986–December 1987.

13. Social Welfare Department programmes include probation, probation homes, and reformatory schools. Probation homes and reformatory schools are referred to as 'residential care' in the text and all juveniles below the age of 16 years are eligible. Correctional Service programmes include detention centres, training centres, drug centres, and prison. These are referred to as 'custody' in the text and all juveniles of 14 years and above are eligible.

14. Community service orders are run by the Social Welfare Department and juveniles of 14 years and above are eligible. Statistics taken from Appendix 9.4, Hong Kong *Annual Departmental Reports* by the Director of Social Welfare, 1977–88.

15. Criminal Judicial Statistics, Statistics Unit, Supreme Court 1988, and (unpublished) *Annual Judicial Statistics*, Departmental Report, 1977–80, Registrar Supreme Court.

16. Juvenile Offenders Ordinance (Cap. 226), Revised Edition 1983, p. 3.

17. Comprises representatives of the Social Welfare and Correctional Services Department. Set up in 1987, the panel recommends whether the juvenile is suitable for probation, residential care, or custody.

18. The research aims to explore how existing sentencing options are used for different types of offenders by following the career patterns of a group of male juvenile offenders up to their current court sentence. The main sample was drawn from two juvenile courts, although a smaller sample was also taken from four of the remaining six juvenile courts in Hong Kong. The researcher traced the career patterns of the juveniles through a content analysis of court records and reports. All juvenile court professionals— such as magistrates, probation officers, and correctional services intake officers—completed unstructured questionnaires or had an interview exploring the rationale behind their recommendation or decision. As the research adopted a qualitative methodology, respondents were encouraged to elaborate on their values and attitudes toward sentencing. It is hoped that the research findings will identify areas in the juvenile justice system where existing resources or new programmes and practices can be developed. At the time of writing, data analysis was still in progress.

19. *Study of Closed Cases of Girls and Boys on Probation in Correctional Institutions*, Social Welfare Department, Research and Statistics Section (1982).

20. From tables 4A and 5, *Annual Statistical Tables*, Correctional Services Department (1988). Detention centre figures include a small number of males aged 21–4.

21. Appendix 9.3, Hong Kong *Annual Departmental Report* by the Director of Social Welfare, 1985–6; and tables 4A and 5, *Annual Statistical Tables*, Commissioner of Correctional Services Department (1988).

4 Drugs

HAROLD TRAVER

LOCAL drug markets typically develop their own special characteristics. From the very beginning, the drug market in Hong Kong has been dominated by an overwhelming preference for opium and its derivatives, especially heroin. Considering that opium consumption was actively promoted by the Hong Kong government for nearly a century, the preference for opiates is to be expected. The fact that Hong Kong has remained virtually untouched by such drugs as cocaine, amphetamines, barbiturates, and marijuana while other parts of the world have been inundated by them, is a testimony to the local consumers' commitment to opiates. Drug control laws, treatment strategies, as well as the general conception of drug abuse as a problem have been shaped by this fact.

Extent of Drug Abuse

The theme of a serious and persistent drug problem is a common feature in most discussions of drug abuse in Hong Kong. Does Hong Kong have a serious drug problem on its hands? The 1959 White Paper on Narcotics in Hong Kong certainly thought so when it reported that drug addiction had been growing at an alarming rate, and that it was then one of Hong Kong's greatest social and economic problems. A second White Paper, in 1974, on Dangerous Drugs in Hong Kong, started off by stating that despite considerable effort, addiction had been contained rather than reduced. Four years later, the Annual Report of the Action Committee Against Narcotics echoed this sentiment when it called drug abuse a 'serious and long-standing problem in Hong Kong' (Action Committee Against Narcotics 1978: 25). Although drug abuse continued to be labelled as a long-standing problem, the 1980s did end on the somewhat optimistic note that there had been a downward trend in the number of new drug abusers coming to the attention of the Central Registry of Drug Abuse. Since 1985, when newly reported cases stood at 3,528, new cases have steadily declined to the point where in 1989 they stood at 2,196. Moreover, with the exception of 1987, when there was a small increase, the number of new admissions for treatment has also gone down from a high of 19,104 in 1984 to 13,157 in 1989.

These decreases are from peak years in the mid-1980s. If one examines a longer period of time, a somewhat different picture begins to emerge. For instance, between 1980 and 1989, while newly reported cases decreased by a hefty 22 per cent (from 2,806 to 2,196), the number of reported cases of drug abuse increased by 16 per cent (from 13,171 to 15,317), and treatment admissions increased by 8 per cent (from 12,156 to 13,175). These figures suggest that despite any declines in newly reported cases there is also a rather intractable group of drug abusers in Hong Kong.

Any attempt to determine the exact, or even approximate, number of drug abusers in Hong Kong quickly runs into some problems. First, most discussions of drug abuse show an alarming tendency to lump the occasional user with the habitual. The result of this lack of precision in terminology is the wildly fluctuating figures that appear in Table 4.1. Depending on what one means by addiction, in any one year estimates of addiction can range, as they did in 1959, from 180,000 to 250,000, and from one year to the next by as much as 50,000. It has only been since the re-organization of the Central Registry of Drug Abuse in 1976 that some consistency, if not accuracy, has entered into estimates of the addict or user population in Hong Kong.

Second, there is marked tendency to categorize all forms of drug abuse as addiction. Occasionally, this tendency can become a clearly articulated policy. For instance, the 1974 White Paper specifically states that for the sake of 'simplicity a person who abuses dangerous drugs is an addict'. Given the addictive qualities of heroin and the fact that over 90 per cent of all cases of drug abuse involve heroin, the margin of error in this assumption may not be too great. It makes less sense to do this when there is any possibility that heroin usage, at least among the young, is being replaced by marijuana, which is acknowledged as not producing any symptoms of physical addiction, or by psychotropic substances such as Mandrax which produce their own special forms of dependence (Barlow 1990).

Types of Drug Abuse

One of the most notable features of drug abuse in Hong Kong is the rapid shift from opium to heroin that occurred in the 1950s; in less than a decade, heroin supplanted opium as the most common abusable drug in Hong Kong.

Table 4.1 Estimates of the Extent of Drug Use, 1909–1989

Year	Estimate	Source
1909	12.94% of adult males smoke opium.	Legislative Council No. 3/1909
1924	20–25% of the adult Chinese population smokes opium. Includes 1–2% of the adult female population.	Legislative Council No. 7/1924
1939	5,577 rationed and non-rationed smokers; 2,500 opium divans x 20 smokers per day = 50,000 users. In addition, there were 30,000 heroin pill addicts.	Report on the Traffic in Prepared Opium, 1939
1959	150,000–250,000 use drugs.	Government White Paper, 1959
1965	100,000 addicts; 12.5% of all adult males.	Way, E. L.
1966	6–10% of the total adult population, 3% of the female population.	Action Committee Against Narcotics
1966/67	30,000–65,000 addicted.	Research Sub-committee of Action Committee Against Narcotics
1977	60,000–100,000 addicted.	Hong Kong *Annual Report*, 1978
1978	35,000–50,000 addicted.	Hong Kong *Narcotics Report*, 1978
1980	Below 40,000 addicted.	Hong Kong *Narcotics Report*, 1980
1985	Around 37,000 addicted.	Hong Kong *Annual Reports*, 1981 and 1986
1988	About 44,000 addicted.	Hong Kong *Annual Report*, 1989
1989	About 42,000 addicted.	Hong Kong *Annual Report*, 1990

The first indication of what was to come appeared in the Commerce and Industry *Annual Report* of 1948/9. The report noted that the traffic in heroin, 'which had almost disappeared after the war, is now steadily on the increase' (Commerce and Industry Department 1949: 5). In 1953, the police reported that increased activity on their part had resulted in the complete elimination of opium divans and went on to comment that morphine and heroin in white powder form were appearing in increasing quantities and that, because neither of these required premises, pipes, or paraphernalia, peddling of these substances in the streets and cafes was on the increase. A year later, it was noted that additional police pressure on the morphine and heroin trade had led to dealers resorting to the distribution of small doses in the street (Commissioner of Police 1954: 36).

Lau and Yap (1967), in the first extensive study of drug abuse in Hong Kong, confirmed the predominance of heroin users over opium users. Between 1961 and 1963, out of 968 addicts only 128 (13.2 per cent) used opium; 501 addicts (51.8 per cent) used opium initially but switched to heroin subsequently; another 339 (35 per cent) used heroin exclusively. Ten years later a similar study (SARDA 1972) found that out of 782 addicts, 87 (11.1 per cent) continued to use opium; another 170 (21.7 per cent) used opium initially before changing to heroin, while 525 (67.1 per cent) used heroin exclusively.

The shift away from opium is also reflected in the arrest figures for narcotic offences in Hong Kong. Between 1952/3 and 1955/6, the number of heroin offences increased from 400 to 11,037 while the number of opium offences remained more or less unchanged (in 1952/3, 4,434 and in 1955/6, 4,264). In 1954/5, the heroin offences exceeded opium offences for the first time and by 1955/6 heroin offences outweighed opium offences by nearly three to one.

By 1974, roughly 79 per cent of all people taking drugs were believed to be using heroin, and since 1978 the reported figures for heroin use have been well above 90 per cent of all drug users. Although concern is frequently expressed over depressants such as methaqualone and quinalbarbitone, opium and methadone abuse account for a greater percentage of reported cases of drug abuse. In 1989, the combined percentage for these latter two drugs stood at 4.6 per cent of all reported cases. Amphetamines and barbiturates accounted for 1.6 per cent of all cases.

The only form of drug abuse that has shown any consistent tendency to increase in recent years is the use of cannabis by

Table 4.2 Seizures of Dangerous Drugs, 1948/49 to 1989[1]

Year	Opium[2]	Morphine	Heroin[3]		Heroin base	Cannabis
1948/49	378	—	0.5		—	—
1949/50	2,989	0.6	14		—	—
1950/51[3]	—	—	—		—	—
1951/52[4]	—	—	—		—	—
1952/53	42	20	5		—	—
1953/54	289	8	10		—	—
1954/55	53	12	8		—	—
1955/56	949	32	19		—	—
1956/57	734	16	22		—	—
1957/58	878	69	29		—	—
1958/59	985	64	37		—	—
1959/60	583	65	54		—	—
1960/61	966	203	64		—	—
1961/62	253	105	32		—	—
1962/63	793	157	83		—	—
1963/64	1,534	92	1		—	—
1965	2,973	185	35		—	—
1966	4,956	407	25		—	—
1967	2,177	120	27		—	—
1968	1,868	81	30		—	30
1969	4,772	187	10		—	23
1970	399	77	14		—	24
1971	5,583	300	55		—	51
1972	5,118	551	73		—	15
1973	2,328	388	69		—	17
1974	4,735	285	95		—	6
1975	422	143	186		—	54
1976	3,553	291	164		—	87
1977	147	98	179		—	19
1978	205	47	285		48	1
1979	125	12	129		19	12
1980	86	2	76		38	39
1981	140	7	77		85	8
1982	187	6	116		232	55
			a	b		
1983	91	trace	151	13	4606	
1984	50	trace	182	48	972	77
1985	104	trace	247	12	113	167
1986	85	1.0	323	79	162	92
1987	179	3.6	358	77	77	285
1988	65	5	625	252	2	55
1989	104	16	458	592	2	445

Notes & Sources to Table 4.2

Notes: 1. All weights are in kilograms.
2. Raw and prepared.
3. Prior to 1978, heroin base figures were combined with heroin. From 1983 onwards, heroin figures separated No. 3 and No. 4 heroin, shown in the sub-columns (a) for No. 3 and (b) for No. 4.
4. There are no published figures for these years.

Sources: Hong Kong Narcotics *Reports*, Department of Commerce and Industry *Reports*, Hong Kong Police *Annual Reports*.

individuals under 21 years of age. In 1989, 40.5 per cent of the 846 cases of reported drug abuse for this age group involved the use of marijuana while another 51.2 per cent involved the use of heroin. Most of the increase in reported cases of youthful drug abuse (that is, use by persons aged under 21) can be traced to the increase in cannabis consumption. Since 1980, reported cases of heroin abuse among individuals under 21 have shown a consistent tendency to decrease. Again, one is talking about relatively small numbers here. Youthful drug abusers only account for 8.2 per cent of all reported cases of drug abuse in 1989 and cases involving cannabis accounted for 4.2 per cent of all reported cases as compared with 2.8 per cent in the previous year.

The extent of Hong Kong's drug problem is indirectly shown by the annual quantities of drugs seized (Table 4.2). Though obviously subject to the vagaries of government interdiction efforts, they do give us some idea of the quantities and types of drugs flowing into Hong Kong in the post-war years. The large quantities of opium and morphine seized in the 1960s and 1970s were largely destined for conversion into No. 3 heroin. When it became difficult or unprofitable to ship opium, attention shifted to the direct importation of heroin or heroin base into the territory. (The latter is used to manufacture No. 3 heroin.) The only other drug of note is cannabis, where seizures have kept in line with reported increases in its use. Depressants, tranquillizers, and stimulants do not appear in Table 4.2. The quantities for these drugs are given in 'tablets' rather than kilograms, and as a result it is impossible to compare the two sets of figures. The quantities of tablets seized in any one year is normally below 100,000, although 1989 saw a record 1.6 million tablets of Valium being seized in Hong Kong. Nonetheless, it is still correct to say that drug abuse in the territory continues to mean heroin abuse.

Methods of Consumption

Narcotics are consumed in a variety of ways. Opium is generally smoked but it can be eaten. Heroin can be injected, which is still the usual method in the West, but it can also be smoked in cigarettes or heated in such a way that the user can inhale the fumes. That fact that Hong Kong had a long history of opium smoking helped to establish smoking and in particular inhalation, or 'chasing the dragon', as the preferred methods for consuming heroin in Hong Kong. Outside observers frequently have been so taken with what, to them, are exotic oriental methods of consumption, that they end up ignoring the fact that the manner in which a drug is consumed is as much driven by considerations of price, purity, and availability as it by culture and tradition.

There are no reliable accounts of how frequently injection was used in the 1950s or even the 1960s, but by all accounts it was uncommon. Heroin was relatively cheap, readily available, and of the highest quality. As heroin prices began to rise in the 1970s the number of users resorting to injection increased steadily and finally peaked in 1980 with 68.4 per cent of addicts using injection. The 1980s saw a dramatic decline in heroin prices and a subsequent decline in injection. By the end of 1985, rates of injection and inhalation were nearly equal. In the years since there has been a trend in the direction of a return to injection. Prices have continued to decline but so has purity. In December 1989, the average purity of No. 3 heroin on sale in the streets was 3.9 per cent, while at the beginning of the decade average purity stood at around 30 per cent.[1] While injection may be a preferred method for high-purity heroin, it is also a way of getting more 'mileage' out of a drug that is expensive, in limited supply or, in the present case, whose level of purity is low.

Opium to Heroin

There is a widely held view that the triumph of the anti-opium movement in abolishing official involvement in the opium trade was a Pyrrhic victory because it encouraged the spread of heroin (Way 1965, Westermeyer 1976). There is every reason to believe that heroin consumption increased dramatically when the government opium monopoly formally ended in 1945 and opium was classified as a dangerous drug subject to the Dangerous Drugs Ordinance of 1935. The argument in favour of a link between restrictive legislation and the switch to heroin is, on the surface, a persuasive one, resting on the relative advantage of heroin in its shipment and, in the case of Hong Kong, on the notion that political unrest in China encouraged an influx of users and manufacturers into Hong Kong from China in the immediate post-war years.

There is undoubtedly some truth in all this, but it also ignores the fact that heroin is not a recent problem in Hong Kong. Even in the days when opium was legally available and the authorities had a financial incentive to suppress competing drugs, heroin consumption gave every indication of flourishing. Throughout the 1930s, official accounts report that opium and heroin were in direct competition. In 1936, it was estimated that between 200,000 and 300,000 pills were being smoked daily by 24,000 addicts. The Dangerous Drugs Ordinance (No. 35 of 1935), which was directed primarily at the manufacture and sale of dangerous drugs, was amended in 1938 specifically to make smoking heroin pills illegal and to strengthen controls on heroin divans (No. 17 of 1938). In that year, more than 2.7 million heroin pills were seized in 671 cases (Hong Kong Government 1938: 4–5). In 1939, there was a dramatic increase in heroin offences. Out of 5,033 opium and dangerous drug offences, 2,196 involved heroin, as compared with 1,291 heroin related-offences in the preceding year (Hong Kong Government 1939: 5–6). It is likely that much of this increase can be traced to the enhanced enforcement powers of the amended Dangerous Drugs Ordinance. Nevertheless, by 1940 Hong Kong had good reason to believe that it had a serious heroin problem, even though opium was readily and legally available to anyone who had the money to buy it.

What occurred in the 1950s was not so much a switch to heroin as a collapse of the opium market in Hong Kong. For the first time, opium and heroin were treated alike. The Hong Kong Government withdrew completely from the promotion and sale of opium. Opium was now forced to compete in a free market. From the standpoint of the supplier, in comparison with opium, heroin was far more profitable; for the consumer, heroin was far more cost-effective. When government intervention in the drug market was withdrawn in 1946, consumer preference for opium quickly ended. Opium consumption persisted as long as it did because of government promotion. The rise of heroin was due to the fact that it made economic sense to everyone concerned, not because of the introduction of restrictive opium legislation or an influx of users.

Drug Legislation

Drug control law in Hong Kong is remarkable both for its severity and for the fact it has experienced few major changes since 1923 when the first Dangerous Drugs Ordinance was passed to bring Hong Kong in line with the requirements of the 1912 International Opium Convention. The Ordinance was primarily directed at the unauthorized shipment and sale of morphine, heroin, ecgonine, cocaine, and medicinal opium. Maximum penalties under this law were a fine not exceeding $10,000 and imprisonment for up to 10 years. Given that the sale of prepared opium continued to be under the control of a government monopoly, this drug was noticeably absent from the list of dangerous drugs. In 1928, in response to the provisions of the 1925 International Opium Convention, the Dangerous Drugs Ordinance was amended to include 'Indian hemp' as a dangerous drug and provisions were introduced to prohibit the cultivation of hemp (*cannabis sativa*).

As mentioned above, the Dangerous Drugs Ordinance No. 35 of 1935 was amended in 1938 to provide more effective controls against the increased use of heroin. Ten years later, in 1948, in an effort to strengthen provisions against heroin, the Dangerous Drugs Ordinance was amended so as to extend controls over the cultivation of the opium poppy (*papaver somniferum*) in Hong Kong and to increase the maximum fine for violating the ordinance to $50,000 (No. 5 of 1948). A number of other amendments were made to the Ordinance in the following years, including restrictions on ingesting or injecting dangerous drugs and an increase in penalties to $100,000 and 15 years' imprisonment in 1962 (No. 4 of 1962).

In 1968, in an effort to bring existing drug legislation into line with concerns about drug trafficking and the treatment of addicts, the 1935 Dangerous Drugs Ordinance was repealed and replaced by a new Dangerous Drugs Ordinance (No. 42 of 1968). The new Ordinance created specific types of drug-related offences. For the first time a clear distinction was made between trafficking, manufacturing, and the possession of dangerous drugs. Criminal sanctions were adjusted accordingly.

The current maximum penalty for drug trafficking is a $5 million fine and life imprisonment, while the maximum penalty for possession for use is a $10,000 fine and three years' imprisonment. Other drug-related offences, such as supplying or procuring a dangerous drug, and cultivating or dealing in opium poppies or cannabis plants, entail a fine of up to $100,000 and 15 years' imprisonment; operating a drug divan carries a fine of $5 million and 15 years imprisonment. The new ordinance is also notable for the inclusion of compulsory treatment for convicted offenders. Depending on the court's judgement of suitability, for simple possession offences the court can make a detention order under the Drug Addiction Centres Ordinance (Cap. 244).

Despite these changes, the Dangerous Drugs Ordinance is essentially a continuation of previous legislative provisions. First, true narcotics, such as opium and heroin, continue to be lumped in with such stimulants as cocaine or intoxicants such as marijuana, although neither of these substances produce symptoms associated with addiction. The proliferation in recent decades of the manufacture and nonmedicinal use of amphetamines, barbiturates, tranquilizers, and hallucinogens has been 'solved' in a similar manner. Wherever there is evidence of widespread abuse of a substance in another country, or when a substance is seen to pose a danger to the health and safety of the community, that substance will be considered for scheduling as a dangerous drug under the Dangerous Drugs Ordinance. As a result, the Dangerous Drugs Ordinance currently lists more than 110 substances as proscribed dangerous drugs in Hong Kong. The list continues to grow.

Second, the policy of applying sanctions irrespective of the drug involved still applies, even though the current ordinance takes pains to distinguish among different types of drug offences. Take drug trafficking. Evidentiary presumption of trafficking comes into effect when the individual is found to possess, among other things, more than 5 grammes of cannabis, 0.5 grammes of heroin or morphine, 2.5 grammes of any mixture continuing not less than 0.2 per cent of morphine, or 10 tablets or capsules containing any proportion of dangerous drug. Other than the occasional nod in the direction of modern terminology, drug law in Hong Kong has been largely untouched by such legislative developments as a distinction between 'hard' and 'soft' drugs or classifying drugs according to relative danger. Hong Kong has been able to do this because it has had to contend with only one major form of drug abuse, opiate abuse. In virtually all cases, trafficking, manufacturing, and possession refer to heroin and before that to opium.

It might seem paradoxical that Hong Kong adopted a punitive approach to the control of dangerous drugs, given that its financial foundations had long rested on the sale of opium. In fact, it was this very involvement that assured that Hong Kong would adopt a punitive approach. Some of the earliest laws in Hong Kong involved setting up controls over the sale and distribution of opium, betel nuts, and hemp derivatives in order to collect revenue from the sale of them. The retail sale of opium quickly established itself as a potentially important source of government revenue and became the main focus of government attention. Suppression of the sale of opium only figured into the law to the extent that concern was directed at controlling the illicit trade in, and unauthorized sale of, opium. In contrast to many Western societies, a moralistic or reformist impulse had almost nothing to do with early drug control efforts in Hong Kong. Instead, legal proscription was seen as a logical and relatively effective way of protecting government opium revenues from competition.

By the beginning of the twentieth century, the anti-opium movement was sufficiently strong to pressure Hong Kong into consolidating and amending its opium laws. The opium monopoly remained in effect, however, and when Hong Kong assumed direct control over the monopoly in 1912, it became an even more profitable source of government revenue. The first Dangerous Drugs Ordinance, passed in response to international treaty requirements, was entirely compatible with the government's desire to continue to derive revenue from the sale of opium. The Ordinance in effect continued the tradition of protecting government opium revenues by legally proscribing the sale of competing drugs.

When the opium monopoly finally ended in 1946, opium was simply classified as another dangerous drug to be subjected to the controls of the Dangerous Drugs Ordinance. The old restrictive legislation and policies still remained in force.

Treatment of Addiction

Prior to World War II, the treatment of addiction was largely a short-term medical problem which involved finding ways of eliminating physical dependency. For instance, in the 1930s treatment was confined to two hospitals in Hong Kong: the Government Civil Hospital (later Queen Mary Hospital) and Tung Wah Eastern Hospital. All treatment was voluntary and was effected either by means of a 'complete and instant withdrawal of opium' or through the use of sedatives and stimulants to effect a more gradual withdrawal. In either case, treatment lasted an average of nine to 12 days and was confined to a small number of individuals (Hong Kong Government 1936: 2). Throughout the 1930s, less than 500 patients were treated in any one year. Moreover, considering the goal was simply the elimination of symptoms of dependency, it should come as no surprise to find that between 70 and 90 per cent of these patients were judged to be relieved of their symptoms. There were, however, no aftercare facilities once these individuals left the hospital and so it was virtually impossible to say to what extent the 'cure' was permanent.

This state of affairs persisted until the 1950s, when the growing heroin problem in Hong Kong became sufficiently serious to create a flurry of official activity. In 1958, as the number of addicts in prison rose to 65.4 per cent of the total prison population, Tai Lam Prison was established for the treatment of prisoner addicts.[2] This facility, the first purpose-built drug treatment facility in Hong Kong, was designed to hold 700 prisoners sentenced for periods of six to 12 months, this being judged sufficient for the complete cure of addiction. Tai Lam Prison may have helped to solve the treatment of addicts housed in Hong Kong's prisons, but it did nothing for those addicts who wished to submit for treatment voluntarily. As a result of this, it was also decided that when the Castle Peak Hospital was completed in 1960 a block of wards with 120 beds (later reduced to 60) would be set aside for two or three years for the treatment of addicts.

Early in 1959, the Governor appointed a Narcotics Advisory Committee to advise on policy, legislation, and campaigns to suppress drug addiction in Hong Kong. At about the same time, a Citizens' Working Committee was formed to study the possibility of setting up treatment facilities for addicts seeking voluntary treatment. Among other things, the Narcotics Advisory Committee made suggestions for legislation regarding basic legal provisions for the voluntary confinement and treatment of addicts. The Committee's recommendations to the government in 1960 formed the basis for the Drug Addicts Treatment and Rehabilitation (DATR) Ordinance (Cap. 326) which provided for the establishment of voluntary addiction treatment centres.[3] While this was going on the Citizens' Working Committee obtained the grant of an island, Shek Kwu Chau, to establish a treatment centre for voluntary patients. In July 1961, the Working Committee was formally incorporated as the Society for the Aid and Rehabilitation of Drug Addicts (SARDA), and the Society took on the bulk of the treatment work specified under the DATR Ordinance. Initially, the Shek Kwu Chau Treatment Centre drew most of its patients from the Castle Peak Hospital. From June 1963 to December 1964, of the 462 patients treated by SARDA, all but eight came from the Castle Peak Hospital. When Castle Peak Hospital was formally closed to drug treatment in 1965, the voluntary treatment of addicts shifted completely to SARDA.

In 1969, the Drug Addiction Treatment Centres (DATC) Ordinance (Cap. 244) was passed, which gave the courts the discretion, in lieu of imposing a custodial sentence, to order that any convicted offender be detained in a designated Addiction Treatment Centre for a minimum of two and a maximum of 12 months. However, when the individual is convicted of a minor drug offence, the court is bound by law to consider such treatment before imposing a custodial sentence. Tai Lam Prison was officially designated as an Addiction Treatment Centre in January 1969, when the new ordinance took effect. In contrast to the voluntary centres established under the DATR Ordinance, treatment centres established under this ordinance are strictly involuntary and custodial. The staff and inmates of treatment centres are governed by the conditions of treatment prescribed by the DATC Ordinance and its subsidiary regulations, which in many ways resemble the Prison Rules.

Table 4.3 Yearly Admissions[1] to Treatment Institutions, Selected Years, 1969–1989

Year	Methadone Clinic	CSD DATC	SARDA	Other[2]	Total
1969	—	1,017	865	118	2,000
1974	1,480	1,976	2,837	167	6,444
1976	10,400	2,160	2,413	172	15,145
1977	9,834	2,269	2,594	42	14,739
1978	10,291	1,999	2,767	—	15,057
1979	10,782	1,655	2,254	—	14,691
1980	8,046	1,518	2,592	—	12,156
1981	9,997	1,675	2,706	—	14,378
1982	11,404	1,783	2,304	283	15,774
1983	11,111	2,116	2,231	356	15,814
1984	14,035	2,577	2,034	368	19,014
1985	13,305	2,621	1,779	374	18,057
1986	10,891	2,547	1,530	388	15,338
1987	11,795	2,036	1,508	476	15,790
1988	8,866	2,318	1,516	496	13,196
1989	8,912	2,128	1,607	51	13,157

Notes: 1. Methadone clinics are operated by the Department of Health. 'CSD DATC' refers to Correctional Services Department Drugs Addiction Treatment Centres. 'SARDA' is the Society for the Aid and Rehabilitation of Drug Abusers.

2. Between 1969 and 1977, these figures refer to persons being treated by the Discharged Prisoners Aid Society. From 1982 onwards, they refer to seven largely Christian organizations involved in small-scale treatment programmes.

In short, by the end of the 1960s, two basic treatment strategies were in place. The first comprised the voluntary in-patient programmes specified in the DATR Ordinance and largely dominated by SARDA. The second consisted of the compulsory in-patient programmes run by the Correctional Services Department under the DATC Ordinance. In the years since, other than an expansion of facilities, there has been little change in this state of affairs. The Correctional Services Department currently operates the Hei Ling Chau Addiction Centre for males, Tai Lam Centre for adult women, and Tai Tam Gap Correctional Institution for young female offenders. The Society for the Aid and Rehabilitation of Drug Abusers (the name-change came in 1979 to conform to contemporary terminology) continues to be the largest provider of voluntary in-patient treatment. In addition to its Shek Kwu Chau Centre for men and the Sha Tin Women's Treatment Centre, SARDA now also operates a series of intake units, Social Service Centres, and half-way houses.

In the 1970s, out-patient methadone maintenance and detoxification became a third, and by far the most popular, basic treatment strategy (see Table 4.3). The possible use of methadone had been discussed in 1968, though pilot schemes to test methadone maintenance were only started in 1972. These schemes, which were scheduled to run for three years, were operated by the Discharged Prisoners' Aid Society (DPA) and the Medical and Health Department. When methadone maintenance was deemed to be a success, detoxification was introduced in 1976. Unlike maintenance, which aims to keep the patient on methadone indefinitely, detoxification is designed to serve as a short-term method for getting the patient totally off drugs. Patients may choose either maintenance or detoxification, but are generally encouraged to opt for the latter. Currently there are 25 out-patient clinics in Hong Kong operated by the Department of Health.

Conclusions

This chapter has presented a broad overview of drug abuse in Hong Kong. In doing so, several features of drug abuse in Hong Kong emerged. First, and perhaps most importantly, drug abuse in Hong Kong has been, from the very beginning, almost completely confined to the abuse of opiates. This simple fact has shaped legislation in Hong Kong, as well as treatment strategies. A second outstanding feature of drug abuse in Hong Kong is the rapid shift from opium to heroin that occurred in the 1950s. The widespread use of heroin, which is generally more addictive than opium, put considerable strain on Hong Kong's treatment facilities and resulted in some major changes in Hong Kong's approach to the treatment of addiction. Heroin abuse, however, had little impact on restrictive legislation in Hong Kong other than to increase penalties. This brings us to the third point, that because drug abuse has been largely confined to heroin, restrictive legislation in Hong Kong has not had to make the distinction between 'hard' and 'soft' drugs that is found in jurisdictions where there are more varied forms of drug abuse. Fourth, as to the seriousness of Hong Kong's drug problem, about all that can be said is that Hong Kong still has a relatively large number of addicts but the problem does seem to have been contained. Finally, in one way or another, all treatment strategies in Hong Kong are aimed at reducing or eliminating physical dependency on heroin. Other forms of substance abuse receive little or no attention. This state of affairs may change if marijuana or other forms of soft drugs, or indeed other hard drugs such as cocaine and 'crack', begin to spread in Hong Kong.

Notes

1. No. 3 heroin is the most common form of the drug in Hong Kong. It varies in purity but averages 25–30 per cent heroin. No. 4 heroin has a purity of about 75–90 per cent and because of this it is more often used for injections ('mainlining'). No. 4 is much less commonly used in Hong Kong.
2. In 1989, the figure was 19.8 per cent. In 1980, it stood at 27.8 per cent, while in 1976 it had been 47.2 per cent.
3. In 1965, the Action Committee Against Narcotics was established, consisting of representatives from all government departments and organizations directly concerned with narcotics in Hong Kong. The purpose of the Committee was to encourage a greater exchange of ideas and information. The Narcotics Advisory Committee was concurrently reorganized so as to confine itself to major policy matters.

5 Vice

Jon Vagg[1]

The Legislative Council is probably not the best source of information on prostitution. But it provides some interesting insights on how prostitution and vice come to be matters of governmental concern. On 21 November 1984, Legco member Pauline Ng asked a question which is coyly indexed in the Legco proceedings under 'control of commercial signboards'. What progress, she asked, had been made since July of that year on the control and content of commercial signboards? The answer stated that 69 dangerous signboards had been found and removed in Yau Ma Tei and Mong Kok, with action pending on others. It went on to imply that in addition to being safety hazards, most of the signboards were in fact advertisements for vice establishments. The underlying point was that vice establishment signs were being controlled principally through legislation directed at public safety. An exchange between the Attorney General and Jackie Chan on 12 March 1986 covered various points, including 'one-woman brothels' and, again, the nuisance created by vice establishment signs. On 21 October 1986, Maria Tam asked for detailed information on the numbers of missing girls and what action was taken when they were found by the authorities. The Secretary for Security obviously divined the motive for the question when he pointed out that only between 3 and 7 per cent of girls found by the police came to light in the course of 'raids', which we may understand primarily to mean raids on vice establishments.

I have begun this chapter with an account of Legco questions because they illustrate one of the key points I wish to make. Almost no public discussion of vice in Hong Kong passes judgement on any moral aspects of the subject. While some pressure groups argue that vice is undesirable, there is no body of 'influential opinion' in Hong Kong that disapproves of prostitution as such. Disapproval is directed at the ephemeral details, such as signboards, rather than the vice business.

Academics are equally tolerant. Ding (1977) claims it is a social necessity, given attitudes towards female premarital sex and Hong Kong demographic factors, with more males than females of comparable ages until the 60–70 age band. Lethbridge (1978a, 1978b) concludes that it is a viable, if stigmatized, occupation for women with no alternative financial support. More recently, Gronewold (1985) points to a long Chinese tradition of officially-condoned and sometimes officially-sponsored prostitution. Women in the 'commercial sex sector' are not regarded with either sympathy or outrage. On the whole, they are invisible to all but their employers, clients, and the police, since one of the few visible forms of prostitution — streetwalking — is virtually nonexistent.

This tolerance has deep roots. In 1858, the Commissioner of Police accepted that it was unseemly for someone in his position to have a direct interest in vice, and sold his brothels (Crisswell and Watson 1982; Sinclair 1983). In 1877, it was estimated that men outnumbered women by four to one, and that about 75 per cent of all women in the territory were prostitutes (Lethbridge 1978a). Between 1857 and 1941, brothels were licensed and regulated, with intermittent arguments about the propriety of this between the Hong Kong authorities and their London masters (Miners 1987). And during the Vietnam war, with Hong Kong a port of call for American servicemen on 'R and R', prostitution prospered. The American servicemen have long since gone, and Hong Kong is not Bangkok, but the issues are still interesting. I have concentrated on four topics: vice establishments and their signboards; young prostitutes; the 'ownership' of vice; and police powers, objectives, and strategies.

The Scene and the Law

Prostitution per se is not illegal, but virtually every activity connected with it is. Soliciting in a public place for immoral purposes is prohibited by the Crimes Ordinance 1984 (Cap. 200), Section 147. Among other things, trafficking in women, harbouring or exercising control over a woman for the purposes of prostitution, causing prostitution, procuring, living on the earnings of a prostitute, and keeping a vice establishment or permitting or suffering premises or vessels that one owns or rents to be used as such, are all offences (Crimes Ordinance 1984, Sections 129–145). Nonetheless, the absence of the act of prostitution itself from this list of offences means that a sexual and financial transaction between, say, a masseuse and a client in his hotel room discloses no obvious offence.

The current commercial sex scene is rather fragmented, but nonetheless caters to almost every need. There are unlicensed massage parlours, providing a more intimate service than the licensed variety. There are a few 'fishball stalls', in which one sits in the dark, on a high-backed bench seat and facing the high back of the seat in front, with one's hostess. More numerous are the 'villas', small hotels which let rooms by the hour. Some are frankly tacky, while the top end of the market is well appointed, with en-suite showers, television sets tuned in to the hotel's porn video channel, and wall-to-wall mirrors — up-market establishments even provide fresh sheets for each client. The girls do not stay on the premises, but are summoned by phone or pager. Some, if not most, hostess night clubs allow patrons to 'buy out' a hostess for the evening, while some hotels cater exclusively for couples staying only a few hours — without offering to provide company for single men. Brothels as such are rare in Hong Kong, although 'one-woman brothels' exist. They are small rooms — some are cubicles — each with a single girl both living and working in it. 'Private brothels' do exist; they take only clients known to the prostitutes, or recommended by the existing clientele. And finally — and much as in other large cities worldwide — one can find in telephone directories advertisements for escort and massage 'outcall services', many of which offer to 'massage your fantasies', or 'escort you into a world of pleasure'.

Most of the establishments that the police would describe as offering 'walk-in sex' are clustered around Yau Ma Tei and Mong Kok. Wanchai is fast being redeveloped as office space; prostitution is moving away from the area. The same may happen in Mong Kok as and when redevelopment takes place. However, many of the services (for example the 'outcall' services) simply require an office with a telephone and could be based anywhere, though their telephone numbers suggest most are in urban Kowloon or around Causeway Bay and Happy Valley.

Tolerance and Signboards

Mong Kok is a comparatively old, overcrowded, working-class district. Vice activities are only one of several issues in the area; residents are equally bothered by traffic noise and fumes, the lack of open spaces, and other environmental problems. But the prevalence of vice led the Mong Kok District Board to convene, in 1982, a Working Party on Vice-Associated Establishments. Its report noted that the 332 vice establishments at that time (the study excluded 'villas') were contained in 164 of the 1,800 buildings surveyed. Thus, at least 9 per cent of the buildings contained at least one vice establishment, and almost all were in residential or mixed-use blocks. The highest concentration was between Shanghai Street and Nathan Road, in an area of about 100 by 1,000 metres.

The report is, in effect, a scrutiny of the environmental nuisances associated with vice establishments. There is no discussion of whether residents disapproved of vice as such. Perhaps the Working Party was simply realistic about the chances of dislodging it. In any event, those interviewed primarily reported three kinds of problems: disturbance, and security problems resulting from many strangers entering the block; enforcement; and embarrassment resulting from the advertisement of vice establishments both outside the building and in the common entrance. Some of the external advertisements were surprisingly large — it would not be uncommon to see signs seven or eight metres tall.

It is unclear whether residents were genuinely concerned only about outward appearances; whether they were asked about more fundamental objections to vice; or whether they feared retribution arising from more direct complaints. But 86 per cent of persons interviewed (the study does not indicate the total sample size or how the sample was selected) had complained to someone about some aspect of the problem.

The Working Party recommendations included: changes in the legal definition of a 'vice establishment'; enforcing license provisions (most of the premises needed but lacked a license for the services under the cover of which prostitution was practised); better entrance security to residential blocks; and the prosecution of the owners of the signs using provisions in the Obscene Publications Ordinance. But developments only appeared in relation to this last recommendation, which gradually became the major issue. Passing through the hands of the Fight Crime Committee and the government, it gradually mutated into the proposition that the police should have powers to remove signboards advertising vice establishments. This issue constituted one-half of the Crimes (Amendment) Ordinance, which passed into law in 1990.

Although this gave the police powers to remove signs appearing to advertise sexual services, it is too soon to assess how effective these new provisions are in comparison with the previous use of laws relating to dangerous signs, and the impounding of signs as evidence for possible prosecution. For many years, Mong Kok police station has had a vast collection of impounded signs in its car park. It may well be that the owners of establishments take the hint and the signboards disappear, to be replaced by other forms of advertisement. Those seeking sexual services are not so shortsighted that they are unable to find newspaper adverts, stickers in telephone booths, red lights in windows, or any of the other ways in which commercial sex is advertised worldwide. The essential aspects of the vice trade will almost certainly not be affected.

Vice and Policing

Police actions in relation to commercial sex are mainly concentrated on 'walk-in sex'; premises where a client can find sexual services immediately available. Thus unlicensed massage parlours, fishball stalls, and 'villas' which call prostitutes for clients are the primary recipients of police attention. The rationale for this seems to be threefold. First and most obviously, prostitution per se is not illegal. An 'outcall' service supplying escorts is a legal business, while employees who offer sex for money on a private basis commit no obvious offence. The only apparent basis for action would be where the firm can be shown to be negotiating sexual services between its employees and clients. Although the Hong Kong police have much experience in surveillance and 'sting' operations designed to gather such evidence, other aspects of the vice trade are higher on the police agenda. Second, since vice establishments contravene the law, and moreover give rise to complaints by residents (admittedly in relation to their signboards), there is a rationale for action against 'walk-in sex' establishments. And third, such premises are probably easiest to deal with in terms of obtaining convictions.

There are two main ways of policing against vice establishments. One is to conduct covert operations to secure evidence in relation to the various offences mentioned earlier. The other is to harass establishments. Harassment is a dirty word in many countries, but not in Hong Kong. The police use it openly; and journalistic and legal sources use it without any evident undertone of criticism. Harassment can be conducted in various ways. One strategy has been to station constables outside known vice establishments and to conduct ID card checks on persons entering them. The current tactic is to conduct raids, using powers provided in Section 16 of the Protection of Women and Juveniles Ordinance (Cap. 213, last amended 1987). In essence, this section empowers properly authorized police sergeants and more senior officers to enter any place where there is reason to suspect that prostitution is taking place, and to interrogate all persons found there.

The largest proportion of raids take place in Mong Kok, where some 1,500 checks take place each month — 13,253 between January and September 1989, in comparison with about 46,000 in the whole territory for the year (see Table 5.1). In fact, given the number of known establishments and police decisions from time to time to 'blitz' particular kinds of premises (in 1989–90 it was 'fishball stalls'), some places can experience three or four raids each night. Nonetheless, it is apparent from the table that, even with the increase in the number of raids in the last couple of years, arrests and prosecutions are comparatively rare. In fact, since most premises have lookouts or closed circuit television cameras, there is usually warning of a raid and women with clients will be able — albeit hastily — to adjust their clothing and leave their clients (who are commonly discovered in various states of undress).

Table 5.1 Raids, Arrests, and Cases for Prosecution in Relation to Vice Establishments, 1978–1989

Year	No. Raids	No. Arrests	No. Cases for Prosection	All Prostitution Offences
1978	17,971	n/a	n/a	3,085
1979	15,460	n/a	n/a	1,219
1980	12,493	n/a	n/a	974
1981	18,364	n/a	n/a	1,146
1982	16,034	n/a	n/a	1,561
1983	17,058	703	188	973
1984	18,231	364	148	1,154
1985	22,094	651	323	1,091
1986	22,960	714	392	1,297
1987	21,361	516	329	800
1988	46,283	513	336	214
1989	45,638	501	298	n/a

n/a = no figure available.

Source: Royal Hong Kong Police.

But this is not the point of the raids. The process of checking business registration certificates (it is common to see fishball stall certificates stating the premises to be anything from a nightclub to a herbalist), employee records, and employees' and clients' ID cards means that the establishment is 'out of action' for about 20–30 minutes. Clients are told that the premises are suspected of being a vice establishment, and advised to leave. Persons arriving at the door will quickly see the situation and leave. The cash flow of the operation is interrupted, and some clients may decide that the experience of the raid is unpleasant enough to dissuade them from future visits.

These raids would run a clear risk of being declared unlawful if the owners of establishments were to apply for judicial review. Tsang (1982) discusses the case of Lee Yin-ping, in which a check made on a fishball stall was held not to be lawful since the police inspector concerned was unable to demonstrate grounds for believing that prostitution *was* going on. The premises were entered in order to check *whether* it was taking place. In short, in conducting harassment actions, the police rely on the fact that the owners are not often prepared to risk exposure and expense in fighting court actions.

Policing and the Ownership of Vice

It is sometimes said that police action against vice tends to concentrate on the lowest level, the 'cannon fodder', rather than the higher-level organization. This is usually followed by one of two arguments: first, that to be effective in dealing with vice, the 'vice barons' need to be rounded up, or second, that the main problem is not the level of vice but the level of exploitation — the conditions of employment, if you like — within the field. In either case, the conclusion is that the focus of policing needs to be shifted from the streets and the fishball stalls to the 'owners of vice'. Two points can be made in this connection.

First, the income from prostitution in Mong Kok alone is estimated by the police to be around $40 million per month; that is, around 15 per cent of the total monthly expenditure on the whole police force. And 'everybody knows', though evidence is rare, that much of the vice scene is associated with Triads, though they do not necessarily own establishments. Police sources suggest it is more common for establishment owners to buy protection from Triads, by employing junior Triad members directly or putting them on a 'retainer'. Clearly, then, ownership of vice is a complex matter and the funds it generates, though large, need to be split several ways.

If the police know more about the Triads than this (and one assumes they do) they remain tight-lipped about it. The 'official' line is that Triads are little more than street gangs. An alternative view is that the street gangs are simply the lowest and most visible level of comparatively sophisticated organizations, the bosses of which are alleged to be wealthy and influential. It is of course possible that both views are true; the 'bosses' may well not have as much control over their foot-soldiers as they had in the past. But it is quite clear, nonetheless, that one would not need a particularly large or complex organization to operate a vice ring. For example: a vice ring bringing girls from Thailand could operate with only one or two 'talent scouts' there and one or two 'minders' in Hong Kong. Obtaining travel documents, visas, and accommodation in Hong Kong is not labour-intensive. The only other link in the chain — between the 'minders' and the outcall agencies or villas — would simply rely on 'business contacts'. Even allowing that extra employees would be hired to escort the girls from place to place and so on, the core of a viable operation might be a dozen people or fewer, spread across two countries, though many more may be receiving bribes or kickbacks. This is not to say that such vice rings are necessarily small: only that their 'minimum viable size' is by no means large, and the degree of organization necessary well within the capabilities of many gangs.

Second, the Crimes (Amendment) Ordinance 1990 strengthened the hand of the police against a wider range of people who have a relatively tenuous connection with vice. The 'ownership' of the problem, as opposed to the ownership of vice establishments, is being extended. Sections 153a–153I of the Ordinance enable the police to apply to a magistrate for an order to close premises or to seize vessels in relation to which two convictions for keeping a vice establishments, or permitting one to operate, have been secured over a period of between four and 16 months. In principle, the effect should be to deprive landlords of the use of premises and therefore of income if they have operated, or allowed the operation of, a vice establishment on their property. But this sanction may not be extensively applied. Thus far, the police have primarily harassed vice establishments, and only occasionally used existing provisions to charge persons with keeping, managing, or assisting in the management of a vice establishment. Making new powers available in the latter domain does not necessarily imply that police practices will change.

Moreover, the ownership of property in Hong Kong tends to rest in the hands of the relatively well-off, and property companies. We might therefore see — to pick some examples at random — lawyers, university lecturers, or real estate companies finding that their investments in property suddenly lead to court appearances and loss of rental income because sub-letting has resulted in vice establishments being able to rent premises clandestinely. And the picture is likely to be complicated by the multiple ownership of some, typically older, residential blocks; by the extent of sub-letting and the use of management companies to arrange leases; and by the relatively rapid turnover of vice establishments. Figures for Mong Kok, for example, indicate that roughly a quarter of all premises known to the police in January 1989 had closed by October of that year, while a quarter of all those known in October had opened since January (Table 5.2).

Table 5.2 Vice Premises in Mong Kok Known to the Police, January and October 1989

	January 1989	October 1989
Villas	246	276
One-woman brothels	88	89
Unlicensed massage parlours	40	48
Pornographic video shops	33	39
Nightclubs/dance halls	11	13
Fishball stalls	9	9
Escort agencies	8	2
'Lady barber' shops	6	0
Total	441	476

Note: Establishments closing during January–October 1989: 103. Establishments opening during January–October 1989: 129.

Source: Royal Hong Kong Police.

It is too early to say whether these new provisions have led to more effective policing of vice establishments; but if they are effective against 'walk-in sex', they may also lead to more 'private brothels', more extensive use of outcall services, and displacement of the current red light districts to other areas. Such a situation would require even more sophisticated policing; and it could also increase the scope for the employment of underage girls. Private brothels, for example, have a relatively small circle of regular clients and accept new clients only on recommendation from existing ones. They are thus less likely to be discovered and raided, and their owners may therefore feel safer in employing younger prostitutes.

Sympathy for Prostitutes?

One topic is obvious by its omission from the discussion so far. The situation of prostitutes in Hong Kong has been extensively covered in journalism but hardly touched by research. There was a 'consensus figure' of around 12,000 for the number of women engaged in commercial sex in the territory in the late 1970s (Lethbridge 1978b). No more recent estimates seem to be based on anything other than idle speculation. Moreover, any useful figures would need to differentiate between occasional, part-time prostitution and professional, full-time prostitution; between 'transients' and those who work in the business permanently; and between different degrees and styles of sexual services — for example between women working straightforwardly as prostitutes and those working in massage parlours.

But concern about young or underage prostitutes has been voiced intermittently. The claim is that young girls, especially those who run away from home, are vulnerable to sexual exploitation and their chances of a 'respectable' life are blighted by an association with vice. Journalistic reporting suggests that a significant proportion of girls involved in commercial sex are under 16, the legal age of consent, and some are as young as 12 or 13. This is in contrast to the figures presented to Legco as a result of Maria Tam's question, in 1986. They suggested that of the 1,200 or so girls reported missing each year, only 50–100 were discovered in situations indicating their involvement in vice or crime.[2] These accounts would be consistent if many girls are routinely involved on a part-time or occasional basis. And there may have been a recent increase in the involvement of underage girls. Notwithstanding that raids under the Protection of Women and Juveniles Ordinance are primarily aimed at harassment rather than the discovery of juvenile prostitutes, in Mong Kok alone, between January and September 1989, 115 underage girls were found during raids on vice establishments. What is not known, of course, is the extent to which individual girls figure twice or more in this total, or might also be counted in the figures for other police areas. Nor do we know whether the majority of girls are in the business only temporarily.

Current legislation is based implicitly on the idea that young girls are forced into prostitution. However, most sources are agreed that while this happens in many parts of Asia, it is now rare in Hong Kong. The only serious study of young prostitutes (Tang 1977) concludes that underage prostitutes were exposed to the idea by friends (of either sex), tempted by the bait of ready money, and gradually encouraged to move from fondling and masturbation into full-fledged sexual activity. Few girls were (or admitted to being) coerced by boyfriends or street gangs. In short, these girls 'learn Hong Kong's priorities early' and do what is necessary to maximize their income at the first possible moment (Grindrod 1988). Tang suggests that such girls may see prostitution as a rational alternative given their educational abilities and future prospects in manual, clerical, or retail jobs — though they may have regretted that it was a rational alternative. In the absence of better data, perhaps the only conclusion to reach is that pathways into vice are, for a significant proportion of young girls, always available and sufficiently attractive in terms of quick returns, especially when compared with unskilled jobs for school-leavers, to ensure a ready supply of recruits.

Some Ways Forward?

There is no clear public demand for, or constituency of interest in, curbing commercial sex as such. The major criticisms of vice seem to relate to matters of decorum, such as signboards, rather than the nature of the business as such. The main forms of policing recognize this. The police, understandably, address only those aspects of vice on which there is pressure for them to be seen to be 'doing something' — even though what are arguably the core problems remain untouched. The major problems relate to the extent of underage prostitution, the exploitation of the prostitutes, and Triad and organized criminal involvement in the control of the business. None of these problems are open to any easy or quick solutions. In consequence, three points are worth making.

First, more research is needed. What changes have really taken place in the forms of vice in the last 10 years? How many women and girls work in the vice trade, and are they part-time or full-time, transients or permanent workers? How much double-counting is there in the figures for underage girls involved in vice? How far are Triads involved? What trends and shifts can we see in the ways that vice has been policed and what prompted them?

Second, police objectives need to be reviewed. The police could have used their pre-1990 powers to police far inside the boundaries of 'acceptable vice'. But they tended to use a relatively small subset of those powers. The police use some of them, in particular those in the Protection of Women and Juveniles Ordinance, for purposes other than those originally intended, and occasionally use more general powers, such as those relating to ID cards, in a strategic manner to discourage potential clients from entering vice premises. There is a question of what the law should be, but equally urgently there is a question of what police policy objectives on vice should be.

Third, if we take the two main problems to be those of underage girls being exploited, and the ownership of vice, then lines of action do suggest themselves, though they would not necessarily be easy to implement. It is unlikely that the number of young girls prepared to enter the sex trade could be reduced, especially since it is a rational alternative for many. But the recruitment of them could be slimmed down by intensified efforts, using existing legislation, to secure convictions against their employers. Deterrence has two aspects. Little can be done to increase the likelihood of detection, which only leaves the level of sanction as a tool. And while the sex market probably cannot be suppressed by police action, its overall shape is clearly determined by the nature of the policing policies applied to it. Realistically, a change in priorities would probably lead to less intensive policing of other areas. Indeed, providing the 'space' for certain activities — and in these include 'walk-in sex' — is probably an essential part of getting across the message that a line has been drawn and that unacceptable practices will call forth a stricter response.

The 'Triad problem' is only one piece of a more complex picture of organized vice syndicates. The main worry seems to be that the more tightly vice is organized, the more potential there is for organized groups, including Triads, to derive large profits that can be funnelled into large-scale operations such as drug-running, or indeed into legal businesses. There are no real solutions to this. But it would be possible for the police to devote resources to checks on the register of companies. Most vice establishments, whatever other legal provisions they may ignore, are registered as companies. Once one company is identified as a vice establishment, it is a relatively simple matter to trace who owns it (often another company) and what other companies are owned by the same person or persons. These 'company trees' could provide other addresses to be checked as a way of keeping track of who owns what in the field of vice, and as a way of trying to keep the vice market a free market, rather than one dominated by a few large 'firms'.

These proposals hardly amount to a total solution. But it makes more sense for the police to take stock of the situation and act in ways designed to shape and regulate the vice market than it does for them haphazardly to harass individual establishments and to leave other sectors of the market untouched, while claiming that more powers, and this time the 'right' powers, will see sweeping reforms of this or that aspect of vice.

Notes

1. This paper draws heavily on conversations and interviews with police officers, and on time spent accompanying the Mong Kok Special Duties Squads on their raids of vice establishments. The statistics were kindly compiled for me by the Royal Hong Kong Police. I would like to record my thanks to all those in the Royal Hong Kong Police who spent time talking to me both on and off the record, and searching out statistics. Responsibility for any inaccuracies in this paper is mine.

2. Hong Kong Hansard, October 1986, 180.

6 Commercial Crime

MARK S. GAYLORD

HONG KONG'S relatively unfettered market economy has created powerful work and investment incentives for its people. 'Positive non-intervention' is the term used to describe the government's preference for avoidance of what might be called unwarranted interference in the marketplace. By and large, this economic philosophy and the policies it has spawned have been remarkably successful. Yet, for all its benefits, I shall argue that the policy of positive non-intervention has largely contributed to the nature and extent of commercial crime in the colony.

The term 'commercial crime' is not a legal one, nor is it particularly precise. White-collar crime, occupational crime, corporate crime, financial crime, and economic crime are other terms also often used to describe crimes committed by persons typically neither poor nor underprivileged. For the purposes of this chapter I shall borrow Coleman's (1985: 5) definition of white-collar crime as a suitable starting-place: 'A violation of the law committed by a person or group of persons in the course of an otherwise respected and legitimate occupation or financial activity'. Nonetheless, the notion of 'commercial crime' is a convenient shorthand for a range of offences, including bank fraud, various forms of securities fraud, and the fraudulent use of letters of credit. And it is often used by the police, the Legal Department, and the judiciary in precisely this way.

It is argued at times that the term 'commercial crime' in actuality includes actions in violation of civil rather than criminal law, and further that because so many commercial offences are handled by civil courts and regulatory agencies, most of the offenders are not 'real' criminals. In terms of criminal convictions, this is so; but in sociological terms it is of less importance. The clear distinction this argument posits between civil violations and criminal offences simply does not exist. The distinction between torts and criminal offences lies not in the acts themselves, but in the administrative response to them. Many commercial offenders violate both civil and criminal laws, and the decision whether to pursue a case in the civil or criminal court is made largely on extra-legal grounds. Where the illegality does not amount to criminality — as for example in 'insider trading' in Hong Kong after 1978 — there are grounds for taking a broader view than the framework of a single legal system, even while recognizing the implications of specific laws.

There are good reasons for urging that Hong Kong's criminal justice system should pursue a more vigorous policy of prosecution and punishment of commercial criminals. First, more is at stake in the regulation of commercial crime than in the regulation of street crime. In making a similar argument in relation to the US, Cressey (1976: 226) argued that what was at stake in America was democracy, not free enterprise. In Hong Kong, one would have to argue the opposite case: what is at stake here is free enterprise, not democracy, something the people of Hong Kong have never enjoyed. Second, it appears that the business world is a high crime neighbourhood, and the need is great for vigorous policing of it if the general public is to maintain its respect for law.

Hong Kong has been, historically, unwilling to regard as criminal or even illegal many sharp business practices outlawed elsewhere. In a number of respects, Hong Kong law is relatively underdeveloped compared to other advanced industrial nations (Chen 1989b: 43). Moreover, many business practices and indeed the business ethos in the territory leave room for offences to go undetected for long periods. These points will be illustrated in the next three sections of the chapter, on bank fraud, insider trading, and money laundering.

Bank Fraud

Despite Hong Kong's claim to being a major international financial centre, the problems created by its *laissez faire* attitude were clearly revealed in the early and mid-1980s, following the many charges of fraud and malpractice leading to the collapse or near collapse of numerous local banks.

There are two major types of bank fraud. One is perpetrated against banks by customers. The other, referred to by auditors and other accountants as management fraud, is perpetrated by bank management. The latter is a deliberate deception by officials that injures others, typically shareholders, through misleading financial statements (Elliot and Willingham 1980: 4). Illegally obtained income is maintained or augmented by the use of false, and thereby fraudulent, accounting practices. Ironically, the techniques that managers use to commit crime on behalf of banks and other corporations are identical to those used by embezzlers in the commission of crimes against the financial institutions themselves (Cressey 1989: 48).

In 1985, Hong Kong's Overseas Trust Bank (OTB) was pushed to the brink of collapse as a result of both types of fraud. Before it was declared insolvent, OTB was one of the three largest local commercial banks in Hong Kong, with a capital base of $500 million, 120,000 depositors, and 44 branches. The government assumed control of the bank in June of that year and is still nursing it back to financial health. Although the total cost of the rescue has not been made public, it is estimated to have cost taxpayers about $2 billion in the first two years of the bailout alone (Wong 1987). In the immediate aftermath of the government's takeover of OTB, a total of 87 writs claiming repayment of almost $1.2 billion were filed by the bank and its subsidiaries naming 55 companies and 24 individuals. The amounts ranged from several hundred thousand dollars to nearly $100 million. In none of these instances did the loan violate the legal lending restriction covering single borrowers as stipulated in the Banking Ordinance, yet altogether the total exposure represented 80 per cent of shareholders' funds, plus retained profits of the OTB group (Ko 1985).

The OTB's troubles began with a vast 'cheque kiting' scheme devised by Hong Kong businessman Simon Yip Chun-ling, chairman of a local deposit-taking company. Cheque kiting is a way of creating cash flow through bad cheques, and relies on the fact that a cheque drawn on, say, a US bank and paid into a Hong Kong account would be instantly credited although it would take several days for the American account to be debited. If a cheque on the Hong Kong account is presented in the US just before the debit takes place, the US account would appear to have funds to cover the debit even though it would again take several days for that cheque to be cleared. And so on. While the perpetrator maintains the scheme, he has interest-free funds at his disposal, and income is thus generated out of what amount to fictitious bank deposits. Once the stream of cheques ends, banks will not be able to clear the last cheques in the sequence and will be faced with bad debts (Leung 1987).

Between 1979 and early 1982, Simon Yip, as a customer of the OTB, had an arrangement with Huang Tiong-chan, then chairman of OTB, by which OTB would purchase cheques drawn on Yip's companies (Chan 1987). This practice of 'cheque purchasing' or 'cheque discounting' is often provided within limits to valued customers. In theory, such limits existed between Yip and the bank. They were, however, grossly exceeded in 1981 and 1982. At the scheme's peak, daily cheques worth nearly US$10 million were being run through Yip's accounts at OTB. Between September 1981 and March 1982, Yip sold US dollar cheques to OTB at face value, allowing him immediate use of the funds. After their purchase, OTB would then forward the cheques to the US for clearance, a procedure that generally took about six to eight days (Chan 1987). Thus Yip had the benefit of this period (called the 'float') to make use of the funds generated by the earlier sale of the cheques. By using funds received from later cheques, he was able to cover earlier ones. It was the time-lag involved in clearing the cheques through the international banking system that made the scheme feasible.

Yip's scheme came to an end in March 1982, when cheques totalling US$66.8 million were returned to OTB unpaid. In a 1983 attempt to make restitution, Yip pledged approximately US$22 million in properties to the bank, a figure far short of the loss suffered by OTB (Wong 1987). In May 1987, he was ultimately convicted of fraud, along with a senior employee in his firm. After the loss had been exposed, it would have been proper banking practice to recover the amount from the customer or write off the loss in the bank's books of account and records, and charge it against the bank's profits. Moreover, the OTB auditors, government officials, and the public should have been alerted to the bank's precarious financial position, none of which occurred (Chan 1987). Following the failure of Yip's cheque kiting scheme, several of the bank's executives, all of whom were Yip's associates in other business activities, conspired with him to cover up the original fraud. This management fraud, involving the falsification of OTB's financial statements, went undiscovered until the bank was taken over by the government in 1985.

At a meeting in early 1982 between Yip and three OTB executives, managing director Patrick Chang Chen-tsong and general managers Dominic Cheung Kai-man and Chung Chiu-fat, an elaborate cover-up was initiated to disguise the loss. It was decided that Yip should form companies as bogus borrowers and then sign whatever documents were required by the cover-up. The conspirators created 'dummy loans' and advances to various customers in the bank's books through various reverse entries. Bogus loans and advances, totally without commercial substance, were thus used to inflate the bank's profits and to reduce the balances of Yip's companies with the bank (Leung 1987). In the course of the cover-up, numerous documents were prepared with the goal of hiding the loss from the bank's auditors and the Commissioner of Banking.

In early 1985, on the advice of Robert Fell, the Commissioner of Banking, Patrick Chang, OTB managing director, retained Hambros Pacific Ltd to examine OTB's books in the hope that an independent financial adviser would help him restructure the bank. Hambros quickly determined that the bank had more than $2 billion in non-performing loans. On 5 June, Chang was called to a meeting with Fell. The meeting ended with Chang agreeing to declare the bank insolvent (Leung 1987). Later that evening, however, he was arrested at Hong Kong's Kai Tak International Airport as he was about to abscond with US$154,000 in cash and US$1.54 million in securities hidden in his briefcase.

Insider Trading

The Stock Exchange of Hong Kong (SEHK) was for many years untouched by any serious legal regulatory activity. Such laws as existed were enforced in a manner that can only be described as lax and inefficient. Only in the last few years has a Securities and Futures Commission (SFC) been set up to bring order out of a situation which has appeared at times as a financial equivalent of the American Wild West.

One major problem arising from commercial crime has been that of dealing adequately with the practice of insider trading (or 'insider dealing' as it is termed in Hong Kong). This occurs 'when a person connected with a corporation who is in possession of information which he knows is relevant information in relation to that corporation deals in any listed securities of that corporation' (Securities Ordinance 1990). In July 1990, the Hong Kong government enacted new legislation, raising hopes among market regulators that it will prove more useful than the law it replaces. It is too soon to draw conclusions about the new law's effectiveness, but in the meantime we can review previous legislative attempts to deal with this practice within the colony.

Prior to 1978, Section 140 of the Securities Ordinance made insider trading a criminal offence. Violators were liable to a fine of $50,000 and two years' imprisonment. Although Section 140 was never invoked before repeal in 1978, the remedy it provided for was at least clear. The government's reason for introducing regulatory changes in the 1977 Securities Bill, as enunciated by the Financial Secretary to the

Legislative Council, was that these sanctions had been ineffective in preventing insider trading since it was often impossible to obtain evidence sufficient for the courts. Subsequently, Part XIIA of the Securities Ordinance, brought into force in February 1978, replaced and repealed the previous Section 140. Section 141B of the new ordinance, which defined insider trading, described a number of actions ('escape clauses') that would not fall within its meaning. For example, trading when in possession of insider information would not constitute an offence if the trade was made for reasons other than gaining a profit or avoiding a loss. Therefore an insider forced to sell a company's shares in order to settle a pressing debt would not be culpable. Subsection 141C(5) also enabled those accused to improve their prospects of being found not guilty by making prompt disclosure of their trading to the Commissioner of Securities (Chan, P. 1986).

The most prominent feature of Part XIIA of the 1978 Securities Ordinance was the creation of an Insider Dealing Tribunal, which could be established by the Financial Secretary to inquire into a matter of suspected insider trading. The Tribunal would be chaired by a judge of the Supreme Court sitting with two members appointed by the Governor. Its terms of reference included determining (1) whether insider trading had taken place; (2) the identity of the persons involved; and (3) the extent of culpability. Unlike the old Section 140, however, the new law contained no criminal sanctions. While this change was made for the pragmatic reason that the previous law could not be enforced, its lack of sanctions left the government virtually powerless to have any substantive impact on would-be insider traders.

From, 1976 to 1990 there were four official investigations into insider trading. The first, in 1976, involved allegations that certain major shareholders in Wheelock Marden were dumping shares in advance of disappointing results. A four-month inquiry by the Insider Dealing Tribunal concluded that insider trading had occurred but 'did not constitute an offence under the existing provisions of the Securities Ordinance'. The second case, in September 1979, involved a probe into the acquisition by Cheung Kong Holdings of 90 million shares of Hutchison from Hongkong Bank (Lai 1989). The third case implicated Li Ka-shing, one of Hong Kong's leading businessmen. The Tribunal found Li responsible for share dealings that enabled a subsidiary of his firm, Cheung Kong Holdings (CKH), to profit from important unpublished details concerning a 1984 property transaction on behalf of a CKH associate, International City Holdings. The fourth case dealt with insider trading in relation to Lafe Holdings Ltd. shares between March and May 1989, and found that Clifford Pang Lun-kee, principal shareholder, chairman, and managing director of the company, 'was involved in such insider trading' (Perkin 1990). In the three most recent cases, despite the fact that millions of dollars were gained from the transactions, the Tribunal's sanctions were restricted merely to public reprimand.[1]

The closing of the SEHK for four days in October 1987 following the near free-fall on the New York Stock Exchange, eventually persuaded the Hong Kong Government and a new team of stock exchange officials to confront the market manipulation, insider trading, and abuse of minority shareholders then prevailing. One outcome has been a new SEHK regulation requiring disclosure of substantial shareholdings (currently 10 per cent) in listed public companies, including nominee shareholdings. This measure greatly eases the task of detecting insider trading and 'creeping takeovers' (Rowley 1987).

The most significant measure to date, however, has been the adoption, in July 1990, of the Securities (Insider Dealing) Ordinance. This law makes it the duty of corporate officers 'to take all such measures . . . for the purpose of ensuring that proper safeguards exist to prevent the corporation from perpetrating any act which is an insider dealing' (Section 9). Just as with the 1978 law, however, an Insider Dealer Tribunal, rather than a criminal court, is empowered to inquire into suspected cases if requested by the Financial Secretary. Any person 'identified' by the Tribunal as an insider trader is subject to fines (up to three times the amount of any profit gained) and banishment from corporate office for up to five years. Yet, just as with the law it has replaced, the new legislation stops short of designating insider trading as a crime.

While the need for a new legal framework may be clear to many observers, there is no consensus within the business community that new laws are necessary or desirable, or that the 1990 Ordinance will prove effective. First, according to political analyst Tsim Tak-lung, local attitudes towards corruption and fraud are blasé:

> More regulation won't matter . . . incidents of corruption will be on the increase [between now and 1997] and incidents of prosecution will decrease . . . because Chinese society is full of double standards (quoted in Bociurkiw 1990).

Second, there is an apparent difference of attitude between the SFC and many local businessmen, some of whom have accused the SFC of imposing 'foreign ways of thinking and doing business' on a market that has developed its own unique ways of operating. One is reported as saying that 'a lot of this protective investment stuff is overdone for Hong Kong . . . the people who have come in really have little sensitivity to the local scene and have little stake in it' (quoted in Bociurkiw 1990). What is needed, say critics, is a recognition that in Hong Kong there is a greater willingness to accept a financial system that is comparatively loosely regulated and thus presents higher risks for investment, but can also promise large rewards. And in late 1989, the convenor of the Legislative Council's *ad hoc* group on the Securities (Insider Dealing) Bill spoke out against what he called the 'wholesale introduction' of legislation from other financial centres without 'proper recognition of the uniqueness of the Hong Kong market' (Yumol 1989).

Third, unlike other major markets, leading shareholders in limited companies in Hong Kong also are often involved in company management. It has long been held that it goes 'against the cultural grain of the local Chinese community to have shareholdings and trading made public, especially as the proprietors of public companies, and their families, usually remain the largest shareholders and wheel-and-deal on a large scale' (Rowley 1987). Hong Kong has traditionally been considered the 'Switzerland of Asia' in preserving confidentiality in banking and share trading. In a market where local companies are tightly held by controlling families, one effect will be that these families will trade their own shares with institutional investors to maintain liquidity in the stock. The potential threat of being accused of insider trading when no such thing was intended could have a chilling effect on the beneficial activities of so-called market-makers who provide the SEHK such desired liquidity. Some brokers argue that controlling families were buying into the crash that followed 4 June 1989, while small local investors and the overseas fund managers ran for cover (Winn 1989).

Some have claimed that international fund managers are far more interested in seeing the local market maintain its liquidity than in seeing the establishment of a 'well-regulated' exchange. In this respect, many overseas institutions will not buy into a family-controlled firm prior to the announcement of company results unless the family is itself accumulating shares. This scenario makes it extremely difficult for authorities to prove that parties are acting on inside information. Special pleadings notwithstanding, it is clear that the SEHK cannot remain aloof from similar insider trading provisions that now govern trading in shares throughout the world's major stock markets if it is to maintain its present position in the region in the future.

Money Laundering

In Hong Kong it is often declared, and as frequently denied, that money is routinely laundered by its financial institutions. Anyone with large amounts of ill-gotten gains, in order to make it appear that the money originated from legitimate sources, is forced to launder it as a precaution against detection and in order to invest the funds openly in countries with strong financial regulatory frameworks, such as the US. Among the main customers for 'money laundries', of course, are drug traffickers.

There is almost no direct evidence of drug money being laundered in Hong Kong. Most of the evidence that does exist is circumstantial and originates from the US. It is true that recent legislative changes in Hong Kong have enabled law enforcement agencies to seize assets worth several hundred million Hong Kong dollars, alleging them to be the proceeds of drug trafficking. (This is discussed further in the next section.) But for the moment I shall concentrate on a review of what appear to have been the golden years of Hong Kong money laundering, 1982–4.

There are two primary strategies for laundering money. In the first, two companies — often 'shell' companies — are set up. One will be in the country where the money will arrive, and the other in a jurisdiction with strong bank secrecy laws. The first company sells goods or services, perhaps fictitious ones, to the second. The second, in the country with the weaker financial regulatory framework, pays for them, often at an inflated rate, with the drug trafficking proceeds. The money thus appears as the profit of a legal business, complete with corresponding invoices. Alternatively, once the money is in the country with weak financial controls it can be used as security for a loan to the firm in the 'source country'. Many variations on this theme are possible (Bartlett and Wallace 1985, US Department of Justice 1983). In the second strategy, the money is transformed into freely convertible goods — gold, jewellry, casino chips, and so on — or into the informal banking sector, where few or no records are kept. Such an 'underground' banking system exists across the whole of Southeast Asia (Lee, Course, and Ng 1988). It operates through gold shops, trading companies, and money changers. Many transactions are run across several countries through individual families. Coded messages, chits, and telephone calls are sufficient to transfer money speedily throughout the system (Liu and Eads 1985). For example, Hong Kong police once seized a document on which was a design of an elephant, alleged to be a collection receipt for $3 million. Penetrating this kind of network requires a degree of sophistication in handling information, and US sources in the mid-1980s were critical of Hong Kong police abilities in this regard (US Department of Justice 1983).

In this scenario, Hong Kong could have been a convenient location for money laundering, since in the early 1980s Hong Kong law declared certain records held by financial institutions, generally describing ownership or control of accounts, to be confidential. Civil and criminal sanctions could be applied for breaches of confidentiality. Although the ICAC had some powers to force disclosure, this was solely in relation to investigations of corruption. In addition, a 'blocking statute' prohibited residents from many forms of cooperation with foreign investigators, including compliance with foreign court orders. Despite exceptions, foreign law enforcement agents were at a severe disadvantage when trying to obtain evidence in relation to international financial transactions.

The aggressive nature of the money markets must also be borne in mind. An American banker, based in Hong Kong, has remarked: 'For banking, Hong Kong is a wild and woolly place. Banking here is very, very competitive. It's tough. There are banks here that are apparently willing to play fast and loose with credit, and even with the law' (quoted in Mann 1985). In such a competitive market, even banks with high professional standards seemed to be reasonably comfortable in the stance that large cash deposits were simply 'black'—untaxed or from the 'underground economy'—rather than 'dirty'. As the managing director of a prominent bank put it: 'It's not our business to inquire into our client's morals' (quoted in Liu and Eads 1985).

In this situation, most of the evidence of money laundering in Hong Kong has been circumstantial. Nonetheless it convinced American authorities of wrongdoing. In 1984, the US President's Commission on Organized Crime requested the Treasury Department to analyze US data on financial transactions with Hong Kong. The analysis displayed US dollars accumulating in Hong Kong in inordinate amounts. One US financial institution in Hong Kong had handled approximately US$700 million in US currency in 1982, more than US$1 billion in 1983, and more than US$600 million in the first half of 1984. Almost all was in US$100 notes or smaller bills. About half of this money was returned to the US in exchange for higher-denomination bills. Most of the balance was shipped to countries with strong bank secrecy laws, such as Switzerland. To see these figures in proper perspective, consider that the volume of small-denomination bills handled in Hong Kong was greater than the total volume of US currency transactions between the US and any European country. Moreover, the amount of US dollars shipped to the US in exchange for larger bills had grown tenfold between 1980 and 1984. The President's Commission noted that between 1982 and 1984 this increase correlated with the amounts of South-east Asian heroin marketed in the US. And it was aware that drug syndicates typically laundered money by depositing cash in small bills in overseas banks (Karchmer 1985), then transferring the funds back to the US. Overseas banks, left with huge stocks of small denomination bills, shipped them to the US in exchange for larger bills (Koepp 1985). This was exactly the pattern observed in relation to Hong Kong.

Alternative explanations for such a pattern have not been slow in coming, often from Hong Kong bankers and government officials. Mann (1985) lists them. First, negotiations on the future of the colony were taking place during these years. The climate of uncertainty led to the flight of capital from Hong Kong. Second, between 1980 and 1983, the Hong Kong dollar fell from about $5.13 to $7.78 to the US dollar (it was only in October 1983 that a fixed exchange rate was established). Many investors moved into US dollar savings. In early 1982, about 17 per cent of all bank deposits in Hong Kong were US dollar accounts. By 1984 the figure had risen to almost 50 per cent. Third, much of the US dollar volume was 'passing through' the territory because of the convenience and efficiency of its financial remittance services; or comprised 'offshore' deposits by investors living in less certain economic regimes.

Each of these enumerated points undoubtedly carried some weight. But it is unnecessary to pick one or other explanation. All of them—including, of course, the money laundering—could contribute to the total picture. But US agencies were not swayed by alternative accounts. In August 1985, the US Treasury Department fined California's Crocker National Bank a record US$2.5 million for violating the US Bank Secrecy Act by failing to report large cash transactions totalling US$3.89 billion during the previous five years. Nearly all the money came from six Hong Kong banks. Crocker's general counsel claimed that there had been 'mistakes in interpreting and implementing' Bank Secrecy Act regulations. The US Assistant Secretary of the Treasury, however, stated that Crocker had 'deprived the Treasury of potentially important law-enforcement leads that could have been useful in drug, tax, money laundering, and other investigations'—thereby implying that the bank had been involved in money laundering and, in effect, also accusing the Hong Kong banks. Crocker Bank officials declared themselves 'outraged' at the accusation (Kaplan, Goldberg, and Jue 1986, Mann 1985). Hong Kong bankers and officials, too, complained that it was baseless: as indeed it was, because Hong Kong bank secrecy laws would have prevented the gathering of evidence to confirm or refute the allegation. It was only as late as 1987 that serious discussions with US officials were begun on the question of how to address the money-laundering problem. And even at that point, a key barrier to progress seems to have been the fear that banking business could be lost to neighbours if the policy of bank secrecy was undermined (Mulcahy 1987).

However, after years of denying that money laundering was occurring, Hong Kong's government has finally begun to acknowledge the obvious. In 1989, police estimated that $6 million in drug money was being laundered in Hong Kong each day (Hewett 1990). That same year, a 30-man special unit, the Narcotics Bureau's Financial Investigations Group (FIG), was established to enforce a significant piece of new legislation, the Drug Trafficking (Recovery of Proceeds) Ordinance 1989.[2] As of April 1990, $375 million of alleged drug money had been seized by the Narcotics Bureau pending the trial of persons charged with trafficking offences. Under the new legislation, assets may be confiscated by the courts following a criminal conviction and a civil proceeding in which the government has won the right of confiscation.

Bank secrecy is not now so strict. The law requires financial institutions under restraining orders to cooperate with the authorities. Inaction can lead an institution to be held in contempt of court, and individuals involved may face criminal charges. As a result, banks and other financial institutions have appointed 'compliance officers' whose job it is to detect and report suspected drug proceeds. Some trust companies now demand bank and character references of new clients, along with financial histories (Hewett 1990). Under the Ordinance, much of the burden of enforcement has been passed on to the banks since they are now liable themselves if they can be shown to have handled drug money, even if unwittingly.

Conclusions

In the past decade, Hong Kong has been struggling to cope with a sharp rise in increasingly complex commercial crime investigations.

Its commercial crime problem is, ironically, largely a product of the colony's recent economic success. Beginning in the mid-1970s, Hong Kong began to develop its financial sector in an attempt to reduce over-reliance on industry. By 1980, it had become Asia's leading financial centre. But as commercial interests have grown rapidly in sophistication, the development and enforcement of business-related laws have lagged behind.

Since the mid-1980s, Hong Kong has tried to dispel its reputation as an easy venue in which to amass huge sums of money, but a less than completely safe place for investment. Nonetheless, after decades of cultivating a *laissez faire* image, Hong Kong faces an uphill battle in its fight to eliminate commercial crime (Wong 1986). Perhaps ironically, major frauds such as the OTB case came to light only because of the sudden economic downturn in the early 1980s, resulting in the collapse of many companies and the ensuing scrutiny of their financial situation by government agencies. It may well be that despite increased regulation, the colony's recent prosperity has enabled other frauds to remain concealed. Moreover, a local think tank, Political and Economic Risk Consultancy, has predicted a rise in commercial crime in the run-up to 1997, as corrupt businessmen try to make as much money as they can before the colony reverts to Chinese sovereignty. It remains to be seen whether the new laws and criminal justice agencies can be effective against crimes in which, ultimately, the rich are robbing the poor.

Notes

1. In Britain, an insider trading law has been on the books since 1980, but there have been few notable prosecutions. Of 27 defendants brought to court, only 12 have been found guilty, and most of these have been given suspended jail sentences or fines of under $40,000.

2. While the Hong Kong government may have wished to jump on this particular bandwagon, they almost certainly were also dragged onto it. There have been a number of international instruments in relation to drug smuggling and money laundering, including the United Nations Convention Against Illicit Traffic in Narcotic Drugs and Psychotropic Substances (1988), to which the UK is a signatory. In addition, a number of other international groups have discussed such problems, including the 'Trevi Group', membership of which comprises the ministers of justice of various European countries, including the UK Home Secretary. In addition, a Financial Action Task Force was set up in 1989 to address the problem, under the auspices of the European Commission. Again, the UK is a member (and the US is also represented). In short, the Hong Kong government must have been under some pressure from the UK to come into line with the thinking of international governmental groups on this issue.

7 Illegal Immigration and Cross-border Crime

JON VAGG

THE YEAR 1990 was an interesting one for law and order issues. There were numerous smuggling incidents, one of which led to the death of a police officer in Tolo Harbour, when his boat was rammed by smugglers. Earlier in the year, Hong Kong police and seamen had been temporarily detained by Chinese authorities, seemingly in the course of a 'sting' operation against car smugglers, an issue which led to a series of recriminations about where exactly the arrest had taken place, and allegations of corrupt Chinese officials. In the spring and summer, there were numerous armed robberies of banks and jewellers' shops; these came amid reports of increased numbers of guns being smuggled from China into Hong Kong, and claims that some of the robberies were being carried out by mainland Chinese who then slipped back across the border to evade arrest. Meanwhile, there was continuing concern about the number of mainlanders who appeared to be coming across the border into Hong Kong to seek work, and new measures were taken to counter illegal immigration.[1]

These three types of offences — smuggling, armed robbery, and illegal immigration — are so different that they can hardly be mentioned in the same breath. But in looking at the way they have developed in Hong Kong, it is clear that they spring from common factors.

First, Hong Kong and China could hardly be more different in terms of their economies and social structures. Hong Kong has a prosperous economy founded upon entrepot trade; and despite occasional lapses, it has a largely effective law enforcement system. China has a developing and still largely rural economy; it has experienced massive migration from rural to urban areas which it has apparently been powerless to stop; and its creaking law enforcement apparatus not only has to contend with high levels of crime, but also appears to suffer high levels of corruption. These differences in themselves provide the motivation and perhaps in some cases the opportunity for mainland Chinese to seek work in Hong Kong, legally or illegally; and indeed for mainland criminals to target Hong Kong, with its comparatively rich pickings.

Second, there is of course a border between the nation and the territory; not only a physical border, but also a set of customs regulations and duties intended, among other things, to protect the Chinese economy (though not that of Hong Kong, which is still largely a free port) and to enable governments on both sides to obtain revenue from international trade. Nonetheless, there is demand in China for many Western goods and demand in Hong Kong for certain Chinese products; and this demand, coupled with the level of the Chinese duties in particular on cigarettes, televisions, and videos, make the smuggling of such items a rather profitable exercise.

The next three sections of the chapter each look at one of the problems — smuggling, armed robbery, and illegal immigration — and the ways in which they are policed. The fourth and last section draws some lessons for the future of cross-border crime and law enforcement. Much of the information presented below comes from the scrutiny of public sources. However some was gathered in interviews with police and customs and excise officers, and I shall cite their perceptions freely and without attributing them to individuals.

Smuggling

Everything from gold to cuddly toys, from watches to cows, have attracted the attention of smugglers (Green 1972). In the last few years in Hong Kong, the range of goods involved has not been quite so diverse. Nonetheless, it has included videos and video cassettes, televisions, cigarettes, and stolen cars from Hong Kong to China, and herbs and antiques in the reverse direction. Mention of herbs in this connection can easily be explained by Chinese export controls, coupled with high demand in Hong Kong for traditional medicinal herbs, and the extraordinarily high prices commanded by some varieties. And this is not to mention the trade in guns and drugs, which allegedly operates through different networks to those used in the consumer goods trade. The reasons why particular individuals become involved in smuggling are under-theorized; the slight academic literature on this topic merely suggests that it is either a matter of economic need (for example on the part of the drug carriers), or of personal connections and opportunities (Adler 1985). However, a consideration of motives need not detain us here. The reason for the smuggling trade, as opposed to the motives of those involved, is quite clear.

In Hong Kong, videos and televisions are plentiful and relatively cheap. However, in 1990 the Chinese authorities were levying import duties equivalent to, for example, $2,666 on a 21-inch screen television, up to $10,000 for a 33-inch screen model; 150 per cent of the price on video recorders; and about $1,500 on a case of Western cigarettes (a case contains 50 200-cigarette cartons).[2] The ability to evade a tariff barrier of this scale is virtually a cast-iron guarantee of profit, even bearing in mind the costs — transport, payoffs, and so on — that would have been necessary. What is less clear is who was making how much profit out of the trade. But the profits must be considerable, since the sheer scale of smuggling indicated the presence of a fairly large distribution and sales operation in China. On the Hong Kong side, since payment for goods was usually in the form of medicinal herbs and antiques, there would also have had to be an extensive 'fencing' operation. Unquestionably, many more people than those actually transporting the goods were making money on the trade.

Bearing in mind Hong Kong's free port status, the significant offence involved (until the summer of 1990) was the rather technical-sounding one of carrying an unmanifested cargo into or out of the territory. Boats and vehicles carrying goods across Hong Kong borders are required also to carry a piece of paper listing the goods on board, where they came from, and their destination (Import and Export Ordinance 1986, Section 17, and subsidiary regulations). This offence in fact carries a severe penalty — a fine of $50,000 and up to two years imprisonment. In addition, it is also an offence to alter a vessel or vehicle to provide a disguised compartment or hiding-place, irrespective of whether the hiding place is actually in use at the time it is discovered.

The situation seen from the perspective of the Chinese authorities is of a wholly different order. A press release from the Xinhua News Agency in Beijing on 5 September 1990[3] asserted that smuggling posed a serious threat to the Chinese economy. It pointed out that of all the cigarettes entering the country in 1989, an estimated 84 per cent had been smuggled in; that in Guangdong province, comparing the first half of 1990 with the same period in 1989, known offences of smuggling had almost doubled; and that the problem was widespread, affecting almost all coastal and inland border provinces. Indeed an earlier report from the Hong Kong journal *Chiushih Nientai*[4] alleged that smuggling networks had become quite sophisticated, with some high-profit items being resold to north-western provinces and even ultimately into the Soviet Union.

At this point, we should turn to the actual mechanics of smuggling and the problems of law enforcement. Goods were being taken by lorry across the land border crossings, and by boat from Tolo Harbour, Tai O, and Tap Shek Kok across either Deep Bay or Mirs Bay. In early 1990, much of the seaborne smuggling was being done in speedboats, often fitted with reinforced hulls and several outboard engines capable of taking them to a maximum speed of about 70 knots — more than sufficient to outrun police and customs vessels.

The legal enforcement problems should not be understated. If intercepted in Hong Kong waters, boat crews could, unless they were rather unlucky, credibly claim that they were delivering the items to another point in Hong Kong. Or alternatively, they could make out a manifest which would simply be thrown away once outside territorial waters. Only if they were carrying cigarettes and clearly heading into Chinese waters would they have been in real trouble if stopped by the Hong Kong authorities, since they would also have needed an export license. At the land crossings, however, the situation was slightly different. While the speedboats relied on power rather than concealment to evade the law, smuggling by lorry relied on, for example, false compartments in containers and in fuel tanks, false fuel tanks, or simply mislabelled boxes in among the legal cargo. Although probably fewer than 5 per cent of vehicles are physically inspected, where goods are found legal action is more certain. Drivers at the border crossing cannot, unlike their seagoing colleagues, pretend to be travelling within Hong Kong, and moreover the presence of a deliberately-constructed hiding-place is itself an offence. Nonetheless, Customs and Excise statistics indicate that in 1989 and 1990 more detections and arrests were made for seaborne than land-based smuggling.

By mid-1990 the smuggling problem had taken on a new aspect. Smuggling of consumer items (unlike, for example, drug smuggling) had not been seen as a major issue by Hong Kong authorities. But opinions changed rapidly after the death of a policeman in Tolo Harbour in June. It appeared that speedboats used for smuggling were not only reinforced (subsequent seizures of boats revealed some had armour-plated crew compartments and bulletproof windshields) but that smugglers were prepared to ram and sink police pursuit dinghies in order to evade capture. This raising of the stakes was quickly addressed by new legal measures. Within a matter of days, two new regulations were promulgated, under the provisions of the Import and Export Ordinance, Section 31. The first, relating to speedboats, had four parts: speedboats were limited to a total engine capacity of no more than 600 horsepower, and a total fuel load of no more than 180 gallons; they were prohibited from operating between sunset and sunrise; and they were no longer allowed to carry more than 200 cigarettes and/or one television or video. The second regulation, relating specifically to televisions and videos, prohibited the export of such items on vessels of less than 250 tons unless a license had been obtained from the Director of Trade. And although the maximum prison term on conviction remained two years, the maximum fine was 10 times higher, at $500,000.

Table 7.1 Customs and Excise Smuggling Cases, 1989–1990

	Detected Incidents	Arrests
Jan–Dec 1989		
Land imports	9	10
Sea imports	21	25
Land exports	35	51
Sea exports	113	169
1 Jan–8 July 1990		
Land imports	14	20
Sea imports	5	9
Land exports	13	15
Sea exports	72	99

Source: Hong Kong Customs and Excise Department, personal communication.

These two regulations had the immediate effect of ensuring that any speedboat operating at night and carrying a cargo of televisions, videos, or cigarettes could reasonably be assumed to be involved in smuggling. It also ensured that smuggling had to be done rather more secretly than hitherto, because any speedboat moored in a Hong Kong harbour and appearing to have several large engines was vulnerable to investigation. What the regulations did not stop, of course, was the smuggling. For one thing, unofficial Customs and Excise estimates were that of around 300 such speedboats operating, only about 60 were Hong Kong-based; the remainder operated, legally or otherwise, out of China. And for another, since smugglers were already breaking the more stringent Chinese laws, which carried extremely harsh penalties, presumably they would not baulk at breaking a few new regulations on the Hong Kong side.

What was happening on the Chinese side and in terms of Hong Kong-Chinese co-operation? First, the Chinese authorities had for some time been seeking to crack down on corruption and serious crime generally; smuggling was only one part of the picture. Indeed, in July 1990, a customs official was executed in Shenzen for accepting bribes from smugglers totalling 464,000 yuan ($578,000) during 1987.[5] Second, the main issue between the two sides — the Chinese treatment of the Hong Kong seamen in the May 'sting' operation that went wrong and the confiscation of the three cars involved — was resolved in July, at a two-day meeting of security and police officials. The three cars were returned and the seamen offered an unspecified amount of compensation for their detention. In addition, information was exchanged on matters including illegal immigrants, smuggling, and gun smuggling in particular.[6] Third, in August 1990, authorities in Guangdong and some other coastal provinces adopted stricter measures on licensing vessels, and speed restrictions on motorboats. Simultaneously, it was announced that stronger enforcement efforts had been made.[7]

Nonetheless, the use of speedboats has not been suppressed. Press reports in November and December 1990 indicated that even items such as stolen cars were still being taken into China by speedboat, and that many smugglers had simply changed their bases and routes to avoid interception (*South China Morning Post*, 29 November and 8 December 1990). Smugglers appear to have adapted to the new conditions. Reports were being received in Hong Kong within a few weeks of that smuggled goods were reaching China by a less obvious route, which required a little more care over the paperwork. Televisions were loaded as manifested goods onto large cargo vessels and dispatched over the side and onto speedboats outside Hong Kong waters. The manifest would be altered, or some other subterfuge employed; and it is not clear how payment for the goods was made. But the lure of quick profit is often a spur to ingenuity, and it seems unlikely that smuggling will be suppressed in the near future.

Armed Robbery

The first few months of 1990 saw a dramatic increase in the number of incidents — mainly armed robberies — involving firearms. Table 7.2 gives data on incidents between 1980 and April 1990 where firearms and 'pistol-like objects' were in evidence. In reading this table, it should be borne in mind that if an offender produces what is apparently a gun, it is recorded merely as a 'pistol-like object' (or

'PLO') unless there is supporting evidence that it is not a fake — for example, if it is fired, or if the police are able to arrest the offender and examine it. The table suggests that although there was an increase in the use of guns and PLOs through 1984, the following year saw a marked reduction, though year-on-year increases have been recorded since then. The sharp rise in 1990 is also quite clear. In addition, the proportion of weapons confirmed to be real has gradually risen, and in addition the police perception is that although in 1980 the majority of PLOs were fakes or starting pistols, by 1990 the majority were probably real guns. Some press reports in early 1990 suggested that a few armed robbers were also carrying what appeared to be grenades.

Table 7.2 Firearms Incidents, 1980–1990[1]

Year	Firearms Incidents	'Pistol-like Object' Incidents	Total	Index (1980 = 100	Percentage Involving Firearms
1980	33	173	206	100	16
1981	53	230	283	437	19
1982	59	240	299	145	20
1983	62	280	342	166	18
1984	49	284	333	162	15
1985	38	143	181	88	21
1986	34	125	159	77	21
1987	40	140	180	87	22
1988	65	179	244	118	27
1989	85	238	323	157	26
1990 Jan–Apr	31	134	165	240*	23

*Estimated; based on four months' figures.

Note: CIB uses different 'counting rules' for firearms and PLOs than does the ballistics bureau, which creates the force statistics for this area. Thus the figures in this table may not tally precisely with those previously published by the RHKP.

Source: Royal Hong Kong Police, Criminal Investigation Bureau.

Prior to 1987, a variety of handguns of different types and calibres appeared to be in use — or at least were being seized by the police in operations. Since 1988, however, the predominant weapon has been the Chinese-style 'T54', the standard People's Liberation Army handgun. And most have almost certainly arrived in Hong Kong from China. Who was using them? In 1988 and 1989, it seemed as though there were a number of mainland Chinese entering Hong Kong, committing armed robberies, and then slipping back across the border. This may still be the case, though the arrest in September 1990, in China, of two mainlanders on charges of committing robberies in Hong Kong may have given others so inclined pause for thought. In this case, the authorities appeared to promise even before the trial that they would be executed. By early 1990, the weapons had become so widely available that the majority of detected offenders were in fact from Hong Kong.

The sources of Hong Kong's sudden spate of armed robberies lie in the wider crime problem across the border. It is virtually impossible to obtain accurate data on crime in China, but accounts from a number of published sources indicate that serious and violent crime has risen dramatically across China in recent years. The Chinese Vice Minister of Public Security, Yu Lei, stated in May 1990 that crime reports had risen 138 per cent, and serious crime had doubled, compared with the previous year.[8] It is unclear which previous year—1988 or 1989—he was referring to. Nor is it clear whether the 138 per cent was the rise (i.e. crime more than doubled) or an index figure (i.e. crime rose by about one-third). In addition, the various figures for arrests are difficult to interpret because of a tendency to have crackdowns and campaigns; it is unclear whether arrest figures reflect actual crime levels or simply a process of 'rounding up all the usual suspects'. For example, a Guangdong anti-crime campaign in the first half of 1990 resulted in some 12,000 arrests and 11,000 prosecutions, but the authorities provided no indication of the time-frame within which offences were alleged to have been committed and very little as to the kinds of crimes involved — though 6,400 prosecutions were said to have been for 'serious crimes undermining social order and endangering lives and property'.[9]

But whatever the problems with the numbers, it is fairly clear from reports of specific crimes and detections that a large number of serious offences are being committed. The Hong Kong *Chiushih Nientai* (1 May 1990) and the Chinese *Renmin Gongan Bao* (20 July 1990) both contain examples of recent serious crimes which, they suggest, are now common.[10] The former mentions robberies with knives, including one case in which the victim was knocked unconscious and strangled. The latter mentions theft from public facilities and a variety of public order offences, describing the situation as 'chaotic'. Both refer to theft and looting from railway trains, in which gangs have invaded trains and systematically robbed the passengers; and this is in addition to reports of barricades being erected on the tracks and cargos looted, and of corruption among railway staff up to and including the Ministry of Railways directorate.[11]

Moreover, it also seems that the use of weapons — mainly knives, but also guns — has become common. There have been attempts in Guangdong to reduce the number of weapons in circulation, and a series of successful police operations against armed gangs and gun smugglers. For example in June 1990, Guangzhou Guangdong Provincial Radio reported that Shantou City police had 'smashed 28 criminal organizations, arrested 284 criminals . . . and captured 42 guns and 118 knives and daggers' in a three-month period. And in August, it reported the detention of a gun smuggler in Guangzhou and the seizure of four military pistols.[12] Nor has Guangdong been immune from the kind of robberies seen in Hong Kong: in July 1990, it was reported that three offenders who had carried out an armed robbery in the centre of Guangzhou had been executed.[13]

There seem to be two reasonably sensible conclusions to draw from the material above. First, we need to reverse the old saying that 'when China sneezes, Hong Kong catches a cold'. In this case, China has an acute dose of influenza; fortunately, Hong Kong has only sneezed. Second, guns have been in wide circulation in China in recent years, and the authorities have only recently begun to attempt seriously to control their availability. Many guns have been smuggled into Hong Kong, where despite what amounted to an oversupply and a consequent drop in price in early 1990, they presumably fetched higher prices than they would have done on the mainland. The drop in price, meanwhile, probably meant that guns became affordable to 'amateurs' who in previous years would have considered it too complex, too expensive, and too risky to 'tool up', and who would not therefore have been in the market for armed robberies.

Illegal Immigration

People do not only smuggle things across the border; they also, sometimes, smuggle themselves or other people. Yet the idea that illegal immigration constitutes a problem for Hong Kong is of comparatively recent origin. Historically, there has been very substantial migration back and forth across the China-Hong Kong border, especially at times of crisis — into China at the time of World War II, back to Hong Kong after the People's Republic was declared in 1949, and a further influx at the time of the Cultural Revolution. Attempts on the Hong Kong side to regulate the flow were only seriously begun in 1938, when an immigration department was set up, though clearly the police and the administration monitored the situation and exercised some controls prior to that time, in particular in relation to 'undesirables' and politically controversial characters. Attempts on the Chinese side to control emigration only started after the establishment of the Communist regime, and since those arriving in Hong Kong are only a small proportion of those making the attempt, the task must have been (and must still be) immense, despite the occasional deliberate lapses, as in 1962—a year of famine in China—when Chinese border guards in effect threw open the border and allowed some 70,000 persons to make the crossing (Hughes 1968).

Table 7.3 Levels of Illegal Immigration from Mainland China

Year	Arrested and Repatriated (average per day)
1975	3.7
1976	2.2
1977	4.9
1978	22.5
1979	246
1980	265[1]
('touch base' policy abandoned Oct. 1980)	
1981	26
1982	29
1983	21
1984	34
1985	44
1986	56
1987	73
1988	57[2]
(introduction of prosecution/imprisonment of IIs found working in Hong Kong, May 1988)	
1989	43[3]

Notes: 1. The average for the month of September 1980 was 450 per day. The average for the months of November and December 1980 (after the 'touch base' policy was abandoned) was 25 per day.
2. The average for the month of April 1988 was 104 per day.
3. Arrested but may have been prosecuted and imprisoned, not immediately repatriated.

Source: Hong Kong *Annual Report*, 1976–90. Figures for 1975–8 based on annual totals. Subsequent figures are the daily averages quoted in the Hong Kong *Annual Reports*.

Nonetheless, strict immigration controls, and with them the need for many would-be immigrants to avoid official regulations, were not introduced until 1974, when about 1,000 people a day were entering from China and settling in the territory. A second baseline for assessing the situation is that there are still large numbers of legal immigrants from the mainland — for example in 1980 and 1989 there were 55,000 and 27,300 legal immigrants respectively. Figures for the number of illegal immigrants (IIs) discovered in Hong Kong are given in Table 7.3. They are approximate since they were given, until 1979, as annual totals and subsequently only as daily averages for either monthly or annual periods. However, they indicate that from a very small baseline in 1975, the numbers detected, arrested, and repatriated to China grew over a relatively short time to an annual rate not far short of 100,000. This of course excludes those entering and remaining undetected. Until 1980, a 'touch base' policy operated; IIs discovered in the border areas were arrested and sent back, while those found in the urban areas of Kowloon and Hong Kong Island were deemed to have 'touched base' and allowed to remain. Around 6,000 immigrants annually, until 1980, were discovered and allowed to remain as a result of this policy. The justification for abandoning it (on 22 October 1980) was primarily that the number of IIs was depressing local wages, especially for unskilled work (Hong Kong *Annual* 1981). From that point on, the policy was simple; all IIs discovered in the territory were repatriated. Not surprisingly, the numbers of IIs coming over the border dropped sharply, though by 1987 it had risen again to its former level. Thus in May 1988,

> In order to curb the influx, stringent measures were stepped up, resulting in many arrests at construction sites, factories, restaurants, and other places of employment. Illegal immigrants so arrested were prosecuted and sentenced to imprisonment ranging from nine to 18 months. As a result, the number of illegal immigrants dropped significantly in the latter half of the year (Government Information Services 1989: 330)

The 'usual' prison sentence was around 15 months for IIs found working in Hong Kong, though others found on the border were still simply repatriated. The Hong Kong *Annual* 1990 credits the 1988–9 reduction in the daily average of II arrests (from 57 a day to 43) to these measures. Even so, in July 1989 the policy was assessed as not stringent enough, and further controls were imposed not on the immigrants, but on their employers, who now risked substantial fines and imprisonment for using II workers. (The penalties on employers were further increased by the Immigration (Amendment) Ordinance 1990 to a maximum fine of $250,000 and three years' jail.) At the time of writing, discussion continues about whether building contractors should be liable if subcontractors use such labour, while the idea has been mooted that all building workers should wear their ID cards while on site.

In reviewing this short history, it seems clear that fluctuations in attitudes towards IIs have often been prompted by fluctuations in Hong Kong's economic situation. In times of full employment and economic boom, illegal immigration has been tolerated and to some extent condoned; many persons entering illegally were subsequently able to become legal residents of the territory. In the late 1970s, the 'touch base' policy, whatever its intentions, was effectively a rationing mechanism. Only a limited proportion of those entering would be allowed to stay. The abandonment of the policy in 1980 was justified on economic grounds, and indeed the territory suffered a recession in the mid-1980s. Only in the last few years have other considerations have entered into the picture.

Conclusions

There is nothing new or astounding in the assertion that the situation in Hong Kong is influenced by the proximity of China. Events in China have always spilled over the border. One indication of this is the 1967–8 'troubles', in which China attempted to destabilize Hong Kong initially through strikes and subsequently by means of bombs. Another, and reverse, case is the 1989 democracy movement, which struck a chord of sympathy in Hong Kong.

It is hardly surprising, then, that current conditions across the border, coupled with the economic differences between its two sides, should play a large part in determining the extent and type of crime in the territory. Smuggling exists so long as it is profitable. Certain kinds of smuggling, such as the international traffic in narcotics, have not been considered here; they exist above and beyond regional economic factors. But the smuggling of consumer goods in the region depends implicitly on demand for Western goods in China and for certain Chinese items in Hong Kong, and above all on the possibility of evading the high level of duties demanded on the Chinese side. Illegal immigration is prompted by the same economic conditions that have resulted in mass migration within China. And so far as the use of guns and the extent of armed robbery is concerned, it is clear that what Hong Kong has suffered is simply a knock-on effect from the ready availability of weapons and the crime wave under way across the border. We might even take the view that we have been lucky in not experiencing its full impact.

What predictions can be made for the future? By late 1990, the 'street price' of handguns had risen sharply in Hong Kong. This can be taken to imply that Chinese and Hong Kong efforts to reduce their availability were having some effect. But it might also have been that the demand was increasing, driving up the price against a more risky supply situation. In police terms, robbery in general is never an easy crime to solve, though ironically the use of firearms not only gives the police more avenues of investigation, but also invites greater police resources in investigation and perhaps increases the motivation of individual detectives. Thus the 1986–8 figures show a relatively high success rate for cases of armed robbery — about one-third to one-half were detected — as compared with other robberies, for which the detection rate was on the order of 20–25 per cent. Nonetheless the number of armed robberies in 1990 must have stretched the detective force, and the continuing availability of guns across the border and in Hong Kong probably means that it will be some time before the wave of robberies dies down.

Both smuggling and illegal immigration are more directly linked to the economic situation across the border, though in different ways. Again, the crackdown on smuggling by using speedboats has probably reduced their usefulness as a means of transport, though other methods have already surfaced. And the economic 'pull' of Hong Kong is and will be as strong as the differential between it and the Chinese economy. The use of prison sentences for IIs as a deterrent has not worked and is unlikely to work, first because of the comparatively small numbers of IIs detected, and second because deterrence requires that potential immigrants know the penalties. It is unlikely that many of the IIs, coming from provinces beyond Guangdong, do in fact know what penalties they can face until they are actually here. In any event, merely moving illegally within China makes them vulnerable to penal sanctions, though the policing of such migration appears to be haphazard and ineffective. Hence, presumably, the move in 1989 to criminalize the employment of IIs in Hong Kong.

In short, all three of the issues discussed above have arisen because of the economic and social differences between Hong Kong and China, and the fact of the border. They are, however, related to the economic situation in different ways. The case of armed robbery is simplest to understand because it is simply a situation in which the prevalence of guns and increased crime on one side of the border have spilled over to the other. The case of smuggling depends on demand, supply, and the level of duties. Given the size of problem on the Chinese side, even though undoubtedly pressure has been brought to bear on Hong Kong, it seems that the willingness of smugglers to engage in violence was a major factor in the decision to step up penalties and widen the scope of the criminal law on this side of the border. In the case of illegal immigration, too, it is clear that the degree to which 'economic migrancy' has been criminalized has been, at least in the past, largely determined by Hong Kong's labour needs. None of these situations lend themselves to easy solutions, not least because the origins of the problems lie outside Hong Kong's jurisdiction. As a result, Hong Kong authorities are left to cope with the results without being able to influence the causes. This they have done, sometimes with reasonable success, using existing laws and policing practices, but often by extending the scope of the criminal law. Meanwhile, it is by no means clear that the Chinese authorities have the capability to address the root problem, which is the parlous state of China's economy.

Notes

1. For the first report of the 'May 3 incident', see the *South China Morning Post*, 4 May 1990. A fuller account was given in the Legislative Council on 16 May 1990 and appears in the Hong Kong Hansard for that date. It was subsequently debated in the Legislative Council on 6 June, and is again reported in the Hong Kong Hansard. The 'Tolo Harbour' incident was reported in the *South China Morning Post*, 5 June 1990. A debate on illegal immigration took place in the Legislative Council on 4 Feburary 1990 and appears in the Hong Kong Hansard.

2. Figures provided by Customs and Excise Department in a personal communication. The Chinese duty on televisions is based on screen size, not price, but would roughly equal the price of a television in Hong Kong. The duty on cigarettes would be in the region of 30–50 per cent of the duty-free price in Hong Kong.

3. Reported by the Foreign Broadcast Information Service 'Daily Report: China' number FBIS-CHI-90-173, 6 September 1990.

4. 1 May 1990; reported by the US Joint Publication Research Service 'JPRS Report: China' number JPRS-CAR-90-055, 26 July 1990.

5. FBIS-CHI-90-136, 16 July 1990.

6. *South China Morning Post*, 28 July 1990 and FBIS-CHI-90-146, 30 July 1990.

7. FBIS-CHI-90-157, 14 August 1990.

8. *Chiushih Nientai*, 1 May 1990 and JPRS-CAR-90-055, 26 July 1990. See also FBIS-CHI-90-133, 11 July 1990 which summarizes a *Renmin Gongan Bao* report asserting the occurrence of a crime wave.

9. Guangdong provincial radio broadcast, reported in FBIS-CHI-90-149, (2 August 1990).

10. See for example the report in *Chiushih Nientai*, 1 May 1990 (which reports a number of PRC newpapers on the issue) and a report of a meeting of Public Security Bureau heads, in *Renmin Gongan Bao*, 20 July 1990 (reported in JPRS-CAR-90-055, 26 July 1990 and FBIS-CHI-90-158, 15 August 1990 respectively).

11. *Hsin Wan Po*, 22 March 1990 and JPRS-CAR-90-042, 31 May 1990.

12. Guangdong Guangzhou Provincial Radio, 14 June and 30 August 1990; JPRS-CAR-90-047, 26 June 1990 and FBIS-CHI-90-171, 4 September 1990 respectively.

13. FBIS-CHI-90-127, 2 July 1990.

8 The Royal Hong Kong Police

HAROLD TRAVER AND MARK S. GAYLORD

IN HONG KONG, as in many other advanced industrial societies, law and order is a matter of public concern and a political issue of some importance. Since the mid-1960s, Hong Kong has experienced an almost unparalleled period of sustained prosperity. Social programmes were introduced and economic changes occurred that, reasonably, would be expected to reduce crime. Moreover, the criminal justice system in Hong Kong has expanded and developed to the point where it now compares favourably to those found in Western societies. Yet, despite everything, the crime rate soared during the 1970s and has remained relatively high throughout the 1980s.

The reasons for, and the timing of, this increase in crime have been examined elsewhere (Lethbridge 1980, Traver 1984) and in Chapter 2. This chapter approaches the problem of crime by examining the ways in which criminal occurrences may be seen to facilitate the achievement of organizational goals by the police. On the one hand, as in Chapter 2, the volume of crime in society may be regarded simply as a dependent variable, to be explained by prevailing social and economic forces or the activities of social control agencies. On the other, crime can be viewed as a potential organizational resource which, if properly utilized under the right conditions, can be used by social control agencies to gain public credibility and justify requests for increased expenditure and manpower.

Police and Crime

The relationship of social control agencies, including the police, and crime is a controversial topic in criminology. The presence of crime is explained by the absence of adequate social control mechanisms, and the expansion of the police force is one of the remedies most frequently advocated. This, in effect, draws a sharp line between the 'authorities' and the 'criminal' and assumes a relentless struggle between the two. Without adequate controls, social behaviour is assumed to be subject to deterioration with a greater tendency on the part of members of society to become involved in criminal activities. Implicit in this position is an acceptance of the necessity for reparative social control responses to law violations.[1]

A more recent interpretation sees social control agencies as an important factor in the production of crime and deviance. The labelling perspective in particular has focused attention on the role of authorities in creating deviance by defining certain behaviours as illegal and selectively singling out for presecution people who violate the law. This interpretation holds that social control agencies create or amplify deviance in their attempts to control rule-breaking. Observed increases in crime are more likely to be due to a 'reporting' or 'control wave' than anything else.[2]

The police in Hong Kong have undoubtedly had a moderating or deterrent effect on the volume of crime in Hong Kong. There is the possibility, as outlined in Chapter 2, that the collapse of the police-Triad alliance in the early 1970s contributed to a dramatic increase in street crimes such as robbery and serious assault in the following years. There is also the distinct possibility, again as outlined in Chapter 2, that changes in police procedures and practices in the 1970s tended to amplify the volume of reported crime in Hong Kong. In any case, most forms of crime were at record levels in the mid-1970s. In the years that followed, the volume of crime declined but it never reverted to its original levels. In the process, Hong Kong had acquired a more or less permanent crime problem. Finding a solution to this problem, or at least being seen to search for one, would become a major preoccupation of the police. The intensity of the search would depend on what sort of crime was observed to be on the increase at any one time.

Police Force Expansion

Hong Kong has traditionally had a relatively large police force, partly because British colonial tradition has always given the police an extensive paramilitary role (Clayton and Killingray 1989, Jeffries 1952). Even so, the rapid expansion of the police in the last two decades has been remarkable. Table 8.1 shows that since 1956/7 the number of police in Hong Kong has grown steadily. With a current establishment of around 27,000 officers for a population of about 5.8 million, the Hong Kong police force qualifies both in absolute numbers and proportionately to the size of the population as one of the largest in the world. Increases in police expenditure are equally

Table 8.1 Police Force Size, 1956/57 to 1988/89

Year	Police Establishment	Police per 100,000 Population	Citizens per Police Officer
1956/57	5,932	226.9	439.76
1957/58	6,874	251.2	397.07
1958/59	7,135	250.0	399.01
1959/60	7,629	257.1	387.96
1960/61	8,135	264.5	377.03
1961/62	8,352	263.1	379.11
1962/63	8,597	256.9	388.28
1963/64	8,753	249.8	399.29
1964/65	9,529	265.1	376.18
1965/66	10,346	280.2	355.88
1966/67	10,966	293.8	339.36
1967/68	11,383	296.9	335.82
1968/69	12,253	312.1	319.45
1969/70	12,512	313.8	317.69
1970/71	13,058	329.8	302.19
1971/72	13,773	340.5	292.71
1972/73	14,963	366.9	271.57
1973/74	16,062	386.1	257.99
1974/75	16,215	375.7	265.15
1975/76	17,124	386.8	258.51
1976/77	18,579	406.9	245.72
1977/78	19,064	410.1	243.80
1978/79	20,894	425.6	234.90
1979/80	21,981	436.0	229.30
1980/81	22,473	435.4	229.70
1981/82	23,477	448.0	223.20
1982/83	24,211	455.0	219.80
1983/84	24,834	462.2	216.40
1984/85	25,397	467.6	213.80
1985/86	25,957	471.4	212.10
1986/87	26,626	476.6	209.80
1987/88	27,367	484.0	206.60
1988/89	27,450	478.7	208.89

Sources: For police establishment, Commissioner of Police; *Annual Departmental Reports*, 1957–90. For population, Census and Statistics Department, *Annual Digests of Statistics*, 1957–90. Calculations by the authors.

Table 8.2 Police Expenditure, 1956/57 to 1988/89

Year	Total Expenditure in Millions of Dollars		Constant 1972 Dollars Per Capita Expenditure
	Actual	Constant Dollars	
1956/57	39.467	58.211	22.3
1957/58	44.272	65.106	23.8
1958/59	49.953	74.558	26.1
1959/60	54.991	76.377	25.7
1960/61	62.366	90.386	29.4
1961/62	62.519	89.313	28.1
1962/63	69.973	101.410	30.3
1963/64	77.520	108.665	31.0
1964/65	91.717	125.640	35.0
1965/66	105.740	144.850	39.2
1966/67	114.081	150.107	40.2
1967/68	125.645	151.379	39.5
1968/69	147.317	179.665	45.8
1969/70	160.248	188.527	47.3
1970/71	173.076	192.307	48.6
1971/72	205.009	218.094	54.0
1972/73	237.733	237.733	58.3
1973/74	309.813	262.553	63.1
1974/75	402.180	297.911	69.0
1975/76	436.353	320.848	73.0
1976/77	514.178	364.665	82.1
1977/78	582.938	391.234	85.3
1978/79	693.952	442.007	94.7
1979/80	912.775	518.622	105.2
1980/81	1,213.490	597.782	118.1
1981/82	1,510.873	645.672	124.6
1982/83	1,745.049	673.764	128.0
1983/84	1,946.967	683.146	127.8
1984/85	2,210.402	717.663	132.9
1985/86	2,517.483	791.428	145.1
1986/87	2,841.509	874.311	158.0
1987/88	3,144.389	916.731	163.3
1988/89	3,867.754	1,051.020	185.0

Sources: For police expenditure, Hong Kong Government, *Hong Kong Estimates of Revenue and Expenditure* for relevant years. For constant dollar figures, price indices in Census and Statistics Department *Annual Digest of Statistics* (1969); Hong Kong Statistics, 1947–67; and Government Information Services, Hong Kong *Annuals* 1956–90. Calculations by the authors.

impressive. Table 8.2 shows that in 1956/7 the annual expenditure of the police stood at $58.2 million (constant 1972/3 dollars) and that by 1989/90 this had increased to $1,051.02 million. In the same period, per capita constant dollar expenditure rose from $22.3 to $185.2. Police expenditure grew roughly twice as fast as per capita expenditure. The most rapid increases occurred between the period 1970/1 and 1980/1. Between these years, per capita expenditure increased by 143 per cent, from $48.6 to $118.2. In contrast, between 1980/1 and 1989/90 per capita expenditure increased by only 57 per cent, from $118.1 to $185.

Did police expansion have any detectable effect on crime? In terms of reported crime, it would appear not. The rate of serious crime increased from 65.13 per 100,000 population in 1956/7 to 147.06 in 1989/90, while in the same period the detection rate fell from 55 to 47 per cent. To put it another way, in terms of constant 1972/3 dollars, each detected crime in 1956/7 cost $4,913 but by 1989/90, this had increased to $25,964. Of course, such a crude cost analysis ignores the fact that by the mid-1980s Hong Kong had become a more complex society and criminal behaviour may have become much more sophisticated and difficult to detect. It also ignores the peacekeeping aspects of police work and the role of the police in maintaining order in society. Still, we are left with the fact that even heroic expenditures of money and manpower have failed to reduce crime.

Police–Community Relations

The fact that until the late 1960s the police force in Hong Kong was essentially a colonial, or alien, presence, meant that it was frequently forced to be more concerned with public acceptance and the maintenance of public order, than with the prevention and control of conventional crime. A concern with legitimacy, or more correctly the lack of it, lies at the back of the increasing importance that the police attached to public relations in the 1960s. At the risk of over-simplifying a complex situation, during this period Hong Kong was rapidly emerging as an industrial society, and there were a number of social transformations associated with this shift that almost guaranteed problems for a colonial-style police force. One explanation that has found official acceptance is that a centralized administration, and the absence of an effective local leadership structure capable of explaining a growing body of policies and laws to the public, created an impression that the Government did not care, and that it 'gave all power to the Police' (Commission of Inquiry 1966). For whatever reason, the police felt, probably quite rightly, that they had an image problem. During the 1960s, they attempted to solve this problem.

In the beginning, public relations consisted largely of keeping the public informed about police aims and methods. It was hoped that the public would be encouraged to cooperate in letting the police get on with the job of maintaining order and controlling crime. To the extent that public relations worked directly at image management, the conduct of the individual police officer was likely to be seen as especially important (Commissioner of Police 1962). Any increase in the number of requests for police assistance and advice was viewed as an encouraging sign that there was growing acceptance of the police as 'servants and guardians' of the public, and recognition that Hong Kong was becoming a community in which the criminal would not find an easy abode (Commissioner of Police 1963: 2).

As well as being a means for increasing public cooperation, public relations could also be useful in countering public criticism. Here the view was that if the public understood the problems of police work they would be less likely to be critical of police aims and methods. When criticism did occur, the police were inclined to see it as arising out of Hong Kong's special problems associated with overcrowding, and the subsequent need to maintain a high standard of public order (Commissioner of Police 1963), or as an unfortunate by-product of unpopular laws the police were required to enforce (Commissioner of Police 1966). In regard to the latter, the clearance of squatters, the restriction and control of unlicensed street hawkers, and the strict enforcement of traffic regulations were cited as some of the reasons why the police were not as popular with the public as they might have hoped.

The first concerted effort to control public relations occurred in 1965 when an officer from the Government Information Services Department was posted to the police and a press section was established to keep the news media informed about various aspects of police work. Emphasis was still on the police and image management, rather than on crime and crime prevention:

> We do not expect to create interest and sympathy in place of apathy and mistrust overnight, but we are confident that by advising . . . people in advance of Police policy and intentions, we shall create an increasing reservoir of goodwill and understanding. There will always be small sections of the community who, out of prejudice, criminal intent, or sheer foolishness will remain beyond persuasion, but if our increasing efforts to communicate adequately with the public lead to greater harmony between the Police Force and the law-abiding majority they will have served their purpose (Commissioner of Police 1966: 3).

Essentially, what the police were trying to do was sell themselves to the public, but as long as all they had to offer were such services as hawker control and the enforcement of traffic regulations, the public would continue to be reluctant buyers. Before the police could be accepted as the legitimate guardians of the public's safety, the public had to feel that it needed guarding. This implied, ironically, that the role of the police as society's guardian and protector depended to some extent on their lack of success in keeping the peace. From the standpoint of police public relations, a general absence of major disturbances and threats to the social order was a mixed blessing. The following states this dilemma quite nicely:

> Hong Kong's recent history has been remarkably orderly and free from major disturbances. This does not mean that the Police Force has been able to rest on its laurels. Experience has shown that it is precisely at these times when the Police Force is able to concentrate upon routine Police work undisturbed by major incidents, that the public for its part has time for reflection and hence for criticism of the Police and of other arms of Government (Commissioner of Police 1966: 1).

The 1967 riots shattered this orderly and peaceful climate. Between May and December of that year, the police were almost continuously involved with riot control, bomb disposal, dramatic raids on communist strongholds, and a variety of other activities that could hardly be called routine or mundane. The riots were of sufficient duration and intensity to affect and threaten nearly all segments of the community (Cooper 1970).

The media were more than willing to capitalize on this situation.[3] Consequently, the 1967 riots became a major news theme. They became a form of street theatre in which the police publicly displayed courage and fortitude in the face of adversity. The public willingly assumed the role of appreciative audience. By the time the riots drew to a close at the end of 1967, the police could reasonably claim to have 'inspired confidence in the minds of the . . . majority of the population, and helped to sustain the resolve of the general public at a time of considerable strain' (Commissioner of Police 1968: 4). Many observers of Hong Kong's history agree that the police emerged from this period with a better public image than when they went in (Sinclair 1983). In short, a riot aimed directly at British colonial rule had accomplished what the police could never have done on their own, namely, increase their acceptance by the public.

The riots also appear to have increased the police's awareness of the importance of the media in the maintenance of effective public relations. In the year immediately following the riots, the Police

Public Information Bureau was established, which took over most of the functions that had previously been carried out by the Government Information Services Department on behalf of the police. With the creation of the Bureau the number of staff dealing with public relations increased from one officer, posted from the Information Services Department, to 10, of whom eight came from within the ranks of the police. The Bureau placed public relations firmly under police control, and it also helped to assure that its services would be expanded and tailored to the needs of the police.

The creation of the Police Public Information Bureau marked the beginning of a new era in public relations. The Bureau would later be enlarged and transformed into the Police Public Relations Branch, and media relations and community relations would be subject to the control of separate bureaux, but in the meantime there was a body within the police force assigned to devote their full attention to media relations and community publicity arrangements in an 'efficient and coordinated manner' (Commissioner of Police 1969: 5). The effects were almost immediately apparent. In 1966/7, the Police Press Office, in collaboration with the Government Information Services Department, issued more than 1,500 news stories, answered approximately 4,200 press queries, and arranged approximately 50 newspaper and radio interviews with police officers. Only two years later, the Police Public Information Bureau fielded more than 22,800 press queries, issued more than 3,000 news releases, and set up more than 1,000 newspaper, radio, and television interviews (Commissioner of Police 1969: 1). In that same period, the Bureau also produced some of the first radio and television programmes covering various aspects of police work, and launched one of Hong Kong's first crime prevention programmes. From that point on, police public relations would never be the same.

From the standpoint of police public relations the effects of the sharp increase in crime in the 1970s were akin to an extended replay of the 1967 riots. The expansion of violent crime became a major news theme during the first half of the 1970s. The Public Information Bureau expanded to meet the increased demand for crime news and, in the year that followed, continued to expand. Currently, the Police Public Relations Branch operates an extensive network of community and school liaison officers to promote public awareness of the problem of crime and to report back to headquarters the problems they have encountered in the field. There are now also well-developed Chinese and English language television programmes conveying the 'fight crime' message and appealing for witnesses to come forward. Moreover, in an effort to develop better relations with young people, the police now operate 'Junior Police Call', which in 1989, with 162,592 ordinary members and 16,683 leaders, is said to be the largest local youth group in the world.

Considering that Hong Kong has one of the highest newspaper readerships in the world, as well as four television channels and four radio stations, media relations are of continuing importance to the police. A police newsroom provides a 24-hour enquiry service to supply the Hong Kong media's vast appetite for news. During 1989, the newsroom staff handled 211,907 enquiries from the media and began to issue photographs taken at crime scenes for use in newspapers. As a result of these efforts, the police now exercise considerable indirect control over what is reported in the media. For the Hong Kong police, media relations has become big business.

Another way in which crime can serve as an organizational resource is to be found in the notion of crime prevention. Crime prevention has been a feature of police work since at least the establishment of the Crime Prevention Office in the 1950s. However, until 1971/2, when a Crime Prevention Unit was formed within the Office, its daily affairs had revolved around the supervision and deportation of offenders, criminal intelligence, and recovering missing vehicles, not the public promotion of crime prevention. The creation of the Crime Prevention Unit, which was specifically assigned the task of promoting crime prevention strategies in the community, formally acknowledged the importance of this aspect of police work. By 1976, plans were under way to restructure and expand the Crime Prevention Office to 100 officers in order to provide an 'expert and aggressive prevention capability' for the force (Commissioner of Police 1977: 22). As a result of these plans, the Crime Prevention Bureau was established in 1977. However, a lack of funds prevented an expansion of the Bureau until 1979, when its phased expansion was commenced. This was completed in 1983. In other words, only in the 1980s did the Bureau start to play a really active part in promoting public awareness and in offering advice on crime prevention strategies. In recent years, the Bureau has become a major force in promoting crime prevention strategies in Hong Kong.

Another important event in the history of police-community relations was the establishment of a centralized Force Complaints Office in 1973. While this does not directly deal with the problem of crime, it has everything to do with the legitimation of the police.

Before that date, all complaints against the police, except for those involving corruption or criminal activities, were the responsibility of District and Branch Commanders, although in practice investigations were normally carried out at a divisional level by the Chief Staff Inspector. Such an arrangement naturally raised questions about the impartiality of investigations. The creation of the Complaints Office not only removed the burden of inquiry from field commanders but more importantly, at least from the standpoint of the police, it was seen to inspire 'greater public confidence in the impartiality of investigations' (Commissioner of Police 1975: 9). This was a further step in the direction of assuring that justice was seen to be done. The Complaints Office was, however, staffed entirely by the police. The next step occurred in 1977 when an independent UMELCO/Police Group was created to monitor and review the operation of the Complaints Office. As its name implies, the Group was originally set up to include representatives from the Legislative Council, as well as from the police. In the years since, the name has been changed to the Police Complaints Committee and police involvement in the review body entirely eliminated. It is now accepted that it is necessary to have an independent body based in the Legislative Council to review the activities of what is now called the Complaints Against the Police Office, in order to assure the impartiality of investigations.

Since the Complaints Against Police Office became fully operational in 1974, complaints increased annually until 1984, when there was a slight decrease. However, they increased again and finally peaked in 1986 with 4,532 complaints. In the following years, complaints declined, to 3,234 in 1988. By way of comparison, in 1975 there were only 814 complaints recorded. The rather dramatic increase in complaints is interpreted, probably correctly, by the police not as representing a deterioration in the conduct of the police, but rather as an indication of the public's increased confidence in the methods of investigation of complaints.

To summarize, the crime wave of the 1970s set in motion policies and actions that persisted. Changes in reporting procedures and a community network of reporting centres did not disappear when violent crime started to decline. If anything, reporting became even more efficient and streamlined. In the 1980s, Mutual Aid Committees were supplanted by an even more extensive Neighbourhood Watch Scheme, and the Fight Violent Crime Campaign was restructured and transformed as a continuous Fight Crime Campaign. From the standpoint of police-community relations, the important thing is that after violent crime increased in the 1970s, the police would never again feel compelled to complain publicly about a lack of cooperation from, or acceptance by, the general public. This was even true when the police were being wracked with charges of corruption. Moreover, a variety of social and economic changes were occurring in Hong Kong society that made it highly unlikely that crime would ever decline to the level seen in the early 1960s. By the end of the 1970s, the police were well on their way to establishing themselves as the legitimate guardians and protectors of society.

There are alternative views on the legitimacy of the police. At various times, police actions have attracted strong criticism (see for example Hong Kong Observers 1981). Yet in the recent past, the police have, on the whole, managed to avoid public controversy: few issues have emerged that have gripped the attention of the public or the media for more than a few days. Nonetheless, some current matters may result in more prolonged discussion, since police powers are extensive, and woven into the political fabric of Hong Kong — a fabric that is rapidly changing in the run-up to 1997. For example, the police have extremely broad powers in relation to demonstrations and marches. Currently, too, the Commissioner of Police acts as the Registrar of Societies under the Societies Ordinance (Cap. 151). As Hong Kong develops political parties and a broader conception of political rights within the framework of the Bill of Rights, both areas of police work may come under closer public scrutiny. The government's consideration of increased powers in relation to electronic surveillance may well also become controversial, again for reasons connected to the Bill of Rights. Equally, the police maintain a large internal security apparatus, the Special Branch, said to number about 1,000 officers (Sinclair 1983). Little is publicly known about it other than the general description of its task as VIP protection, counter-terrorism, and security co-ordination. However, the fact that it has had a considerable say in the political security of the territory has never excited much public interest.

Conclusion: Controlling Crime versus Selling Crime

To the extent that crime rates are driven by such forces as unemployment, inequality, and urbanization, they are to a large extent beyond the control of the police. In fact, serious questions can be raised as to whether crime control or crime prevention are realistic goals of police work. Even in theory, crime control is a responsibility that the police share with other sectors of the criminal justice system. In the final analysis, the police are only responsible for the apprehension and arrest of offenders. Subsequent actions by prosecutors and the courts are beyond police control. In Hong Kong, as elsewhere, with the exception of the occasional crackdown on vice establishments and the like, police efforts are typically reactive in nature. The police normally respond only when a crime is reported or when its commission is observed. Yet despite clear limitations in their ability to control crime, the police claim to offer a solution, possibly the only solution, to the problem of crime in society. Solutions must, however, be seen to work before they can bring credit to the organizations that supply them. Fortunately for the police, the problem of crime, like most social problems, is largely a matter of perception and, therefore, open to interpretation and redefinition.

First, the effectiveness of control efforts is not always readily apparent. Crime is subject to annual fluctuations and, at least on some occasions, control efforts are almost bound to be associated with a reduction in crime. Moreover, in many instances it is difficult to determine clearly the direction in which crime is moving. One crime, or type of crime, may increase while another appears to decline or at least remain stationary. As the major source of information about the incidence of crime in society, the police have considerable power to channel and shape the perceived significance of crime trends. This power is appreciably enhanced if, as in Hong Kong, the police have also managed to establish close relationships with the media.

Second, as with many other powerful social institutions, the police have both the ability to raise anxieties, in this case meaning the fear of crime, and the authority to propose solutions — including a call for more resources. In such a situation, the police cannot lose. Rising crime provides the police with an opportunity to call for more resources. If crime continues to increase, the police can simply claim insufficient resources and call for yet more. Once crime decreases, with or without the assistance of the police, the police can point to their success. In the unlikely event of a clear decline in the volume of crime, the police can still reasonably claim the need for continuing high levels of aid to assure that the low crime levels are maintained.

Third, the police are not faced with controlling the uncontrollable. As long as they are seen to respond quickly to calls for assistance, they can claim to be doing their job. A defensive response to crime also has its pragmatic advantages. The police do not — and arguably cannot — attack the root causes of crime. Rather, all the police need to do is 'keep the peace'—which in practice means confining disorder to certain parts of the city. While neighbourhood watch schemes, police patrol strategies, and the like are designed to deter potential offenders and to diminish the public's fear of crime, such measures largely displace, rather than reduce, crime.

Notes

1. Efforts in the US to establish a systematic inverse relationship between police and crime levels have been less than successful. Swimmer (1975) has established an inverse relationship between the two. But Greenwood and Wadycki (1973), Huff and Stahura (1980), and Humphries and Wallace (1979) have established either reciprocal or positive relationships.

2. The literature on this has been growing since the 1960s. See for example: Bittner (1967), Ferdinand (1989), Marx (1981), Piliavin and Briar (1964).

3. There is an extensive literature on the ways in which journalists seek and create news themes as means of organizing what otherwise would be disparate incidents of limited significance. See for example Cohen and Young (1973), Fishman (1978), Molotch and Lester (1974).

9 Victims of Crime

CHAN WAI-TO

VICTIMS of crime play an important role within the criminal justice process. They detect unlawful acts, report offences to the police, provide evidence, make statements, attend identification parades, check photographs of known criminals, and attend as witnesses in court. Regrettably, however, the importance of the victims' role does not guarantee them a central position within the criminal justice system. Most of the attention is directed to the offence and the criminal, through the various stages of arrest, charge, prosecution, sentence, punishment, and treatment. The contemporary justice system has been created primarily to punish wrongdoers. It pays much less attention to the injury, rights, and dignity of victims, who are marginalized and whose feelings and needs are neglected by the criminal justice professionals.

In the light of the above, whom can the victim turn to for support, help, or care? The present situation in Hong Kong can easily be stated: there is no comprehensive provision for victims. Therefore, it is essential to identify the limitations and ideological currents of the various existing programmes and to establish a sound philosophical basis for action. The major victim provisions discussed in this paper are either statutory—compensation orders and the Criminal and Law Enforcement Injuries Compensation Scheme—or schemes operated by welfare agencies. They are largely focused on 'conventional crimes' as defined by the criminal codes. (Arrangements for victims in police stations, courts, clinics, and so forth are excluded from this discussion.)

Who Are the Crime Victims?

It may be surprising that the term 'crime victim' can mean several things. A broad legal definition would be that crime victims are persons who, individually or collectively, have suffered harm, loss, or damage through acts or omissions which are in violation of criminal laws. A social process definition is wider: it would include all those who have suffered pain as a consequence of social interaction. This second definition is often used to argue that what happens to victims at the hands of criminal justice agencies—for example, unsympathetic police questioning, delays in trials, aggressive examination in court, and lack of information about the progress of the case—often amounts to a 'second victimization' (Maguire and Pointing 1988).

Moreover, neither the legal nor the social process definition has much to say about 'indirect' victimization. This term, despite the lack of an easy definition, can be simply illustrated. The Hong Kong victimization surveys (Census and Statistics Department 1979, 1982, 1987, and 1990a) distinguish between 'household crime' and 'personal crime'. In a 'household crime' such as burglary, a complete listing of victims might include all persons living in the same household. Equally, no conclusion can be reached on the question of whether family members of victims of serious crimes of violence might also be considered as crime victims since their lives, too, will be radically affected by the victimization.

As a final word on definitions, even international bodies like the United Nations and the European Committee on Crime Problems have different emphases in their conceptions of crime victims. The UN considers crime victims within the legal framework or criminal justice system, while the European Committee refers more broadly to the civil law concept of the 'damaged person', which covers all persons who have suffered any form of damage or pain arising out of an offence (Colvin 1988: 57). The lack of a unified formal definition of a 'crime victim' poses considerable problems within criminal jurisprudence in general and the field of victimology in particular.

In reality, the number of crime victims is one of the 'dark figures' in criminology. Many crimes and therefore many victims do not figure in the official criminal statistics. Some victims may fail to realize that an offence has been committed against them. This might be the case in relation to failed attempts of vehicle theft or successful shoplifting. Second, the victim may not be competent to recognize the criminal implications of an act against him or her. Sexual assaults on children would belong to this category. Third, the victim may be a willing party to the offence. Illegal abortion, underage sexual relations, and underage drinking can be offences of this nature. Fourth, a range of other considerations may lead to non-reporting, including feelings of helplessness and the perceived powerlessness of the police, the threat of further retaliation, and fear of 'secondary' victimization from the authorities (Kidd and Chayet 1984). Fifth, the damage may be too trivial for the victim to feel it warrants reporting.

And lastly (though of decreased importance in Hong Kong since the advent of computer logging of phone calls, including crime reports by telephone), it may be that offences reported to the police are not recorded by them.

The four victim surveys mentioned above provide a partial picture of who victims are, though it serves my purpose here to deal only with the latest published survey, the data for which was collected in 1989. The picture is incomplete because the surveys distinguish between 'personal' and 'household' victimization, the former referring to rape, assaults, robbery, theft, and so forth, and the latter including burglary, vechicle theft, criminal damage, and so on. Demographic information—age, sex, and so forth—is only available in the case of personal crimes, which accounted for 54 per cent of all victimizations in the 1989 data. At this point, it becomes helpful to express victimization in terms of rates; that is, the number of victimizations per 1,000 persons in the relevant age or other social categories. On this basis, in 1989, personal victimizations were most common against persons aged 12–19 (31.4 per 1,000 in the age group) and 30–39 (30.3 per 1,000 in the age group), and were lower among older people. Both the 12–19 and the 30–39 age groups primarily suffered thefts. Snatching and pickpocketing accounted for most of their victimzations. However, in the younger age groups, victimizations involving violence were more common. There were also differences based on the sex of the victim. Women were much more prone than men to theft from the person, presumably because many such offences involve stealing, or snatching handbags. In the 30–39 age group, for example, women, who had the highest overall victimization rate of 35 per 1,000 among all age-sex groups, were more likely than men to suffer this form of victimization. However, both males and females aged 12–19 were by far the most likely groups to be victims of violent offences, with, respectively, 16.6 and 10.9 victimizations per 1,000 persons in the age group.

Information on physical injuries as a result of violent crime also show an interesting picture. In general, 25.4 per cent of male but only 23.4 per cent of female victims of violent crimes received some injury as a result. However, for both men and women, the majority (about 85 per cent) received only minor injuries, while some 15.7 per cent sought medical attention. Where victims in fact sustained physical injuries and sought medical attention, it seems that most needed only a small amount of treatment. Only 10.7 per cent were hospitalized for one or more nights; 59.3 per cent had medical expenses of less than $50. Only 13 per cent had medical bills over $950.

In short, victimization data suggest that victims of violent crimes are more often young and male; that persons in the 12–19 and 30–39 age groups, if victimized, would more often experience theft rather than violent crime; that women are disproportionately targets of theft; and that the majority of injuries sustained by victims are comparatively minor. None of this, of course, detracts from the needs of those victims who are seriously injured; nor does it address the emotional or psychological needs of victims, which are independent of the extent of actual harm suffered; and finally, it does not address specific problems such as battered women, who may not even have reported their victimizations to the survey.

Provision for Victims

Presently, there are both statutory provisions for victims — the Compensation Order and the Criminal and Law Enforcement Injuries Compensation Boards — and efforts sustained by welfare agencies such as Harmony House for Battered Wives, and Services to Victims of Rape rendered by the Family Planning Association.

Compensation Orders

The use of court-ordered compensation is, perhaps, the most direct way for offenders to recompense their victims. The courts can require the offenders to pay compensation to the victim for any injury, loss, or damage resulting from the offence of which he or she has been convicted and any other offences taken into consideration. There are no figures for the number of compensation orders made annually or their amounts. But the inherent constraints on this kind of court-ordered compensation cannot be concealed.

First, compensation orders can only be imposed after the defendant has been convicted. If an offender is acquitted, for example on technical grounds, no compensation order can be made. Also, the offender in a large number of criminal cases is neither identified nor traceable. In reality, the clear-up rates for notifiable offences recorded by the police vary significantly. In general, it is around 45 per cent but for some property offences it is much lower. For burglary it is around 11 per cent.[1]

Second, the offender's means must be taken into account. Full compensation may not be possible, and the courts may require payment through instalments over a specified period. Thus, it could be the case that the compensation is a small amount, paid over a period of some months. To aggravate the situation, some offenders may need to be pursued for failing to comply with the court requirements. Moreover, compensation may not be paid in serious cases; the courts should not impose an order when the offender is sentenced to a period of imprisonment.

A third and related criticism is the irregular use of compensation orders. Compensation is not awarded equally in all types of criminal cases. Quite often, the number of compensation orders made against the criminal damage cases is much greater than in cases of assault, robbery, and so forth, precisely because such serious offences often result in imprisonment.

From the victim's perspective, compensation orders are of marginal relevance. Not only are they applicable to just a small minority of victims, but also the whole system is court-focused and in the hands of professionals whose priorities lie in dealing with offenders rather than victims (see the discussion in Chapter 10). In reality, victims have very little opportunity to express their own views on what compensation is appropriate.

Criminal and Law Enforcement Injuries Compensation Schemes

The schemes were first introduced in May 1973, immediately after the publication of the Five Year Plan for the Social Welfare Department in Hong Kong, 1973–8. They are operated by Boards appointed by the Governor and administratively serviced by the Social Welfare Department. By implementing them, the government assumed some responsibilities for compensating victims sustaining personal injuries in crimes of violence and law-enforcement exercises (Social Welfare Department 1974). The objective is to provide *ex gratia* compensation to all qualifying victims or their dependents without any age limit, residential qualification, or test of means, and on a non-contributory basis.

Specifically, the schemes administered by the respective Boards provide monetary compensation to victims suffering personal injury arising out of the following:

(a) a crime of violence (including arson and poisoning);
(b) an arrest or attempted arrest of an offender or suspected offender;
(c) the prevention or attempted prevention of an offence;
(d) the giving of help to any police officer or other person who is engaged in arresting or attempting to arrest an offender or suspected offender or preventing or attempting to prevent an offence (Social Welfare Department 1974: Chapter 3, Annex F).

Regarding the basis of payment, both Boards have full discretionary power to assess eligibility. For the Criminal Injuries Compensation Scheme, grants from the Emergency Relief Fund are made in respect of burial expenses, loss of life, injury, or disability; and interim 'adjustment payments' may be made in recognition of total or partial loss of income. For the Law Enforcement Injuries Scheme, compensation is assessed on the basis of either common law damages, or in accordance with the Emergency Relief Fund rates, whichever is greater.

During the first year of implementation, only 282 applications were received. Yet in recent years, the number of awards went up from 654 in 1984/5, to 690 in 1985/6, and reached 933 in 1986/7. Although the figure dropped to 824 in 1987/8 and 887 in 1989/90, the projected five year demand (1989/90 to 1993/4) has been estimated for budgetary purposes in accordance with the 1987/8 level (Social Welfare Department 1989: 16–17). On the face of it, the schemes seem to be a success. Yet, upon closer scrutiny, they still have significant shortcomings.

First, compensation is paid to claims of personal injury directly attributable to a crime of violence. Property loss, even if it occurred as part of the same incident, is not included. Yet property crime constitutes a substantial proportion of all crime. It may be argued that victims' recompense should be via property insurance or compensation orders. However only a very small proportion of victims currently obtain court-ordered compensation.

Second, the Boards operate with a conception of the 'deserving' or 'reputable' victim. They may refuse a claim or reduce the amount of payment if the victim's conduct or activity has contributed to his own injury. It is by no means certain that victims with previous or recent convictions, or who are 'disreputable' (prostitutes assaulted by clients, for example) would be considered eligible for compensation.

Third, in cases of family violence, there is a general condition that the offender should have been prosecuted. Since prosecution is likely to be an alternative to family counselling and attempts at reconciliation, it follows that the schemes are not compatible with family social work practices.

Fourth, victims are only eligible for compensation subject to satisfying the Boards that 'the circumstances of the injury have been the subject of criminal proceedings, or were reported to the police without reasonable delay' (Social Welfare Department 1989: 13). This implies that failure to report and cooperate with the police would likely lead to no award being made. It may also raise problems where injuries only become apparent some time after the offence; a situation which is, surprisingly, quite common (Shapland, Willmore, and Duff 1985). Such restrictions may be justified on the grounds that they are the government's principal safeguard against fraudulent claims. There may be problems in checking the validity of claims or the circumstances in which alleged offences were committed. But at the same time, they mean that no adequate compensation is available where victims are reluctant to report crimes due to factors such as fear, the threat of further retaliation by offenders, or anticipated 'secondary victimization'. In other words, victims' needs or difficulties have not been recognized by the professionals within the criminal justice system.

Fifth, injury compensation is only available where 'the injuries inflicted are sufficiently grave that sick leave of three days or more is recommended by registered doctors' (Social Welfare Department 1989: 12–13). While recognizing this rule does not apply to cases where the victim sustained injury as a result of resisting or preventing crime, the only rationale for it can be one of economizing. There is no other reason why victims with less serious injuries should not receive equal treatment as regards financial compensation.

In brief, the major criticism of the schemes lies in the value stances of the Boards. Rather than focusing attention on victims' needs, the Boards implicitly support the notion that only 'deserving' or 'innocent' victims warrant the government's sympathy. Moreover, compensation is provided as a discretionary welfare measure for which victims should feel thankful; it is not in any sense a right. Of equal significance, the Boards look more favourably on victims who cooperate with criminal justice agencies, who are strangers to the offender, whose needs can be delayed, and who manage to establish social support on their own initiative or from their personal resources. But this is a controversial stance: should victims be penalized for being 'uncooperative' within a criminal process that consistently disregards victims' dignity, fails to satisfy their needs, and thereby adds a further burden to their victimization?

Houses for Battered Spouses

In recent years, there has been a marked increase in concern about domestic violence. Most victims are women. They have a range of needs which can be met in a variety of ways, including telephone 'hotlines', temporary shelter, and practical assistance, both financial and in the form of counselling.

The voluntary welfare sector has been most responsive to problems experienced by victims of family violence, mostly battered wives and/or their children. In 1985, Harmony House, with a capacity of 40, was established to provide a retreat for women, with or without children, in immediate danger of violence. Its first task is to provide for the safety of the victims and to give them financial and practical support, while the ultimate goal is 'to help battered spouses find the strength, self-confidence, and resources to live a life free from the threat of violence' (Harmony House 1990: 5). In late 1986, the government also began to assume responsibility by running a similar refuge, Wai On Home for Women, under the administration of the Social Welfare Department. The admission criteria, apart from battered spouses, are extended to girls aged 13 and over who are ill-treated or sexually molested, or in an emotional crisis resulting from serious conflict with their family members and needing temporary shelter, or without a home to go to due to the death of their parents or unexpected hospitalization of parents/guardians. The design capacity is 40, broadly categorized into the family section for spouses and children (24 places) and single-person section for the girls at risk (16 places) (Social Welfare Department, no date).

Both houses operate round the clock. While the physical accommodation is offered free of charge, the residents may be required to pay for their meals and daily necessities. They are rendered individual counselling and a supportive group. Essentially, this kind of victim programme is a crisis service, and the victims are anticipated to be reintegrated into their own families rather than becoming dependent on the services. The length of stay varies, however, though the maximum period of residence is three months.

But despite the growing concern for domestic violence both from government and voluntary sectors in recent years, and the facilities now in place, developments in this area can still be considered sluggish. The provisions fail to reach the vast majority of the victims. The figures on the number of admissions to Harmony House has been quite steady: 166 in 1987/8, 105 in 1988/9, and 141 1989/90; and the cases known to the Social Welfare Department decreased (685 in 1987/8, 433 in 1988/9 and 252 in 1989/90) (Shin 1990). It is very difficult to know the full extent of violence against wives, since it is probable that many incidents go unrecorded. This may occur because women feel ashamed or guilty about confessing that their marriage has gone wrong. Alternatively, they may fear that self-disclosure would lead to further attacks or that nothing can be done to help them.

In short, the official statistics provide no real indication of the extent of the problem and the majority of victims can hardly be contacted or helped.

On the other hand, the current provisions very likely reflect society's view of these victims' status. In all likelihood, they are most widely perceived as (a) a humanitarian response to people in trouble; (b) the fulfilment of the need of the victims; and (c) an indispensable crisis service provided by groups of welfare personnel. But this perception fails to appreciate that a wider response is necessary. Focusing on psychosocial dimensions is probably less important than seeing the more diffuse and subtle relationships of power and oppression between both sexes in society.

Services to Rape Victims

Services to rape victims have been rendered by the Youth Advisory Service of Hong Kong Family Planning Association since 1977. The Service was started for adolescents and young adults with problems concerning their sexual development in general, as well as the victim programme related to rape or sexual assault in particular. The Association has so far recorded 1,114 clients, an average of about 80 per year from 1977 to 1989 (Kwan 1990).

The victim programme includes a hotline handled by a trained worker during office hours, while messages are recorded after service hours and subsequently followed up. Five further kinds of services are currently on offer: the prevention of pregnancy with post-coital contraceptive methods and medical checkups; examination and treatment for venereal diseases; termination of pregnancy by legal abortion as a result of rape; counselling on the serious psychological after-effects of rape; and referrals to the police through a special arrangement by which the victim's first statement to the police can be taken by a woman detective at the Association's offices.

In all likelihood, service statistics, like police statistics, bear no relationship to the extent of the problem. In the initial five months of this victim programme in 1977, only 18 clients solicited assistance. However, the figure increased to 91 in the subsequent year (25 per cent reported to the police). With the help of protection of victims' privacy through legislation since 1978—the reporting of the identity of victims and questioning on the sexual experience in court proceedings was strictly forbidden—more victims appear to be willing to report to the police. For instance, more than 50 per cent of the victims reported to the police in 1984 and 60 per cent in 1989. Of the cases that come to light, it seems that about half involve rapes by acquaintances of the victim, and that many victims — or at least many who come forward — are quite young. In 1985, 22 (28 per cent) of victims were under 16, and 29 (37 per cent) were between 16 and 20. In 1989, the figures were 32 (36 per cent), and 30 (30 per cent) respectively (Kwan 1990). But since only a miniscule proportion of rapes are reported, either to the police or the victim scheme, we are left with the dispiriting prospect that many more victims exist than this or any other voluntary sector scheme could hope to deal with.

Moreover, it is likely that severe under-reporting will continue. In Hong Kong's ethical and cultural context, rape or serious sexual assaults bring about disgrace, misfortune, or guilt to the family and/or community. It may also be that even the limited programme now on offer provides criminal justice agencies with an excuse for not according rape victims and their needs a higher priority. The argument would be that if they need help, they should approach the existing scheme.

In brief, this victim programme is generally considered to be a humanitarian response to people who are in trouble. It partializes the problem, looking at the psychosocial dimension of the individuals rather than challenging the inadequacy of the justice system and structural or societal forces which constitute the social problem of sexual assaults.

Ideologies and Victims

The victim provisions described above vary in their objectives, structures, and forms of help. Where do they fall within the range of ideological approaches to victims that have been developed in Western countries in the last few years? Victimology is now a broad area of study, with a wide range of views (see for example Schneider 1982). But generally speaking, three broad approaches to crime victim issues can be identified: one based on 'care' or 'welfare', one on restitution, and one on victim rights.

The 'care' or 'welfare' model is mainly based on the principle that the community should, as far as possible, absorb the burden of severe hardship suffered by individual citizens as a consequence of misfortunes like illness, accidents, or unemployment (Mawby 1988). Emphasis is placed on providing for victims rather than on the criminal nature of the offence. The problems of crime victims are perceived to be a manifestation of stress, psychological trauma, or economic needs. No particular reference is made to the moral aspect of crime or to the punishment of the offender, providing that the victims' injuries or traumas are treated professionally and hardship is alleviated. However, services are not provided as a right, but according to perceived need, often on an *ex gratia* basis. The Criminal and Law Enforcement Injuries Compensation Schemes, refuges for battered spouses, and services for victims of rape and sexual assault bear some characteristics of this model.

Models based on restitution often ride on the shoulders of retributive sentencing philosophies, which have been resurgent in recent years (von Hirsch 1976; for an example of recent moves towards retributive policies, see Home Office 1986). The retributive approach in general seems to have wide support from the Hong Kong public (Lau and Kuan 1988). Within this approach, the general principle is that the offender should be punished in proportion to the seriousness of the offence, and that while the punishment reflects the harm done to society, there should also be compensation to the victim for harm done to him or her. Court-based compensation orders thus stand within this ideological framework. However, this is not to say that individual victims share the same view as the general public about their case, for example in relation to the punishment of the offender and the extent of compensation, if any.

The third, rights-based, model has not yet taken hold in Hong Kong. There do not so far seem to be any advocates for it. In other jurisdictions, however, demands for victims to have rights in relation to court proceedings, compensation, and even sentencing have become major issues (Mawby 1988, van Dijk 1988). In this approach, the argument is that victims should have some ability to influence key decisions — that their case is, in Christie's (1977) word, their 'property' and they should be able to exercise choices as to how it is disposed of. In addition, they should have the right to participate in court hearings as aggrieved parties and not simply as witnesses in the state's case against the offender; and should be entitled to not only compensation but also other forms of help from welfare agencies.

Current practice in Hong Kong, so clearly based on the 'welfare' view of victim needs, presents several challenging questions. For example: should the needs of crime victims be viewed as problems of a more general psychological or economic nature? Would these services avoid such unintended side-effects as generating expectations among victims that cannot be satisfied? And would these services be free from the stigmatizing features of the established welfare institutions as victims might often be unduly labelled as persons in need of treatment? In short, victim programmes characterized by the 'care' ideology bear moralistic overtones. Many are reserved for certain categories of what are considered to be 'deserving'. This model represents a form of charity, or a humanitarian response to people in trouble. In no way does it promote social justice for victims.

However, the outlook is cloudy rather than sunny. For example, the government's current philosophy of welfare provision is to reduce government commitment, to direct attention toward the voluntary sector in the community, and to encourage counselling rather than financial provisions in the welfare service field (Hong Kong Government 1990). None of this suggests that victims are likely to be significantly better cared for in welfare terms, nor that they are likely to be accorded any entitlements. At another level, Smale (1984) points out a core problem of crime victims seems to be their loss of social trust and their feelings of alienation from their community, and this urgently calls for a re-development of 'community' which could be achieved through the mobilization and integration of a diverse range of organized social resources, both voluntary and government-financed. Yet it is difficult to see how this could be done, not only because of the current financial climate, but also because entrenched 'welfare' attitudes towards victimization individualize the problem and do not encourage it.

Conclusions

To protect society, the main emphasis of the criminal system is 'to sustain the rule of law by preventing crime wherever possible; by detecting the culprit when crimes are committed; by convicting the guilty and aquitting the innocent; by dealing firmly, adequately, and sensibly with those found guilty; and by giving proper effect to the sentences or orders which are imposed' (Home Office 1986). By contrast, much less attention is paid to the victim. Indeed, the victim's needs and feelings are ignored by the professionals at various stages in the criminal justice process. The victim, in general, has no accepted role to play other than being functionally and legally 'just another witness in court' (Shapland 1982).

The possible consequence is that the victim does not always co-operate in an effective or useful way. More essentially, the victim has to rely on the support, help, or care from the family and/or community because his or her needs cannot be fully met within the criminal justice system. Community care is important to victims not only because they are marginal members of the criminal justice system, but also because they are often the forgotten people in the field of social services or welfare provision. More crucially, in view of the government's current philosophy of minimizing its welfare obligations, crime victims cannot expect much from the government's intervention on the basis of a collective well-being. Rather, individual crime victims have to solicit assistance from statutory and voluntary resources. The basis for a more trenchant rights-based model of victim assistance does not yet exist in Hong Kong.

Current victim schemes and programmes have grown in a haphazard fashion, some perhaps as the result of developments in Britain, some in response to local needs. There has been no systematic thinking about victim provision in Hong Kong. As a result, schemes operate with different and possibly incompatible theoretical assumptions, objectives, and 'target groups'. In some cases, the schemes' objectives and operating assumptions were imported wholesale and may not fit with Hong Kong's needs.

Three developments would be of use in sorting out this situation. There should be joint planning in need assessment for victims, which would begin to identify priorities. At the current level of provision, coordination of service delivery is almost irrelevant, since there is too little to coordinate. In the case of injury compensation for battered wives, for example, there needs to be further discussion of the apparent incompatibility of the approaches of the compensation scheme and social work assumptions and objectives. In addition, further talks between agencies on ways to avoid 'secondary victimization' would be a major advance. Third, the lack of published — or perhaps even any — monitoring and evaluation of programme effectiveness is alarming. Programmes run the risk of operating without reference to real needs, or indeed without due regard for the wider research findings in the field of victimology.

Last but not least, the current major provision of victim programmes seems to be hampered by the absence of a really sound philosophical basis. Neither of the two models now apparent in Hong Kong — 'welfare' and 'retribution/restitution' — can be considered entirely satisfactory. The first represents a form of charity or a humanitarian response to people in trouble, and in no way can this promote social justice. The second remains focused on the offender, without genuine consideration of victims' needs and participatory rights within the criminal justice process. There are problems, too, associated with the 'rights' model; primarily they are that victim rights can become treated by the criminal justice system as though they are duties, so that victims become caught up in the bureaucratic processing of their case and suffer continuing trauma as a result (van Dijk 1988). But it has to be said that in Hong Kong, even though victims may be spared this problem, they have none of the benefits it brings either.

In conclusion, attention must be paid to the fact that crime victims have the right to services aimed at addressing the difficulties and inconveniences caused by crime. This includes at least four areas of concern: (a) the victim's right to play an active role in the process of the criminal justice system; (b) the right to knowledge of the process of a criminal case at various stages; (c) the right to financial help, and; (d) the right to advice and support. People involved in various programmes must see themselves not as offering charity or professional counselling, but as making a collective effort to 'reconstruct a caring community'.

Note

1. These percentages can be calculated from data published annually in the Hong Kong *Annual Digest of Statistics*: see for example Census and Statistics Department (1990b).

10 The Courts and the Judiciary

Lo Man-chiu

Law courts are not constituted by legal rules alone. They are situations in which working relationships are formed and maintained. Such relationships are not only incidental to, but constitutive of, the court process. So long as human actors are involved, such relationships are inevitable. Legal rules are important, of course. The law is intended to be impartial, and legal justice largely consists in the production of similar results in similar cases irrespective of persons. The courts are intended to be impersonal settings where impartiality prevails. Yet there is no doubt that a purely legalistic picture of the court process is unrealistic. The law has to be applied in concrete situations, where the court is required to decide publicly who and what to believe, what is relevant, and what, in the circumstances, is just. Decisions are routinely made on the credibility of witnesses, the probability of allegations and promises, and how people appear, behave, and relate to others. While these decisions are made in the light of legal rules, they are made by people. Ultimately, it is human judgement, not the law, that must produce these decisions. Moreover they are not just produced by the judge or magistrate. Other actors, in particular the lawyers and the defendants, can play a significant part in shaping the final decision.

Lawyers usually become aware of the unreality of the legalistic conception by experience. At law school, aspects of this are sometimes presented in the context of advocacy skills, to which law students are introduced towards the end of their training.[1] For most of the time, however, the substance of legal training is only the legal rules. The danger, of course, of emphasizing non-legal aspects too much is that it threatens the whole basis of legalistic justice. It is not surprising that the importance of the non-legal aspects of the court process is seldom acknowledged by practising lawyers.[2]

The focus of this chapter is on the Magistrates' Courts where the bulk of criminal work is done. In 1988, for example, the magistrates heard 525,786 cases, the District Court had 1,514 criminal cases filed, and the High Court heard 296 criminal cases and 1,814 appeals from magistracies (Census and Statistics Department 1989). Although the District and High Courts handle the most serious cases, the number of people attending the Magistrates' Courts each day — defendants, witnesses, police, lawyers, and law officials — make them the most important in the Hong Kong system.

No attempt is made here to cover the legal rules, which are contained in law textbooks. The legal rules are always in the background, but they do not cover everything in court. In fact, most participants are not expected to have any proficiency in them. For those who are proficient, the discourse of legal rules can be a powerful front behind which legal actors unwittingly fall prey to the maze of informal non-legal relationships. Making explicit the fact that the world of legal discourse is not the only level of reality would certainly help the actors to make more rational decisions.

The account provided in this chapter is theoretical. It is more an account of what can be than what is the case. Until recently, there has been no significant sociological study — indeed not much study of any kind — of Hong Kong law courts.[3] In consequence, it is necessary to draw on studies in other Common Law jurisdictions. There are two reasons why such an exercise may be worthwhile. The first is that Hong Kong courts do share a common tradition with courts in England and Wales, Australia, and, to an extent, the United States and Canada. Research results in these other jurisdictions may serve at least as a spur to empirical research in Hong Kong. Second, like other common law jurisdictions, Hong Kong courts are mostly open to the public. Although not everything is visible in a personal visit to the courts, much of what is said in this chapter can be observed and verified.

The Setting

The law court is an assemblage of actors for the disposal of cases. Each actor has a pre-defined role to play in the process. Their motives, ideals, and perceptions may differ. Some may see their job as dispensing justice, some as avoiding the stigma of a criminal conviction or a jail sentence. Structurally, the process has an objective of its own — the processing of cases. The law court ceases to exist as such if it stops dealing with the cases brought before it.

The pressure of this objective is especially visible in the Magistrates' Courts, where most of the criminal cases are processed. Very often, routine cases are dealt with in such a summary way that most defendants new to the courts find it very difficult to adjust to. The magistrate, on the other hand, cannot afford the time to attempt to 'convert' every defendant to the court's own definition of the situation. With this productive imperative in mind, it is easy to notice in the court setting that some actors are more familiar with the prevailing rules than others. These 'regulars' are there every day because their jobs require them to be there. It is usually these actors who must form working relationships with the others in order to meet the productive imperative. Others, such as lawyers, may or may not be 'regulars'. Some solicitors, for example, may spend most of their time in courts; most, however, do little criminal work and appear in court rarely. There are also the defendants who are there under compulsion. A few are 'regulars', but only in the sense that they are frequently prosecuted. They are not committed to maintaining any working relationships; their concern is probably to get out of the situation as soon as possible.

It makes a difference whether a certain actor is a 'regular' or 'non-regular'. It is the 'regulars' who know, give practical effect to, and sometimes even help to form, the rules, both formal and informal, of the court process. Their main orientation is toward each other and the smooth running of the courtroom. Regulars try to maintain workable relationships with other regulars, may be cooperative with them, and in turn expect a degree of trust and cooperation. The non-regular is a stranger and is regarded as such. His unfamiliarity with the rules makes him liable to disrupt the regulars' 'definition of the situation', perhaps unwittingly.[4] Rather than being a candidate for cooperation, he is potentially in need of control. With these points in mind, the following sections discuss the roles and characteristics of some of the major actors in the 'courtroom drama': magistrates and judges, defendants and defence lawyers, and — of particular significance in Hong Kong — the interpreters.

Magistrates and Judges

Much has been written on judges in common law jurisdictions, and a large proportion of it is critical (see for example Griffith 1985 on British judges). But there is little of substance on the Hong Kong judiciary. Hong Kong judges do not exactly fit in the modes characterized by studies because they are not recruited or dismissed in the same ways and are subject to different conditions of employment. However, they identify themselves with the same tradition, being required to take cognizance of or be bound by English case law. They are mostly trained in the United Kingdom, or at least in the English common law tradition.

As in the UK, judges are more and more constrained to take a 'public view', giving more weight to administrative policy, rather than a 'private' view, which puts the individual citizen's right before the demands of the state.[5] They are required to give effect to the ever-increasing volume of statute law, and to laws initiated by the executive to enforce policies— such as immigration or deterrence of crime— which often favour administrative feasibility or expediency. The courts often regard themselves as constrained to interpret these statutes in order to give effect to these policies. Higher courts have felt it necessary to set sentencing guidelines in certain cases, such as those involving dangerous drugs, illegal immigrants, or support of a policy of deterrence.[6] By contrast, common law notions of individual liberty nowadays are less important and always qualified or eroded by statute. Common law protections are mainly procedural or negative in nature, and may now be insufficient to safeguard the citizen against the state.

The Hong Kong judiciary is peculiar in a number of respects. Magistrates in particular are potentially subject to a number of administrative incentives and disincentives. Unlike the English situation, in which the majority of magistrates are appointed from among the community and serve on a voluntary basis, in Hong Kong they are almost all 'stipendiaries'—professional, salaried civil servants.[7] Yet they do not enjoy the special security of tenure given to judges of the Supreme Court and the District Court. Some are engaged on fixed-term contracts with no automatic right of renewal. Long-serving magistrates may suddenly find their contracts not renewed.[8] On the other hand, they have the prospect of promotion to the positions of principal or chief magistrate, while appointments from among magistrates to the District Court bench are not infrequent. Yet some magistrates are promoted sooner than others and some not promoted at all. Cases like these have led to a belief that 'those who don't toe the line won't be tolerated'.

Due to a substantial gap in income between local private practice and a judicial appointment, a substantial proportion of Hong Kong judges and magistrates are recruited from the government's own legal officers, or from overseas. There is no precise figure for the number of expatriate magistrates, but in December 1989, of 44 sitting magistrates (excluding the Chief Magistrate, coroners, and tribunal officer), only 13 had Chinese names.[9] By and large, the following characterization, attributed to Sir Denys Roberts, a former Chief Justice of Hong Kong, is still applicable:

Generally a judge is middle-aged and, by comparison with most of society, well paid and enjoying a comfortable middle-class standard of living. His ways of thought and pattern of life, even assuming, as is usually not yet the case in Hong Kong, that he is of the same race as the defendants, are very different from theirs.[10]

Judges and magistrates are indeed likely to be middle-aged, because it is the practice that candidates must attain the age of 35 before being considered for appointment as a magistrate. The age requirement had been 40 for many years, a requirement relaxed recently due to difficulty in recruitment. Moreover, Sir Denys' reference to the judge as 'he' is apt, since the judiciary is overwhelmingly male. The High Court and Court of Appeal do not yet have female judges, although in December 1989, there were six females among the 44 sitting magistrates. And it must be true that the contrast between the magistrate and the defendant is even more pronounced where the magistrate is of a different race and is recruited from overseas. Not only are his ways of thought and pattern of life vastly different, but the language barrier makes positive adjustment difficult.

In a Magistrates' Court, structurally it is the magistrate's definition of the situation which prevails. He has the ultimate responsibility for, as well as control of, the court business. Yet in order to exercise such control, the magistrate has to form a working relationship with the officials. The working rules of the court are the result of an implicit negotiation of the magistrate's own definitions with the prevailing bureaucratic ethos. The magistrate may know the legal rules better, but has to rely on the court officials — mainly his clerk and sometimes the prosecutor — to figure out the administrative procedures not only of the court, but also of other government departments. He relies on his clerk to provide information which is not available to him in his chambers and to be familiar with the formal and informal means of moving the bureaucratic machine of government departments. An omission to sign a form may result in defendants being sent to wrong places, or not being brought to court, or interpreters not being available.

In addition, one of a small group of prosecutors also works with the magistrate every day. The police witnesses and police prosecutors would also make frequent appearances.[11] A magistrate sitting for some time will come to know their practices and will be in a better position to judge whether and what they present is trustworthy. Similarly, the magistrate will also come to know and understand, directly or through his clerk, their administrative problems.

The magistrate is both a judge of law and of fact. Legal arguments are infrequent before magistrates. For most of the time, the magistrate has to decide what the facts are, based sometimes on evidence (as in trials) and sometimes on allegation or even common sense (as in bail applications). In the busy environment of a Magistrates' Court, an inarticulate defendant who is a virtual stranger to the court is potentially at a disadvantage. What he says may not make much sense to anyone in court except himself because he does not know that a lot is being taken for granted. The prosecutor very often does not even have to say anything to have his position understood. The following (English) example recorded by Pat Carlen (1974: 106) in the Metropolitan Magistrates' Courts may serve as an illustration:

Magistrate: Are you asking for bail?

Defendant: I have been in custody for three days without being charged.

Magistrate: I can't go into it. I am going to remand you in custody.

Defendant: But what I am saying is that I haven't been able to contact my solicitor, and if I had . . . .

Magistrate: It's not my job. You tell everything you have to complain about to your solicitors.

Defendant: [leaning forward and speaking slowly and with emphasis] But I understand that I have legal rights. I have been in custody three days without having the charge read out to me.

Magistrate: I am remanding you in custody and, as I have told you, you can tell all this to your solicitor. You have a right to appeal to a judge-in-chambers.

The repeated reference to the absent solicitor, whom the defendant had been unable to see, is interesting. The solicitor is apparently referred to as someone who would be expected to understand the rules better and would have agreed with the court. He is certainly not seen as someone who would have stated the defendant's position more clearly and would have made a difference in the court's decision. His absence, although noted repeatedly, did not therefore worry the magistrate.

Defendants

Statistics in Western capitalist countries show that defendants are disproportionately likely to be young, male, and of a lower social class. Hong Kong has the same pattern in relation to youth and sex, and though there is no systematic data on the social class of defendants in Hong Kong, it is very likely that most come from lower-class background.[12]

In the court setting, the defendant is a stranger. The ideal of 'equality before the law' is enshrined in legal rules which deliberately exclude his personal history except at a standardized minimum. The massive turnover of cases means that he is liable to be treated as one of a number of similar cases which the court processes every day. A defendant who asserts himself as an individual case would be administratively disruptive.

If the magistrate finds it necessary to make a judgment on, for example, a person's credibility, or the likelihood that he may abscond, he is often forced to go by appearance and demeanour, and probably a scheme of stereotypes acquired by experience.[13] A defendant may of course bring the court's attention to aspects of his personal history, as is often done by defence lawyers at the sentencing stage. At other times, this may be seen as irrelevant. Especially in a court of summary jurisdiction like the Magistrates' Court, the concept of relevance often restricts the court's attention on 'what happened on this occasion' (McBarnett 1981: 16). Asking the court explicitly to take into account who you are may appear to be an affront to the impartiality of the court. For an inarticulate defendant who is unrepresented, there is even less chance of presenting himself as a person. Even for an articulate and highly intelligent defendant, the chances of being able to present himself effectively are slim, since the court uses a jargon and follows rules which only court regulars would understand. Moreover, it is in fact not necessarily to the defendant's advantage that he exhibits any familiarity with the jargon, since the court may suspect that he has been in trouble before.

Statistically, the great majority of defendants charged in Magistrates' Courts are convicted. In 1988, the conviction rate was roughly 88.4 per cent; in 1987, 94.8 per cent (Census and Statistics Department 1989: 258). Some convictions are a result of guilty pleas, but it seems likely that such cases constitute less than half the total number of convictions, while in contested cases, the chances of acquittal seem to be slightly higher (Law Society of Hong Kong 1989). The high conviction rate may be read by some as indicating that most defendants in fact have committed crimes. The number of guilty pleas tends to reinforce such a reading. What is often forgotten is that this presupposes that court proceedings are an effective and reliable means of finding the truth. This presupposition, however, has been widely questioned, even by some senior judges (Frankel 1980,

McBarnett 1976). Without such a presupposition, the high conviction rate would mean that in the majority of cases, the court tends to believe the prosecution's case.

Even a guilty plea does not necessarily mean the crime was in fact committed by the defendant. It is recognized by the courts that sometimes a defendant may plead guilty for convenience and perhaps without legal advice.[14] In many jurisdictions, 'plea bargaining' is common (Bankowski and Mungham 1976). The defendant agrees to plead guilty after taking into account such factors as the prosecution's promise to drop charges or accept lesser charges, the expectation of a lighter sentence, the defendant's perceived likelihood of conviction, saving of legal costs, the avoidance of publicity, and the stress of a full trial.

Finally, a plea of guilty from a defendant is administratively advantageous for the regulars. Too many pleas of not guilty create a backlog of trial cases for the court. Guilty pleas ease the productive pressure in the processing of cases. The prosecutor gets his job done with a conviction. The defence lawyer, even if he has advised his client to plead guilty, may be able to present himself as having obtained the best possible outcome under the circumstances. At the same time, he is often also seen by other regulars as being 'sensible'. In short, the lawyer may be called upon to play a 'confidence game' in which he serves as 'double agent' (Blumberg 1971).

Defence Lawyers

The Hong Kong lawyer belongs to a small and relatively young elite.[15] In December 1989, there were about 2,100 solicitors and 384 barristers.[16] It is generally acknowledged that the lawyers are well paid and the public sector is continually suffering from an outflow of lawyers to the private sector (Matthews 1989). Although entry to the legal professions is open to all in a publicly funded system of legal education, a few years' practice would in a majority of cases provide a middle class or higher standard of living. Class differences may make it difficult for the lawyer to identify with the client and lawyers may find it 'easier to identify with fellow lawyers, including prosecutors and judges' (Galliher and McCartney 1977).

Criminal litigation is not the most attractive kind of work for lawyers. Solicitors prefer conveyancing and other more profitable work. Contrary to popular perception, the bar traditionally see that their practice comes more from civil than from criminal work. The preference for civil over criminal work is also noted in other common law jurisdictions (Galliher and McCartney 1977: 241, Zander 1988: 34). In large part, this may be because the average criminal client cannot afford high fees; for most cases, fees are paid from public funds according to a set scale by the Legal Aid Department for defence work and by the Legal Department for prosecution work. There are certainly lawyers who do criminal work by choice — but there are also many who would rather do some other kind of work.

Lawyers are subject to the same productive imperative of the court as other officials, although in a more indirect way. Solicitors are officers of the court and owe a duty to the court as well as to clients. Barristers see it as their duty also not to waste the court's time, and competence in advocacy 'above all makes for swift and efficient dispatch of cases' (General Council of the Bar 1989: 49). Lawyers who are regulars would be familiar with the formal and informal rules of the court. They would be 'able to administer justice much more speedily and much more efficiently than those who lack this expertise'. This would mean that in the Magistrates' Courts in particular, proceedings tend to become 'repetitious and boring' with events and outcomes becoming mostly predictable (Bankowski and Mungham 1976: 98). It is this predictability that makes the efficient functioning of the court possible. The kind of understanding between the advocate and the bench is appreciated by all other court regulars. The lawyer who is 'reasonable' rather than 'fierce' (Blumberg 1971: 326) is more likely to have their cooperation. Frequently, he would be allowed more latitude in procedural matters, such as getting the court to schedule his cases to suit his convenience, and he often gets real concessions for his clients from the prosecution, such as having an additional charge dropped (Galliher and McCartney 1977: 245). An experienced lawyer who shows an understanding of the court's 'public' view on the bench is likely to be trusted and his submissions would be taken sympathetically.

Despite the apparent fact that all qualified lawyers are in some sense competent advocates by virtue of their qualifications, some lawyers are better than others. People with means are able to afford better lawyers. Even so, given the relative closeness of the lawyer to the court, especially as a court regular or potential regular, having a lawyer is still better than having none. On the whole, legally represented defendants do better than unrepresented ones in terms of acquittal rates and severity of sentences. In one English study of the Magistrates' Courts, those represented were statistically more than twice as likely to be acquitted as the unrepresented (Zander 1972). An Australian study of petty session cases showed that those represented have a better chance of being found not guilty or having the case dismissed, while the unrepresented are three times more likely to be sent to prison (Vinson and Homel 1973).

Interpreters

Among the court officials, the interpreter merits separate discussion. Perhaps in no other jurisdiction is an interpreter used so routinely and regularly. Almost all law courts use interpreters, except courts presided over by lay (or 'special') magistrates (there is one such lay magistrate in each magistracy and his power of sentencing is limited). In a sense, though, the interpreter is not eliminated in these courts. The lay magistrate in fact doubles as his own interpreter, because the legal rules which he has to apply and the court records which he has to keep are in English. A number of the lay magistrates are in fact former court interpreters. In other courts, even though the judge or magistrate may be proficient in both Chinese and English, the court is still bound to use an interpreter if any defendant or witness chooses to speak Chinese.

Structurally, the interpreter should ideally not count as an 'actor' at all. He should be a medium through which messages are transmitted. He should be transparent, so that the messages pass through him almost entirely intact.

This is impossible in reality. The languages themselves do not permit a mechanical translation because of radical differences in structure and cultural content. Moreover, the words are not the only thing in a message. Non-verbal elements in a message cannot be translated and will be mostly lost in translation. The interpreter is therefore left with a thankless task. His translation is inevitably a product of his own judgement, since there are no objective standards by which a translation can be said to be only correct one. It is this judgement, however, which makes him liable to criticism.

The great majority of defendants are Chinese, speaking the Cantonese dialect, usually called 'Punti' in the courts. The language of the courts is English. There is a genuine need for interpreters if the members of the judiciary are overwhelmingly non-local and do not speak the dialect. In such cases, the magistrate is heavily dependent on the interpreter, who thus assumes considerable importance. Not only does he interpret defendants' words into English; he also speaks with the authority of the magistrate as his mouthpiece. He becomes another court official with whom the magistrate must form a satisfactory working relationship.

The situation has changed in recent years. As more magistrates are recruited locally, more interpreters find themselves interpreting for bilingual magistrates. Increasingly, defendants who prefer to speak Chinese are in fact bilingual. More lawyers are now locally educated and bilingual. The role of an interpreter in a court in which everyone is bilingual is rather reduced. What he does becomes a mere legal formality. In addition there is a significant loss of power, with the magistrate no longer dependent on him. The special relationship between him and the magistrate is entirely transformed. It is now possible for the magistrate (and other actors) not just to ignore him, but also to criticize him. What was previously exclusively the domain of his own expertise is now liable to be trampled on.

The gradual loss of the magistrate's dependence does not mean that the interpreter's relationship with him must suffer. What is missing now is a powerful structural factor in the relationship. He is still an official. He is a regular and there is an administrative need for the magistrate to form a satisfactory working relationship with him, as with other officials. Some interpreters, in the role of court official, will help the magistrate and his clerk in minor administrative jobs in and around the court. His relationship with the non-regulars, such as witnesses and defendants, is unlikely to change. It would still be easier for the interpreter to side with another regular like him, such as the magistrate, than with many defendants.

The interpreter is familiar with the vocabulary of the court and with its Chinese translations. He would also be used to the magistrate's usual choice of words. In most cases, he would be able to render a full and satisfactory translation of what is said by the court. His familiarity with court procedures also helps him to form a view as to what is relevant and irrelevant. Continually translating irrelevant speech is an even more immediately frustrating thing than the general futility of the job itself. The temptation to do some editing must be tremendous. A student observer noted the following exchange in a Hong Kong court:[17]

Court: Where were you when you felt you were indecently assaulted?

Victim: [giving evidence in Chinese] That day, I went window shopping with my husband. We spent a few hours at the Yaohan Department Store in Sha Tin. Then we walked out to the park opposite the store. It was then that he indecently assaulted me.

Interpreter: In the park just outside Yaohan.

The sentence given by the interpreter was perhaps the only answer the court wanted to know. The interpreter, in editing out what the victim said, would have saved the court a lot of time. The alternative would not just mean the interpreter translating a lot more sentences. The court will have to record the translations. Then the court will probably spend some more time telling the witness to listen to the questions and answer them directly. This would have to be repeated many times with some witnesses who are not used to the communicative style of the court. One finds the productive imperative for efficiency once again at work here.

For the victim, all was perhaps relevant. All such detail formed part of her perception of the incident. It was perhaps a sense of grievance or outrage which she wished to convey. She was not there to be indecently assaulted. She was in fact doing what ordinary housewives do on a holiday, innocently window shopping and walking in the park with her husband. The sudden offensive act probably felt more offensive when presented in such a context.

The interpreter in this case had unwittingly sided with the court rather than with the witness. He was interpreting for the court. He apparently did not see his job as interpreting for everyone. The court's business got done efficiently at the expense of the victim's wish to present her case. The interpreter affirmed his status as a court official and his relationship with others as a court regular.

Blindfolded Justice?

Lau and Kuan (1988) found a fair amount of legal alienation among the Hong Kong public. An absolute majority (75.4 per cent) thought the legal system as a whole was just but a similar percentage (73.4 per cent) thought that court trials were unfair. The figures concerning the fairness of the substantive law were not as clear-cut. About a third of the sample gave the reply 'don't know' and the proportions of 'fair' and 'unfair' opinions were roughly one-third each.

The researchers found the figures puzzling and attempted an explanation based on the probable personal experiences of the respondents of substantive laws. This explanation does not make a distinction between substantive law and procedural law. It may be true that regarding substantive laws, the public has varying degrees of personal involvement. It may be also true that a great majority of the public do not have such personal involvement. Nevertheless, the respondents were apparently not asked about their personal experience of court procedure. The striking contrast in the figures in relation to the procedural aspects of the system therefore remains unexplained.

The analysis in this chapter in fact is confirmed by such 'puzzling' figures. The legal procedural rules such as 'equality before the law', 'everyone is presumed innocent until convicted', and the requirement of proof (beyond reasonable doubt in a criminal case) embody values which the public could perceive as fair. This was what 75.4 per cent of the respondents did. The reality in practice is, however, not simply the procedural rules. A court trial must involve human judgement in a context of social relationships. It is perhaps this aspect about which the respondents tended to be more suspicious and cynical.

Space does not permit a detailed account for every court actor. Nor is this necessary for the purpose of this chapter. It should be clear from the above analysis that court regulars, including the magistrate, the clerk, and lay prosecutors, basically are subject to the same pressures. There is the productive imperative of the court's business. There is also the organizational need to form satisfactory working relationships with each other. These in turn have an effect on other actors who may find it expedient or necessary to conform to the social rules of the court.

Legal rules belong to the realm of 'ought'. They work only through being applied to people and situations. This chapter is about people and situations in the criminal judicial process. The legal rules may embody values such as equality before the law, symbolized by blindfolded justice. But the human system through which such rules are applied cannot be ignored. This is not to deny that legal rules have a central place in the process. However, a better understanding of the human system and its actors will help to ensure that they do.

Notes

1. See, for example, Evans (1983).
2. A prominent exception is the American Realist judge Jerome Frank. See Frank (1970).
3. An empirical study of the jury in Hong Kong is in progress. See Chan, T. F. and others (1989, 1990).
4. See for example Carlen (1974).
5. A UK example of the 'public view' in relation to prison overcrowding is *R. v Bibi* [1980] 1 WLR 1193, 1194.
6. Examples of such guidelines are found in: *R. v Lau Tak-ming*,

unreported, Criminal Appeal 1989 No. 230; *AG v Ng Kin-hung and others*, unreported, Application for Review No. 5, etc., of 1990; and in the inflexible 15-month imprisonment guideline for Chinese illegal immigrants.

7. Certain candidates without legal qualifications but with considerable experience in law related to government service are appointed as lay magistrates (officially, 'special magistrates'). Lay magistrates sit alone without the assistance of legally qualified clerks.

8. Under Article XVIA of the Hong Kong Letters Patent, judges of the Supreme Court or District Court may only be removed in accordance with a special procedure, for inability to discharge the functions of the office or for misbehaviour. The situation as regards magistrates is altogether different. McGivering and Green (1990) discuss the implications of a case where a magistrate's contract was not renewed after nine years' service. He had refused to apply sentencing guidelines set by the Court of Appeal.

9. Information from the Hong Kong Government telephone directory, published in December 1989. This of course is not a completely accurate picture since some Chinese may be non-locals (for example Singaporean), while some Chinese, for various reasons, bear Western surnames.

10. Quoted in Wesley-Smith (1987: 95).

11. The same applies, although to a lesser extent, to prosecutors from other services such as the Customs and Excise, and Immigration Departments.

12. On the UK situation, see Lea and Young (1984: 97–9). Hong Kong statistics show the highest prosecution rate for those aged 16–20, and the second highest for those aged 14–15; at all stages in the criminal justice process, men vastly outnumber women; but data on social class are not available (Census and Statistics Department 1989). Of course, those arrested and prosecuted, and those who have committed crimes, are not necessarily the same persons. A recent British MORI survey shows that the middle classes are disproportionately law-breakers (*The Times,* 10 April 1989). Of all those who admitted breaking the law, 22 per cent came from the upper-middle class, which comprises only 17 per cent of the population.

13. The appearance and demeanour of witnesses is regarded as 'real' evidence; see Cross and Tapper (1985: 41).

14. *Lui Yim-po v Chow Moon Tong* [1980] HKLR 84, 85–86.

15. More than 60 per cent of the barristers practising in Hong Kong are of under 10 years' call. See Robert Tang's paper at the Conference on the Future of Legal Education and the Legal Profession in Hong Kong, December 1989.

16. These figures are quoted by Donald Yap, President of the Law Society and Robert Tang, Chairman of the Bar Association, at the Conference on the Future of Legal Education and the Legal Profession in Hong Kong, December 1989.

17. This was recorded in April 1990 by a student of the Chinese University of Hong Kong taking course LAW 101 (Law and Society), in the second term of 1989–90.

11 Corrections

Jon Vagg

British colonial rule goes hand in hand with prisons. Commodore Sir Gordon Bremner took possession of Hong Kong on 26 January 1841. Captain Charles Elliot, the head of the colony (Sir Henry Pottinger was the first governor, two years later) appointed a Chief Magistrate, Captain William Caine, on 30 April. Caine's first task was to create a police force, but in a matter of months he had also created the colony's first jail. (Victoria Prison, behind Central Police Station on Hong Kong Island, is on the original site, though it was built a few years later. It remains in use to this day.) The prison service remained a police function from that time until 1938, when a separate department was set up, headed by a Commissioner of Prisons.

A detailed history of Hong Kong's prisons would undoubtedly be interesting; and one has never been written. But for the purposes of this chapter it suffices to move history along to 1982, when the Hong Kong Prison Service was reborn as the Correctional Services Department (CSD). It was held that this name better reflected the intentions of the service which were, broadly speaking, to reform and rehabilitate offenders. It is not, of course, the only agency in Hong Kong that deals in 'corrections'. The Social Welfare Department (SWD) has largely similar aims both for its non-custodial work in probation and community service orders, and for the custodial institutions for juveniles that function under its auspices. These, however, will have to await another account. The following sections of this chapter briefly describe CSD organizational arrangements, prison regimes, current operational problems, and 'outcomes' in terms of recidivism rates.

The Organization of CSD

In 1989, about 12,500 persons were, on conviction, given custodial sentences; this figure includes slightly over 2,000 individuals sent to drug addiction treatment centres operated by CSD. In addition, about

3,100 offenders were given probation orders, served under the supervision of probation officers employed in the Social Welfare Department. The vast majority of offenders, including about two-thirds of those convicted of serious offences, thus received some 'non-correctional' sentence from the courts. In most cases, this would have been a fine. The size of the 'correctional sector' should not, therefore, be exaggerated. However, the concept of 'prison' stands in penal thinking as the last resort of criminal justice outside of the death penalty. As Winston Churchill is reputed to have said, prison conditions are an indicator of the humanity of the criminal justice system as a whole, if not society as a whole.

Correctional Services operate five distinct types of institution: adult prisons, young offender training centres, a detention centre, drug addiction treatment centres, and a psychiatric centre for mentally abnormal offenders. These neat labels are slightly confused by CSD's description of some establishments as 'correctional institutions', but they will suffice here.[1] Prisons deal on the whole with adults (i.e. aged 21 and over), though prison sentences can be passed on persons under this age. However the custodial sentences passed on young offenders are usually detention centre or training centre orders. Sha Tsui Detention Centre accepts males aged 14–24, and the training centres accept males and females aged 14–20 (with separate institutions for the two sexes). The drug addiction centres and Siu Lam Psychiatric Centre both deal with highly specialized segments of the offender population.

Descriptions such as 'prison', 'training centre', and 'detention centre' are poor guides to what goes on in the institutions. Establishments described as prisons vary greatly as to their physical environment, the types of inmates housed there, and their specific functions within the prison system as a whole. Moreover, what prison actually means for an inmate is likely to vary, depending upon factors such as his or her own security classification and the level of security — maximum, medium, or minimum — of the institution. The same is of course true for treatment centres and to some extent for the detention centre, which is split into two halves catering for different age groups.

The three pieces of legislation central to CSD — the Prisons Ordinance (Cap. 234), the Training Centres Ordinance (Cap. 280), and the Detention Centres Ordinance (Cap. 239) — like the British models they are based on, say comparatively little about the actual running of penal establishments. The Prisons Ordinance contains three main provisions — for the Governor to appoint the

Commissioner of Correctional Services and other officials, the Secretary for Security to designate places as prisons, and the Governor in Council to make rules concerning the regulation and government of prisons. Most of the other clauses in the Ordinance deal with matters which, while important, are rarely burning issues; offences against prison discipline by staff, exemption of staff from some forms of jury service, the medical treatment of inmates, the Prisoners' Welfare Fund, and the like. More specific provisions are in the Prison Rules and their training centre and detention centre counterparts, and in unpublished, internal Standing Orders and other documents. Nonetheless, most rules and regulations are worded in ways that allow the Department substantial flexibility about matters such as the ways in which particular inmates — for example, those alleged to constitute a security risk — are dealt with. Moreover, and notwithstanding the implementation of Hong Kong's Bill of Rights, inmates have and will probably continue to have few legally-enforceable rights of any real substance in relation to their treatment by CSD.

Regimes[2]

Visitors to CSD establishments will usually see a high degree of order and purposeful activity — much higher, in fact, than one sees in any English or European establishment. Inmates will be busy in the workshops, some admittedly only folding and gluing government envelopes, but many engaged in modern industrial processes. Inmates march smartly in line from one activity to the next; and while waiting for meals, or in recreation periods, there will be no lounging around and no idle conversation. Staff come to attention and salute as senior officers pass by — and inmates, too, stand at attention until they are told to 'carry on'. In centres for young offenders, a visitor may well pass by a group of inmates being given military-style parade drill, or listening attentively to a lecture on the rules they must observe and privileges they may receive. Vocational training and educational facilities, while variable, are generally good. Stanley, Shek Pik, Lai Chi Kok, and Siu Lam — the two long-term prisons, reception centre, and psychiatric centre respectively—accommodate almost all their inmates in cells. Other establishments are mainly or entirely dormitories. If the visitor is shown a dormitory, it will invariably be spick and span, with the blankets folded military-style into 'bed boxes' and inmates' possessions neatly placed into small wooden lockers. Personal belongings are few; often only a toothbrush and toothpaste, a few books, and maybe a small transistor radio. The best comparison that comes to mind is one of military discipline and the spartan conditions of army barracks for new recruits.

Training centre regimes are even more regimented, though with a strong orientation to vocational training and education; inmates spend half the day working and half in educational or vocational classes. They operate a 'progressive' system, in which inmates can be promoted through several grades, offering successively more opportunities and fewer restrictions. The detention centre runs on similar lines but is even stricter than the training centres. Both training and detention centre orders are indeterminate. Detention centre sentences run for a minimum of one and a maximum of six months; training centre sentences for a minimum six months to a maximum three years, with the point of release being determined, not by the court, but by the Senior Superintendent on the advice of an institutional review board. In practice, most training centre inmates are released after serving about 15 months.

Daily routines vary with the institution, and weekend routines are different to weekdays. And in young offender institutions, more time is given to education. But, broadly speaking, they follow this pattern: get up at 0630, wash, and fold blankets and sheets ready for an inspection at 0700. Inmates then have a substantial breakfast and exercise, starting work at 0830. They cease work at midday, have a light lunch, and resume at 1300. Work finishes at 1630 and they have an evening cooked meal, exercise, and a period of relaxation (not necessarily in that order). They may attend evening classes but will, in any event, be given a supper of bread and milk and then locked up for the night at about 2100, with 'lights out' about an hour later.

Two further points are also worth mentioning. First, communication with the outside world is rather limited. Convicted adult inmates are entitled to two visits per month (though usually receive more in practice). Since they have no direct access to telephones, other communication must be by mail. Second, while there is a system of one-third remission for good behaviour for prison sentences and a nascent parole system for medium and long-term offenders, for offenders sent to other CSD facilities, the sentence does not end at the point of release. On completion of training centre, detention centre, and drug addiction treatment centre sentences, there is a period of post-custody supervision (three years for training centre, one year for the others) intended to ensure that the ex-inmate has indeed reformed — with the threat of recall to the institution hanging over his or her head.

The system has not always been so strict or so orderly. Much of what now exists has been either created, or implemented if it previously existed on paper, since 1973. On 19 April 1973, there was a major riot in A block of Stanley prison. Some 390 inmates took part, holding three prison officers hostage for about three hours. They were, fortunately, released unharmed and the riot quelled by teargas. Subsequent official accounts of the incident (Commissioner of Prisons 1974, Government Information Services 1974) alluded to the changes in the prison population, with an increase in the number of young violent offenders; prison overcrowding; staff shortages leading to problems in maintaining the regime; and the riot being sparked by a crackdown on drug trafficking in prison. All these problems were substantiated both in the official accounts and in the press and undoubtedly did contribute to the riot. However, subsequent events demonstrated that they were not the full story. By August 1974, it emerged that some 26 officers at Stanley — almost 10 per cent of the staff — had either been suspended from duty, dismissed, or arrested for a range of disciplinary and criminal offences. In October, it was disclosed that an ICAC investigation had identified several rackets, including collaboration between staff and some inmates to extort money from the families of other prisoners (*South China Morning Post* 5 August 1974, 10 September 1974, 5 October 1974).

This brief account of the 1973 riot serves two purposes. First, it is a tribute to the prison management of the time that such a situation was turned around, apparently in the space of a couple of years. Second, it suggests that much of the discipline that was instituted in prisons after 1973, and which still prevails, is backed by fears that a similar loss of control could happen again.

Current Operational Problems[3]

The two major operational problems in 1989–90 were overcrowding and staff shortages.

In mid-1990, the prisons, training centres, and detention centre had a combined capacity of 8,039 persons; their combined population was 11,147. The correctional system was holding 39 per cent more inmates than it was designed for. But overcrowding was not spread equally across institutions. It was highest (at 88 per cent) in the detention centre, though here again it was much higher for some categories of inmates in the institution than it was for others. Overcrowding was higher than average (at 48 per cent) in maximum security prisons, and therefore lower in medium and minimum security prisons and in training centres. Nonetheless, specific institutions, such as Lai Chi Kok Remand Centre and Pik Uk Training Centre, were much more overcrowded than other broadly comparable institutions.

The reasons for this overcrowding are twofold. First, prison accommodation had, in previous years, been turned over to house Vietnamese boat people. For example, in 1980 the CSD lost the use of Chi Ma Wan, with a capacity of more than 1,000. The system's total capacity is less now than it was in 1985 when 9,397 places were available. Second, the policy change of May 1988 in relation to illegal immigrants from China had begun to bite by the beginning of 1989. The new policy was to prosecute illegal immigrants (IIs) and give an average 15-month prison sentence on conviction. This resulted in the prison population increasing by about 9 per cent in the first six months of 1989. By mid-1989, the intake of illegal immigrants was being balanced by the discharge of those who had been sentenced in 1988. Nonetheless, by mid-1989 CSD had about 11,500 inmates to deal with and, following further increases in the numbers of illegal immigrants from the second quarter of 1990, the penal population rose to just under 12,000 by the middle of that year. In almost every establishment, IIs constituted a significant proportion of the inmates. While prison systems in England, France, and some states in America currently have much greater levels of overcrowding, their experience demonstrates the rapid decline in prison regimes that crowding entails. In short, by late 1990 the pressure of numbers in Hong Kong prisons was intense, and in need of correction.

Meanwhile, staffing has been problematic. At the end of 1989, the authorized staffing level was 7,050, with 6,578 staff in post. This may not sound a particularly bad situation, but it is not good either. In crude terms, in 1980 there were 4,189 staff looking after an average of 9,765 inmates on any one day; that is, one officer for every 2.3 inmates (Commissioner of Prisons 1981). The situation had improved by the middle of the decade, with the staff strength increased to 6,335 and the average daily prison population fallen to 8,209 by 1985 (Correctional Services Department 1986). The ratio was thus one officer for every 1.3 inmates. By 1989, however, the 6,578 staff in post were supervising an average daily population, swelled by sentenced IIs, of 11,530 (Correctional Services Department 1990). This gives a ratio of one officer for every 1.8 inmates. The gains made in the first part of the decade were partly wiped out in the second half. Moreover, these are crude figures. They do not, for example, take account of the CSD commitment to staffing Vietnamese detention centres. Whitehead, for example, reputedly has a staff requirement of nearly 300 officers. In practical terms, then, CSD is probably almost back to the position it was in 10 years ago.

It may come as a surprise that prisons require such a high staffing ratio; but in fact the figures, in comparison with other developed countries, are not particularly good. Such comparisons are problematic for a number of reasons: prison officers do not work the same hours, and prison systems have different staffing commitments. Nonetheless, the ratio is about the same as England, which itself has experienced severe staffing problems, and only just over half the ratio of countries we like to think of as penologically advanced, such as the Netherlands and Denmark (Brydensholt et al. 1983, King and McDermott 1989, Netherlands Ministry of Justice 1984). They suggest, in short, that the system is understaffed.

Meanwhile, prison administrators in Hong Kong have just begun to experience litigation about inmate rights. Prison litigation is now well established in many jurisdictions, where it has resulted in the gradual development of recognized inmate rights (Morgan and Bronstein 1985, Richardson 1985). The kind of legal challenge that we may see more of in the future is illustrated by the case of Sakchai Suwannapeng.[4] A Thai citizen, he was arrested on 21 October 1989 on arrival in Hong Kong and remanded to Lai Chi Kok two days later, pending extradition proceedings in relation to drug trafficking. The Correctional Services administration gave him category 'A' security status and placed him in solitary confinement forthwith. He was held in the 'close supervision unit' at Lai Chi Kok, locked up for about 23 hours a day, and denied association with other inmates. He was also denied his privileges as an unconvicted prisoner—for example, to have food brought in and to have beer or wine. He made an application for judicial review of the decision to segregate him.

The Correctional Services were required to explain their decision to the court. At various times, they asserted that it was for 'management reasons', 'security reasons', and to prevent an escape attempt, to prevent his corrupting other inmates, to prevent his corrupting prison staff (he was alleged to be extremely wealthy), and to protect him from assassination. The judge gave all these arguments short shrift; but the case turned on a specific legal issue, namely whether there was in law a provision for an inmate to be held in segregation on any of the grounds cited by CSD. The judge determined that while Hong Kong Prison Rules provide for an inmate to be segregated as a punishment, this inmate was not undergoing punishment; and while they provide for segregation at the request of the inmate, he had not requested it. However, there is no provision for inmates to be segregated for 'operational reasons' or for the purposes of good order and discipline. When CSD argued that the segregation of subversive inmates is authorized under Standing Order S796, the judge's response was that the Prison Rules made no provision for such authorization and that the Standing Order must perforce be unlawful. In short, the judgement was that the Correctional Services (a) cannot, under the current rules, segregate inmates unless it is for punishment or unless the inmate requests it; (b) had no reasonable grounds for segregating the inmate in terms of the existing provisions; and (c) appeared to have a Standing Order which was incompatible with the law. This judgement may well be taken as a precedent enabling inmates to challenge other administrative decisions made about them, for example security classification.

Rehabilitation and Outcomes

A commitment on the part of CSD to rehabilitation permeates all its written reports. It is clearly implied by the level of resourcing that has gone into prison workshops and educational and vocational training. It is present in the formal legal structures of the sentences it administers, not least the supervision of detention centre and drug addiction treatment centre inmates for one year and training centre inmates for three years following release.

Ironically, there has been a major retrenchment of the rehabilitative ethic in Europe and the United States. Accumulated research evidence suggests that most correctional programmes are rather poor at reforming and rehabilitating offenders; while the change of name from, for example, 'prison department' to 'correctional service' has in many American jurisdictions been no more meaningful and rather less amusing than that other attempt to sanitize the world—the progressive re-designation of lavatories into 'restrooms'.

Nonetheless, rehabilitation is not only alive but in vigorous health in Hong Kong. Correctional Services officials might claim that the real problem with the 'treatment model' was that other prison systems treated it in a shallow fashion, and it often existed on paper but not in practice. They would be right. They might go on to say that in Hong Kong it has been taken seriously, and they would again be right. Rehabilitation has been treated in a more thoroughgoing fashion, and more efforts have gone into it, here than in almost any other jurisdiction worldwide.[5] At the same time, Hong Kong has a very particular brand of rehabilitative practice. It is carried out in the context of strict and paternalistic discipline, surveillance, and control.

Table 11.1 Success Rates of Inmates Released from Training Centres, 1985–1989

Supervision Expired in	Cumulative Figures		Annual Figures		
	Expired by Year End	Successfully Completed Supervision	Expired by Year End	Successfully Completed Supervision	Annual Success Rate(%)
1984	1,654	1,047	*	*	*
1985	1,912	1,240	258	193	74.8
1986	2,228	1,467	316	227	71.8
1987	2,587	1,707	359	240	66.9
1988	2,875	1,904	288	197	68.4
1989	3,152	2,087	277	183	66.1

* Figures not calculated (1984 data are only included in order to make calculations concerning 1985).

Source: Correctional Services Department, *Annual Reviews*, 1984–9 (calculations by the author).

One consequence of the rehabilitation ethic is that those who espouse it are apt to be judged on the basis of their success. What counts as success is a thorny question, but the commonly-used criterion (because it is the most easily measured) is the proportion of released inmates convicted of another offence within a given time period. Hong Kong figures are unconventional in that they give success rates—that is, successful completion of the mandatory supervision period following detention centre, treatment centre, and drug addiction treatment centre orders—rather than failure rates based on reconviction. However, since someone who is reconvicted while on supervision is not deemed to have successfully completed it, the difference between the two measures is not worth extended discussion here.[6] The only practical point to note is that the published statistics, not being produced for comparative research purposes, are based on the supervision periods, which vary with the type of custody. Moreover they are not annual figures, but cumulative statistics giving the total proportion of persons who have successfully completed supervision since the programme in question (detention, training, drug addiction centre) was instituted. Since there is no supervision period following imprisonment (unless by virtue of early release on parole) no statistic is published for prisons and the discussion below revolves around training centre inmates.

A feature of using cumulative statistics is that even quite a large change in the rate for one year will not greatly affect the cumulative figure. This can be illustrated by a hypothetical example. If the same number of inmates are released each year, and the rehabilitation 'success rate' over a nine-year period is 90 per cent, but in the 10th year it is only 50 per cent, the success rate for the whole 10-year period is 86 per cent—and in such a case that would be the figure published. In fact, most of the figures are rather stable. From 1980 to 1989, detention centre figures ranged from 94.1 to 95.0 per cent for younger offenders and 94.1 to 95.8 per cent for the older group. The training centre figures for males range from 62.1 to 66.2 per cent, with 1980 a rogue year, showing a rate of 52.6 per cent. In this series, the higher rates come in the latter years. Since raw numbers are published each year along with the rates it is possible to investigate this a little further. Table 11.1 indicates that the rate of successful completion of supervision since 1985 has been in the range of 66.1 to 74.8 per cent.

Undoubtedly, the detention centre success rate is higher than the others largely because the follow-up period is one rather than three years. But even so, all these figures—for training, detention, and drug addiction centre success rates—are high in comparison with correctional services in other countries. In England, for example, reconviction rates within two years of release are about 60 per cent for all offenders, and much higher—between 65 and 80 per cent—for young offenders and juveniles. The high Hong Kong success rates, if translated into failure rates, suggest only 5 to 10 per cent of detention centre leavers are reconvicted within one year and only about 30 to 35 per cent of training centre leavers are reconvicted within three years.

This is, therefore, a feature of CSD work which demands further attention. How has CSD been so successful when other countries have not? While a definitive statement will have to await detailed research, three broad reasons for this are at least plausible. First, the regimes are much stricter in Hong Kong correctional facilities than in almost any other developed nation. It may be that this exerts a substantial deterrent effect, with young offenders not wishing to experience such regimes again. Second, it was mentioned earlier that the rehabilitation ethic seems more deeply entrenched in Hong Kong than it now is in most other countries. One possibility may be that Hong Kong is simply doing right what other countries have not seriously tried to do. But third, it may well be that the process of supervision results in many supervisees, including a proportion of those who might re-offend (or who have re-offended but escaped conviction), being recalled into custody. In short, the high success rates may be influenced at least in part by the extensive use of recall. This is a relatively technical factor and worth explaining, though for the sake of simplicity the discussion below concentrates on males released from training centres.

Table 11.2 Training Centre Recalls into Custody, 1984–1989 (males)

Year	Discharged Under Supervision	Supervision Completed During Year	Caseload on 31 December	Successfully Completed During Year	Recalled During Year
1984	370	*	836	*	53
1985	287	258	829	193	64
1986	297	359	776	240	61
1987	322	316	797	227	103
1988	295	288	815	197	78
1989	384	277	919	183	114

* 1984 figures for completed supervision and successfully completed supervision are not included in the table since inferences based on them would have to refer to earlier years.

Source: Correctional Services Department, *Annual Reviews*, 1984–9 (calculations by the author).

During 1986, 297 male trainees were released under supervision (Table 11.2). Their supervision period would have ended during 1989. Of the 297, 183 had successfully completed their supervision. Since this is defined as not having been reconvicted during the period, it implies that 94 had in fact been reconvicted. However, recall to training centre does not affect the success rate. It is difficult to say how many of the 1986 'cohort' had in fact been recalled. Persons under supervision can be recalled at any time during the supervision period, and so some of those released in 1986 would have figured in the recalls for each year from 1986 to 1989. Nonetheless in 1987–9, the number of recalls was about 10 to 13 per cent of the annual caseload, which translates into the likelihood that something like

20–30 per cent of trainees were in fact recalled during their supervision. Over the period covered by the table, 1,955 trainees were released and 473 recalled, a rate of 24 per cent. Some of the 1984 and 1985 recalls would have been trainees released in earlier years, just as some released in 1989 will be recalled in 1990 and 1991. But the system as a whole increased in size over time, so that using the caseload in any one year as a 'baseline' against which to index recalls of persons released in previous years is likely to result in underestimations of the proportions actually recalled.

The notion that CSD is identifying and recalling persons under supervision who are likely to re-offend, and thereby preventing them from featuring in reconviction figures, is not particularly plausible. Criminologists worldwide have so far had little success in making such predictions. However, if a relatively large proportion are in fact being recalled, it is likely that at least some of them would have been re-offenders; and the recalls would thus make some contribution to the maintenance of high success rates. Having said this, it will be interesting to see how the year-on-year (rather than the cumulative success rates) change in the years to come, since it will only be by about 1992 or 1993 that the effects of the current CSD operational problems will appear in the supervision statistics.

Summary and Conclusions

Prison discipline in Hong Kong is undoubtedly much tighter than in most developed, Western countries. Part of this may derive from the paternalistic way in which the business of rehabilitation is conceived. Part probably also derives from the measures taken after the 1973 riot, which occurred at what seems to have been a 'low point' in terms of discipline, violence, drug trafficking, and staff corruption.

There have been a number of relaxations in regimes over the last 10 or so years. More letters and visits are allowed, a greater variety of personal effects may be received from relatives, the range of canteen goods has been extended, the types of recreation available has become more varied, more hobbies are allowed, and inmates are no longer made to squat during assemblies and are called by their names rather than their prison numbers. But the nature and extent of further liberalizations will undoubtedly depend on at least three factors.

First, penal legislation, like all of Hong Kong's laws, will have to be scrutinized in the light of the Bill of Rights. It may well be that some current practices will have to be changed to conform with the Bill. In addition, now that a judicial review of a CSD decision has been successful, there may be more. In other countries, liberalization has come in large part from inmates mounting court cases against the correctional authorities.

Second, while CSD is not necessarily opposed to further liberalization of regimes, some improvements are directly linked to matters such as staffing levels. For example, increases in recreation facilities and time require increased staffing. In the current climate of staff shortages, they are unlikely to materialize. Other liberalizations, such as relaxations of censorship of mail or the availability of telephones to inmates, are probably unlikely to occur because of fears about the ways in which some inmates may abuse them. Such improvements will probably only occur if or when they are held to be implied in the Bill of Rights.

Third, it may be that Hong Kong has been successful in the area of rehabilitation, while other countries have not, partly because of the discipline in its young offender institutions. There is no evidence to support this view but it is nonetheless widely held. Further liberalization of young offender institutions would, on this view, go against the grain of the rehabilitative task. Other factors clearly also figure in the question of rehabilitation, not least of which is the extent to which treatment and detention centre recall is used. Perhaps the only safe conclusion on this whole issue is that published data raise intriguing questions about how the high success rates are achieved, and further study of the area should be on our research agenda.

Finally, it is quite clear that CSD has been massively and adversely affected by the need to keep large numbers of illegal immigrants in custody. The introduction in 1988 of prison sentences for IIs was announced as a deterrent measure, in the light of a rise in illegal immigration. All it has done is to choke up the prison system. And in the light of continuing illegal immigration, the policy has failed. It should be scrapped, and the burden lifted from the shoulders of CSD. Unfortunately we will not know for another couple of years what the effects of the policy have been on the work of CSD. We typically only know that correctional authorities cannot cope at the point where services have actually begun to break down. Moreover, in so far as any breakdown is reflected in recidivism rates, it will only become apparent in the years to come.

Notes

1. I have given no figure for the number of institutions, since it is no reflection of the number of separate regimes for inmates. Some establish-

ments are multi-purpose. Some are not prisons in the full sense of the term. There are for example three 'half-way houses' administered by CSD but accommodating persons released under supervision. Moreover, some establishments have been turned over to use for Vietnamese asylum-seekers.

2. There are no detailed studies of correctional regimes in Hong Kong. This section of the chapter is largely drawn from an earlier paper, now published (Vagg 1991), based on visits to a number of CSD establishments, and originally delivered at a conference 'Prisons Today and Tomorrow' at Buchenbach, West Germany, in September 1989.

3. Unless otherwise indicated, data for this section were kindly supplied by CSD in response to the author's enquiries. Calculations based on the data, and the implications drawn from them, are of course the author's responsibility.

4. High Court Miscellaneous Proceedings No. 157 of 1990; judgement delivered 23 January 1990.

5. I have no particular source for this statement. It is based on personal knowledge of the English, French, Dutch, West German, and Hong Kong prison systems, and indirect knowledge (through documentary sources and meetings with personnel) of many more.

6. In fact, counting success and failure is slightly complicated by the following considerations. First, if a person undergoing post-sentence supervision is detected or confirmed to have committed a breach of supervision conditions, he or she is recalled but this is not counted against the failure rate. The exception is drug addiction treatment centre inmates, who are counted in the failure rate if they are found to have breached their supervision conditions by taking drugs. Second, if a person under supervision is reconvicted, this counts as a failure and he or she is vulnerable to recall following the court decision. It is possible that a person who is reconvicted and given a fine may also be recalled. It is also possible that a person recalled for breach of supervision conditions (thus not counting against the failure rate) may subsequently be released, still under supervision, and commit an offence resulting in a further conviction, at which point he or she is counted as having failed supervision. I am indebted to CSD for this information.

12 Enforcing Workplace Safety Legislation

DAVID A. LEVIN AND STEPHEN CHIU

IN HONG KONG, as in other industrial societies, workplace safety and health have come to be defined as problems that require ameliorative action by the state. From its origins in pre-war Hong Kong, a public policy has evolved along three main lines: (1) the setting of workplace safety and health standards through legislation and regulations, (2) the creation of a Factory Inspectorate for monitoring and enforcing compliance with these standards, and (3) a system of employees' compensation for injury and death at the workplace.

Of these three elements of public policy, the first and third have received the most attention (Chen and Ng 1987, England 1989, England and Rear 1981). Relatively less attention has been given to how the observance of safety and health standards is monitored and enforced. This is not surprising since laws on safety standards and employees' compensation are in documentary form and are thus readily accessible to interested observers whereas the activities and decisions of those working in administrative organizations are much less visible. Yet it has been argued that administrative behaviour is crucial in determining the effectiveness of laws and hence what difference they make to the lives of individuals whom the laws are intended to protect or benefit (Edelman 1977: 77).

And it is lives that are at stake. While murder and armed robberies capture more attention from the media, occupational safety is arguably a much more serious problem. Its magnitude can perhaps best be grasped by comparing government figures on injuries and fatalities due to occupational accidents with crimes against the person. In 1989, there were 216 fatalities from occupational accidents compared with only 102 cases of murder and manslaughter and five attempted murders. During the same year, there were 97,234 injuries from occupational accidents compared with 9,194 serious assaults and 667 other reported offences of crimes against the person (Census and Statistics Department 1990c: 17, 96–7). Some writers have argued that a substantial proportion of occupational fatalities and accidents in industrial societies result from employer negligence in failing to follow legally required safety standards and consider such cases as falling under the rubric of 'organizational crime' or 'corporate crime' (Hagan 1989: 4–5).

In focusing on the Factory Inspectorate as the administrative agency for monitoring and enforcing compliance with workplace safety standards, our first aim is to describe how it is organized and how it operates in practice. Our second aim is to assess the effectiveness of the Factory Inspectorate in monitoring and enforcing workplace safety and health standards. In the process, we will identify some of the problems that have arisen in attempting to regulate the behaviour of employers and workers through administrative means. A concluding section considers the potential for, and constraints on the ability of, the Factory Inspectorate to enhance the quality of work life in Hong Kong. Our main argument will be that the Factory Inspectorate operates within the framework of a broader political economy that imposes severe limitations on its ability to improve the record of industrial safety.

Three limitations to our paper should be noted. First, our time frame is confined mainly to developments in the 1980s. Second, we focus on workplace safety and ignore issues relating to workplace health. Third, we concentrate mainly on manufacturing and construction.[1]

The Origins of the Factory Inspectorate

The first law concerned with industrial safety in Hong Kong was the Factory (Accidents) Ordinance of 1927, the purpose of which was 'to provide against accidents in factories'. Among other things, the Ordinance defined a factory and empowered the Governor in Council 'to make such regulations as he may think desirable for the purpose of preventing accidents in factories, of relieving persons suffering from the effects of accidents, and requiring notification to be made in relation to accidents occurring in factories.' It further empowered the Governor to appoint Inspectors and Assistant Inspectors of Factories with specified powers including the power 'to enter, inspect, and examine' any factory and the 'power to make such examination and enquiry as may be necessary to ascertain whether the requirements of the Ordinance are being complied with'.

This Ordinance was replaced by a consolidating Factories and Workshops Ordinance of 1932 that combined industrial safety matters with those concerning safety and welfare of women and children employed in manufacturing. An important new feature was the requirement that factories and workshops be registered, an essential step for keeping track of factories but one that was subsequently to prove difficult to enforce (Chan, S. 1986). Other legislative changes followed in the 1930s, and by the end of the decade the basic features of a factory inspectorate system had become institutionalized. There were factory inspectors, bylaws dealing with dangerous conditions in factories, procedures for notification of accidents and investigation of these accidents, and the collection of statistics on industrial accidents (Butters 1939).

The pre-war legislation remained in effect after World War II but as Hong Kong's postwar industrial take-off began, the government recognized that the legislation on industrial safety needed to be updated. This led to the enactment in 1955 of the Factories and Industrial Undertakings Ordinance (Cap. 59: hereafter referred to as the FIUO), which amended the laws relating to factories and industrial undertakings (and also to the employment of women, young persons, and children) and empowered the Governor to appoint a Chief Labour Inspector, Senior Labour Inspector, and Labour Inspectors, to carry out the purposes of the Ordinance.[2]

The original mission assigned to the Factory Inspectorate — to provide against accidents in factories — has broadened since the late 1960s. New safety regulations have come into effect for specific technologies, materials, and processes used in industry.[3] Regulation of safety has been extended to the construction industry beginning with the Construction Sites (Safety) Regulations of 1973. In 1983, these regulations were further amended to provide for more detailed regulation of safety at construction sites. In 1990, new provisions were enacted to make the FIUO and its subsidiary regulations applicable to the industry of preparation of food for consumption and sale on the premises where the food is prepared.

At present, the Inspectorate is 'responsible for ensuring the safety, health, and welfare of workers in industry through enforcement, education, and publicity' (Commissioner for Labour 1989: 46). However, this broad mandate carries no specification of precisely what level or degree of safety and health is to be deemed acceptable, what means are to be used to ensure safety and health, how resources should be prioritized among the sub-goals of enforcement, education, and publicity, or what performance standards should be used to judge the effectiveness of the Factory Inspectorate in achieving its goals. This leaves considerable flexibility in operationalizing the mission assigned to the Factory Inspectorate. We turn next to the way in which this mission has been translated into an administrative system.

Organizational Dimensions of the Factory Inspectorate

The pre-war Factory Inspectorate was reconstituted immediately after World War II but has undergone changes over the years in terms of size, status within the Labour Department, and internal structure.

In 1965, when the title of Factory Inspector was officially distinguished from Labour Inspector, the approved establishment of the Factory Inspectorate was 50 positions. In 1970/1, the approved establishment had risen to 84. A decade later, the establishment had more than doubled to 178, with much of the growth taking place between 1976 and 1980. During the 1980s, the Factory Inspectorate continued to grow but at a much slower pace, so that the establishment stood at 228 by the end of 1989.

Prior to 1977, the Factory Inspectorate was located in the Industrial Undertakings Unit as one of three units under a Senior Labour Officer (Industry) who in turn reported to an Assistant Commissioner of Labour. In 1977, the position of the head of the Inspectorate was retitled to Chief Factory Inspector (CFI) in acknowledgement of the increased responsibilities of the post, and the CFI became directly responsible to an Assistant Commissioner of Labour (England and Rear 1981: 302). In 1979, the Industry Division was retitled the Factory Inspectorate Division.

The internal structure of the Factory Inspectorate can be described in terms of two dimensions: the vertical rank structure and the horizontal grouping of staff. The hierarchy of ranks in the Factory Inspectorate has remained unchanged since the late 1970s except for the lower ranks. At the top is the Chief Factory Inspector, then Deputy Chief Factory Inspectors, Superintendents of Factory Inspectors, and Divisional Factory Inspectors. In line with the general growth in the size of the Factory Inspectorate, the number of Divisional Factory Inspectors has increased substantially from an approved establishment of 15 in 1975 to 44 by the end of 1989.

Divisional Factory Inspectors supervise the rank-and-file Factory Inspectors. Since the latter are the 'street-level bureaucrats' who carry out much of the fieldwork involving monitoring of compliance with factory regulations, a closer look at this group is warranted. Most

Factory Inspectors are grouped horizontally into geographical divisions, which may be sub-divided at the discretion of the Divisional Factory Inspectors into districts. Divisions are grouped together under regions headed by Superintendents of Factory Inspectors. In addition, there are two specialist units. After the Construction Sites (Safety) Regulations was enacted in 1973, a Building and Engineering Division was created to specialize in monitoring safety standards on construction sites. This division had 30 inspectors in 1985 and 40 by 1990 (Safety Bulletin 1990). The other specialist unit is for noise control.

Since 1983, Factory Inspectors have been sub-divided into two ranks: Factory Inspector I and Factory Inspector II. Recruitment into the entry rank of Factory Inspector II is normally directly from school, with matriculation as the minimal entry requirement. Applicants must achieve a pass in two subjects of which one must be chemistry, physics, or maths. Three other subjects at grade C or above in the Hong Kong Certificate of Education, or a Diploma or Higher Certificate in relevant subjects from the Hong Kong Polytechnic or Technical Institute, are also required (Audit Department 1987: 23). This minimum entry level has implications for inspections which are discussed below.

A final point concerns the social composition and attitudes of the Factory Inspectorate. After World War II, it was comprised of expatriates as well as locals but since 1979, the Inspectorate has been fully localized. Little is known about attitudes of the members of the Factory Inspectorate. It was alleged by observers in the 1970s that some staff engaged in corrupt practices but evidence of this behaviour is lacking (Easey 1977, England and Rear 1975).

Monitoring and Enforcing Compliance

A core task of the Factory Inspectorate is to monitor employer and worker observance of standards set by the FIUO and subsidiary regulations. This task has become increasingly complex for three reasons. First, the number of undertakings and workers covered by the FIUO has expanded due to the growth of the Hong Kong economy and also to changes in the law. One indicator of these changes is the growth of the number of workplaces that come under the purview of the Factory Inspectorate. In 1977, there were 45,325 notifiable (then called registrable) workplaces. By 1980, the number had risen to 63,634 and by 1989 to 91,722.

A second factor complicating the work of the Inspectorate is the growing number of regulations to be enforced. Between 1976 and 1989, the number of sets of regulations under the FIUO increased from eight to 25. Each new set of regulations increases the number of items that inspectors must pay attention to and requires more time to prepare for factory visits. The Labour Department's 1980 manual of the most common compliance requirements for industrial establishments already numbered some 58 pages of fine print. New regulations and constantly changing technology mean that the skills of Factory Inspectors must be continually upgraded.

A third factor adding to the burden of the Factory Inspectorate was the formation of the Committee on Industrial Safety and Accident Prevention (subsequently renamed the Committee on Safety and Health) in 1978 under the auspices of the Labour Advisory Board. Inspectors had to devote increasing efforts to providing back-up services to the Committee such as assisting in formulating codes of safe working practices for a range of trades and industries and in industrial safety promotional activities.[4]

Because the establishment of the Factory Inspectorate has not kept pace with the growth in the number of notifiable workplaces, the intensity of monitoring has declined. Between 1977 and 1985, the ratio of notifiable workplaces to the total number of inspectors rose from 378 to 407 (S. Chan 1986). In 1989, the ratio had further risen to 441. Another indicator of the declining intensity of monitoring is the ratio between the number of factory inspections and the number of notifiable workplaces. In 1977, there were 0.70 inspections per notifiable workplace. This improved to 0.86 in 1985, but had fallen back to 0.72 in 1989. Given the large number of notifiable workplaces relative to the number of inspectors and the number of inspections that they can make, decisions therefore must be made on how to allocate scarce manpower to this task.

Different strategies are possible. One is to concentrate on the investigation of formal and informal complaints from employees (Smith 1986). A second strategy is 'targeting': bureaucratic criteria are devised to assess the degree of risk or hazard posed by particular types of industries or by particular technological processes. Those that are considered to pose relatively greater risks are then inspected more frequently. This is usually defended as a cost-effective way of using resources.

The Factory Inspectorate in Hong Kong has generally adopted this targeting strategy. Three criteria are apparently used to assess the degree of risk posed by an industrial undertaking: the size of establishment, the type of technology used, and the attitude of the employer. The working assumptions underlying these criteria appear to be that larger workplaces carry the potential for harming more persons than smaller workplaces, that certain types of technology are more hazardous than others, and that the cooperativeness of an employer is likely to be an indicator of his or her willingness to comply voluntarily with safety and health standards.[5] One result of targeting criteria is that construction sites are inspected relatively more frequently because of the industry's relatively poor record on industrial safety. In addition to 'targeting', the Inspectorate will also investigate complaints received, whether verbally or in writing, with identities of complainants kept anonymous.

The manner in which Factory Inspectors carry out the day-to-day monitoring of factory compliance with safety regulations involves a considerable degree of routinization of procedures, as would be predicted from a bureaucratic model. Inspectors enter a workplace with a standard form, the 'Factory Inspection Report' and have available the reference manual for factory inspection reports. This manual lists 'matters requiring attention' under the FIUO, with each requirement given a code number in the manual. The one-page Factory Inspection Report provides columns for matters to be drawn to the attention of the proprietor/manager. Each noted violation of a regulation is given the corresponding code number from the reference manual. There is a small space for the inspector to provide a brief description, and for an action code for each separate item listed as requiring attention. There are three action codes. A single 'X' means 'matters not attended to, you are now warned'. A double XX means 'matters not attended to, prosecution is being considered'. A single X with a circle around it means that 'a legal notice in respect of these matters is being considered'. These Factory Inspection Reports are given to the management of the industrial undertaking. The contents are explained to the management, and any problems or queries that they may have are also discussed.

Although these procedures are superficially routinized, they leave considerable room for discretion in decision-making on the part of inspectors in the field (Lipsky 1980). When there are violations of laws, an inspector has to consider the nature of the offences, whether there are mitigating circumstances, the safety performance of the offenders, and the appropriateness of legal sanctions. In deciding whether to recommend prosecution, an inspector has to take into account the seriousness of the offences and whether there is evidence to establish *prima facie* cases under the laws.

Investigating Accidents

In addition to decisions on allocation of scarce resources for the task of factory inspection, the Inspectorate also has to make decisions on which accidents to investigate. Accidents which result in fatal or serious injuries and those which are likely to have serious consequences will be investigated. Of 56,493 industrial accidents in 1989, 4,365 or 7.7 per cent were followed up. Though this ratio has been rising since 1984, it is still below the peak figure for the decade of 9.4 per cent in 1982, and well below the performance standard that 10 per cent of notified accidents should be investigated (Audit Department 1987: 22). When fatalities are involved, they are typically investigated by the Divisional Factory Inspectors, who will visit the site where the fatality occurred, investigate the circumstances, and photograph the scene. In exceptional cases, the investigation of accidents may be undertaken by the Chief Factory Inspector.

Monitoring and Enforcing Compliance

What is meant by the effectiveness of an organization and how it should be measured are controversial issues (Child 1984, Scott 1987, Wilson 1980). However, if the principal objective of the Factory Inspectorate is defined as reducing occupational fatalities and accidents, then the picture is mixed. On the one hand, occupational fatalities have declined. The average number of 213.6 fatalities per year during the decade 1980–89 is substantially lower than the average number of 277.7 per year during the decade 1970–79. By contrast the number of non-fatal occupational accidents has continued to increase more or less steadily over the past two decades from 24,351 in 1970 to 70,386 in 1980 and 97,234 in 1989.[6] Yet while total non-fatal occupational accidents increased by 38 per cent between 1980 and 1989, non-fatal industrial accidents (accidents occurring in industrial undertakings as defined under the FIUO) increased by only 20 per cent over the same decade.[7] However, non-fatal accidents in construction rose by 41 per cent between 1980 and 1989 compared with only 16 per cent for other industrial undertakings.

The rising number of industrial accidents, at a time when Inspectorate resources were increasing, have presented problems for the Labour Department. The Director of Audit, in his review of the efficiency and effectiveness of the Factory Inspectorate Division, sought to examine the 'reasons for the failure to achieve the Division's objective of reducing the number of industrial accidents' and focused, among other things, on the entry qualifications and training for the Inspectorate and its operational procedures (Audit Department 1987: 22).

The quality of those recruited into the Inspectorate was seen to be one source of the problem. In 1973, a Labour Adviser (A.J. Lineham) was appointed from the UK to study ways to improve the efficiency and effectiveness of the Factory Inspectorate. In his 1976 report, he stressed the need to recruit better trained inspectors with more industrial experience to be recruited. In 1977, the Commissioner for Labour reported to the Legislative Council that he had taken steps to implement the recommendation that new recruits to the factory inspectorate should have at least three years' industrial experience and proposed that incremental credits should be given for this industrial experience (Hong Kong Hansard 1976/7: 467).

Shortly afterwards, the Standing Commission on Civil Service Salaries and Conditions of Service considered the need for higher entry qualifications to the Inspectorate but took the view, later supported by the Secretary for the Civil Service, that the existing matriculation entry qualification was 'adequate to enable recruits to complete the required training satisfactorily' (Standing Commission 1979: 84). The result of maintaining this recruitment policy was that in 1986 some 46 per cent of the Factory Inspector grade had only the minimum qualification of matriculation while only 3 per cent were university graduates. About 70 per cent had no industrial experience when they joined the Factory Inspectorate (Audit Department 1987: 23).

A second focus of the Director's report was on the operational procedures of the Factory Inspectorate and in particular the failure of the Factory Inspectorate to meet its own performance standards. One of these standards concerned the allocation of the time of the inspectors between field inspections and office work. The Labour Adviser appointed from the UK in 1973 had noted that Factory Inspectors in Hong Kong spent only about 30 per cent of their time inspecting factories compared with a figure of about 65 per cent by their counterparts in the UK (Audit Department 1987: 22). On the basis of a 1974 Organization and Methods survey commissioned on the work of the Inspectorate, the Commissioner of Labour reported in the Legislative Council that 'the most significant improvement to be obtained will be to increase substantially field inspection time as against time spent in routine office procedures' (Hong Kong Hansard 1974/5: 847).[8] The performance standard eventually set for the Inspectorate was that Factory Inspectors should spent 50 per cent of their time on field inspection work. However, a 1981 review by the Management Services Division of the Finance Branch found that an excessive amount of time was still being spent in report writing. It was recommended that Factory Inspectors should concentrate on reporting exceptional cases only and stop minuting normal cases in files. In 1986, it was found that Factory Inspectors still spent only 33 per cent of their time on inspecting factories (Audit Department 1987: 21-2).

The Divisional Factory Inspectors also came under criticism for similar reasons. The Labour Adviser had considered this rank to be an inspecting rank that should not be confined to supervision of other inspectors. He therefore recommended that Divisional Factory Inspectors should spend more time inspecting larger and technically more difficult factories under their jurisdiction. To enable them to do this, it was recommended that the average number of subordinate staff should be reduced from eight to five. The performance standard set for Divisional Factory Inspectors was that 29 per cent of their time should be spent on factory inspections, to be allocated among visits to supervise the work of their subordinates and inspection visits to larger factories and those with poor accident records. The 1981 Management Services Division study found that the Divisional Factory Inspectors were still spending an excessive amount of time reading minutes and reports prepared by their subordinates. The Director of Audit found in 1986 that they were spending on average only 10 per cent of their time on factory inspections (Audit Department 1987: 22).

Another failure cited by the Director of Audit concerned the frequency of factory inspections and the number of factory visits to be made by each Factory Inspector/Divisional Factory Inspector per year. Factories were supposed to be inspected on average three times a year but in 1986 the average number of inspections for each industrial undertaking was reportedly only 1.23. Moreover, the average number of factory visits a year made by each inspector had fallen from 660 in 1980 to 560 in 1986, short of the standard of 715 factory visits for each Factory Inspector/Divisional Factory Inspector set by the Commissioner for Labour (Audit Department 1987: 22).

Further hampering the effectiveness of the Factory Inspectorate in the late 1980s is the problem of under-staffing. In an interview, the Chief Factory Inspector acknowledged the loss of many experienced staff due to emigration. Some 35 inspectors reportedly resigned from the inspectorate in 1989 (*South China Morning Post*, 19 April 1990, 28 June 1990). This has resulted in a drop in the ratio of the strength of the Inspectorate to the approved establishment from 99 per cent in 1983 to about 90 per cent in 1988 and 1989. The exit of Factory Inspectors has also led to the aging of the Inspectorate, since it is mainly the younger staff in the Factory Inspector I and II ranks who have left. This is of considerable concern to the Inspectorate because an aging staff is less easily retrained to keep up with the technological changes in the private sector, thereby creating problems for monitoring compliance with safety standards (*Sing Tao Jih Pao,* 8 January 1990).

During the first half of 1990, the turnover problem seems to have worsened. The strength of the Factory Inspectorate fell from 208 at the end of 1989 to 202 in June 1990. Even the approved establishment has been cut, from 228 at the end of 1989 to 221 in mid-1990. The Chief Factory Inspector has claimed that even if all vacancies were filled, the numbers would still be insufficient. In his view, a figure of 300 would be more realistic to enable the Inspectorate to cope effectively with its workload. He has accordingly pressed the Civil Service Branch and the Finance Branch to consider increasing the size of the Inspectorate in order to alleviate the problem of understaffing (*South China Morning Post*, 28 June 1990, *Sing Tao Jih Pao*, 8 January 1990).

Sanctions

The principal sanction for failure of employers (and workers) to comply with relevant provisions of the FIUO and subsidiary legislation is prosecution resulting in fines. Table 12.1 shows that the number of prosecutions by the Labour Department for violation of safety and health regulations has declined during the 1980s from the figure of 4,082 in 1980 to 2,542 in 1989. Prosecutions as a proportion of industrial accidents dropped from 8.4 per cent in 1980 to a low 3.8 per cent in 1985, though it climbed back to 4.5 per cent in 1989. Selectivity is clearly operative in decisions to prosecute. According to the Chief Factory Inspector, 'our policy is to prosecute blatant offenders; we throw the whole book at them . . . we don't want our factory prosecutions to develop to the state of parking ticket or unlicensed hawker' (*Sunday Standard,* 19 October 1986). One of the considerations in deciding whether to prosecute is perceptions of how magistrates will view and deal with contraventions of regulations. This is one implication of the Chief Factory Inspector's comment that 'it is not the number of cases but the gravity and seriousness of the case we take out which will make a good impression on the magistrate.' The decline in the number of factory prosecutions may be interpreted as the Inspectorate's strategy for coping with the strain of having inadequate resources, so that only the cases where the probability of successful prosecution is high will be prosecuted.[9]

Table 12.1 Summary of Labour Department Prosecutions against Safety and Health Provisions, Selected Years[1]

Year	Fines ($1,000)	No. of Cases	No. of Cases Convicted[2]
1980	4,303	4,082	3,955
1983	4,735	3,134	3,000
1985	4,836	1,951	1,896
1987	6,799	2,216	2,163
1989	10,537	2,542	2,504

Notes: 1. Refers to cases reported in Part 1, Table 7 of the annual reports.
2. Excludes cases convicted but discharged.

Source: Commissioner of Labour, *Annual Report*, various years.

One of the problems the Labour Department faces in enforcing safety regulations is that even when prosecutions are successful, magistrates seldom penalize offenders to the full extent of the law under which, for contravention of certain regulations, the maximum fine can be $50,000.[10] The Director of Audit in his 1987 report drew attention to this 'inadequate deterrent' when enforcing safety laws. The average fine for convictions in 1986 was only $2,700 and 'factory operators would have little difficulty in absorbing such fines in their operating expenses' (Audit Department 1987: 23). In 1989, the average fine for convicted cases had risen to $4,208, a figure that reflects an average annual increase from 1986 of 14 per cent.[11] While higher than the rate of inflation over the same period, it is still arguably too low to have much of a deterrent effect on most employers.[12]

In response to this inadequacy of deterrence through fines, the Factories and Industrial Undertakings (Amendment) Ordinance of 1989, in addition to setting out general obligations of employers and employees for work safety and health at industrial undertakings, introduced custodial penalties for serious offences, a measure favored by the Labour Department though opposed by employers. Thus, the proprietor of an industrial undertaking who contravenes the general obligations — such as failing to provide and maintain plant and systems of work that are, so far as is reasonably practicable, safe and without risks to health — commits an offence and is liable to a fine of $30,000 and to imprisonment for six months. To the maximum fine of $50,000 for certain offences has been added a maximum custodial sentence of 12 months for contravention of specified regulations made under the principal Ordinance.

While the number of safety and health requirements under the FIUO and its subsidiary legislation runs into the hundreds, relatively few are frequent sources of summonses leading to fines. Prior to 1985, a frequent offence was the operating of an unregistered workplace that was required under law to be registered. The switch from a registration to a notification system in 1985 cut the number of such cases sharply. The other frequent sources of summonses involve contraventions of the Guarding and Operation of Machinery Regulations, the Fire Precautions in Registrable Workplaces Regulations, and the Construction Sites (Safety) Regulations. Under each of these sets of regulations, certain requirements are more frequent sources of summonses than others. For example, in the case of Fire Precautions, failure to construct fire-resisting exit doors, failure to maintain exit doorways free from obstruction, and failure to comply with fire precaution orders are frequently cited contraventions. Under the Construction Sites (Safety) Regulations, a frequently cited offence has been failure to ensure that working platforms, openings in floors, and dangerous places are securely fenced.

The Political Economy of Enforcement

Our discussion of the monitoring and enforcement of workplace safety regulations has thus far focused mainly on the internal organizational features of the Factory Inspectorate and some of their implications for the Inspectorate's ability to improve the quality of worklife in Hong Kong. The effectiveness of the Inspectorate has been hampered among other things by the expansion in the scope of its duties and number of establishments under its purview. Yet this is only one component of what Tombs (1990) calls the 'vicious circle of regulatory non-enforcement' that underlies the increase in industrial injuries. What therefore needs to be considered is the political economy of regulation — the wider economic, social, and political contexts of industry and how they impinge on the enforcement of safety regulations (Carson 1989, Noble 1986).

One economic factor that makes the monitoring and enforcement of safety regulations exceedingly difficult is the structure of Hong Kong industry. The majority of manufacturing establishments are very small and the sheer number of establishments is a hindrance to effective monitoring of compliance with regulations. This compels the Inspectorate to 'ration' its visits among different firms.[13] The small size of the average firm also means that large numbers of employers are unlikely to be willing or able to spend money on the improvement of the safety conditions at the workplace. Furthermore, because of the ease and frequency of inter-firm mobility in the manufacturing sector, workers are less likely to pay much attention to the safety standards in any particular firm.

Construction has been the most accident-prone industry in Hong Kong. In 1989, it accounted for more than a quarter (27.6 per cent) of all non-fatal occupational accidents and more than a third (34.3 per cent) of all fatal occupational accidents (Commissioner for Labour 1990: 155). The construction boom in the latter part of the 1980s and the use of immigrant workers have undoubtedly contributed to this situation. However, a more fundamental cause of the high accident rate is the prevalence of subcontracting in the construction industry, a point on which both factory inspectors and trade unionists agree.[14] It is very difficult to monitor the operations of a large number of unrelated work groups on any construction site. The casual nature of the employment relationship under subcontracting also blocks official efforts at promoting safety consciousness among subcontractors and their workers.[15]

Second, the social structure of Hong Kong's industries is such that trade unions exert only marginal influence at the shopfloor level. Not only are unions overall weak due to low union density, especially in manufacturing and construction, but their top-heavy structure and the absence of shopfloor organization is inimical to the effective enforcement of safety regulations.[16] Factory Inspectors themselves have acknowledged that the weakness of trade unions has made their job more difficult.[17] Without union support, individual workers are afraid to refuse to work under dangerous conditions or to report violations of safety regulations by their employers. Without an active union organization on the shopfloor, the Labour Department's attempts to promote 'tripartite cooperation' of workers, employers, and the government as a strategy for raising safety consciousness and reducing accidents is unlikely to prove very effective.

Last but not least, the Hong Kong Government's adherence to an economic philosophy of *laissez faire* has also been a hindrance to the more effective enforcement of safety at the workplace. Because of its commitment to this approach to economic management, the Hong Kong Government has been reluctant to impose many restrictions on the internal management of private firms because they are perceived as adding unnecessary burdens and discouraging investment. While the government has since the late 1960s come to recognize that for its own political survival it has to pay some attention to moderating the worst social consequences of an unregulated market economy, it has nevertheless continued to follow a labour policy described as 'voluntarist' and 'abstentionist' in which the 'self-regulation' of the employment relationship of employers and employees is deemed to be desirable (Ng 1982). Given that the Hong Kong Government as a whole lacks a commitment to reshaping the existing imbalance of power between labour and employers, it means that whatever reformist intentions labour administrators may have, they do not normally carry sufficient political clout within the broader policy-making and budget-making processes to obtain the resources necessary to enable them to achieve the level of monitoring and enforcement of safety regulations they might wish.

Consequently, it is no surprise that the priority given to labour administration is declining, as indicated by the Labour Department's share in the government's overall budget allocation. The share of the Labour Department in the total government expenditure has declined from 0.51 per cent in 1980 to 0.44 per cent in 1988.[18] This budgetary position of the Labour Department means that steps aimed at improving the effectiveness of the Factory Inspectorate can hardly be implemented. Funds are simply not available, for instance, for a major expansion of the Factory Inspectorate establishment or to attract better qualified people to join the ranks of the Inspectorate.[19] Even though the 1989 amendment to the FIUO stipulated that 20 new inspectors should be hired in order to administer the new provisions, only eight were in post in late 1990.[20]

Thus the Inspectorate is in this sense trapped between the Government's need to ensure a congenial investment atmosphere at a time of economic stringency on the one hand and the pressure to maintain levels of monitoring and enforcement of more safety regulations over an increasing number of establishments with fewer personnel and resources. Recently the Inspectorate has sought to find a way out of this dilemma by 'privatizing' the responsibilities for industrial safety. One example is the Factories and Industrial Undertakings (Safety Officers and Safety Supervisors) Regulations of 1986, which require the compulsory employment of Safety Officers and Safety Supervisors in designated industries. (Thus far, only the construction industry has been designated for this purpose.) Another example is the attempt to promote tripartite cooperation on safety matters, culminating with the establishment in 1988 of the Occupational Safety and Health Council as a statutory body 'with the purpose of fostering, through education, training, promotion, and research, safer and healthier working conditions in Hong Kong' (Commissioner for Labour 1989: 21).[21]

Yet spokespersons for labour have repeatedly warned that these efforts are unlikely to have much of a payoff because they neglect the need to 'empower' workers at the shopfloor level.[22] In their view, the present movement of tripartite cooperation is overly concentrated at the economy-wide or industry level. The safety promotion campaigns that take the form of variety shows, talks, and media commercials may raise safety consciousness, but the message tends to be rather remote from the daily experiences of workers. In any case, the imbalance of power at the workplace would still likely deter workers from responding to these messages even if they wished to do so. Labour spokespersons have thus argued that the only way out of the present impasse is to empower the unions to conduct inspections of the workplace, and to establish statutory shopfloor safety committees with elected workers' safety representatives to enforce safety regulations. Such advice is unlikely to be heeded, given the government's desire to preserve management prerogatives in the workplace. Any proposals for change that might activate discontent and opposition from the employers and jeopardize Hong Kong's 'prosperity and stability' during this crucial period of transition to 1997 are unlikely to be welcomed.

Notes

1. A few of the figures reported in the text are based on unpublished data from the Labour Department. We gratefully acknowledge the help of Yip Yuk-lun, Chief Factory Inspector of the Factory Inspectorate Division of the Labour Department, and the Association for the Rights of Industrial Accident Victims in the writing of this paper. Any errors are solely our responsibility.

2. The 1955 Ordinance extended the requirement for annual registration from factories to mines and quarries and all premises in which dangerous or potentially hazardous trades were carried on. The definition of 'factory' was widened to include establishments formerly classified as 'workshops' under the Factories and Industrial Workshops Ordinance, but only establishments employing more than 20 workers or power-driven machinery were required to register (Commissioner of Labour 1956: 35–6). In 1965, the Ordinance was amended to define inspector to include all ranks of factory inspectors.

3. These include regulations for woodworking machinery (1971), electrolytic chromium process (1972), lifting appliances and lifting gear (1974), abrasive wheels (1975), spraying of flammable liquids (1976), goods lifts (1976), dry batteries (1976), guarding and operation of machinery (1976) and cartridge-operated fixing tools (1977), fire precautions (1981), safety of persons working at electrical installations in industrial undertakings (1982), the use of ear protectors (1982), the use of asbestos (1986), and the labelling of dangerous substances (1988).

4. According to the Commissioner of Labour, Factory Inspectors were spending between 12 and 16 per cent of their time on promotional and publicity activities (Public Accounts Committee 1988: 23). The Committee on Industrial Safety and Accident Prevention was renamed as the Industrial Safety and Health Committee from January 1987, in preparation for its eventual development into the Occupational Safety and Health Council.

5. The precise weighting of criteria is a closely guarded secret. This seems to be one way to avoid politicization of the way in which bureaucracy allocates scarce resources to enforcement activities.

6. According to calculations made by the authors, controlling for the number of employees also shows that while the fatality rate per 1,000 employees has been falling, the rate of occupational injuries per 1,000 employees has been rising since 1975.

7. According to Labour Department figures, the rate of accidents (including both fatal and non-fatal) per 1,000 employed in all industrial undertakings rose from 45.9 per cent in 1980 to 58.15 per cent in 1989.

8. At the end of 1975, the Labour Department launched a pilot scheme based on the Government Secretariat's Organisation and Methods survey in a bid to improve the operational effectiveness of the Factory Inspectorate. These recommendations were fully implemented from January 1977. As a means of monitoring its efficiency, a number of performance standards were set and in 1978 an Implementation Plan was prepared by the Factory Inspectorate Division. See the Commissioner for Labour (1976: 17, 1977: 21).

9. One indirect indicator in support of this argument is the increase in the proportion of convictions to the total number of prosecutions from 95.7 per cent in 1983 to 98.5 per cent in 1989.

10. The present level of fines was last revised in the early 1980s. The maximum fine upon conviction of $50,000 applies to safety violations that pose imminent danger to lives. For those violations that can cause injuries but are

not life-threatening, the maximum fine upon conviction is $30,000. For violations of health standards that can be injurious to employee health in the long term, the maximum fines range from $20,000 to $30,000. For personal offences by employees of safety regulations, the maximum fine is normally $10,000.

11. The average increase of the GDP deflator per annum was 7.6 per cent from 1986 to 1989. See Census and Statistics Department (1985: 112) and *Hong Kong in Figures* (1990).

12. An example of the discrepancy between the maximum possible fine upon conviction and average fines is the case of safety helmets. Under the Construction Site (Safety) Regulations, a proprietor who fails to provide workmen with safety helmets and to ensure the wearing of such helmets is liable to a maximum fine upon conviction of $50,000. By comparison, the average fine for the 189 summonses heard for this offence in 1989 was $5,191.

13. In 1987, out of a total of 50,756 manufacturing establishments, some 65.8 per cent were employing less than 10 workers, and 92.6 per cent were employing less than 50 workers (Census and Statistics Department 1989: 56).

14. For many construction projects in Hong Kong, the principal or main contractor usually subcontracts out the jobs to a number of subcontractors, who in turn will further sub-contract to sub-subcontractors. The bottom level subcontractors normally hire only 10 to 20 workers and the turnover rate of their workers is very high. For a glimpse of these arrangements, see *John Lok/Wimpey Joint Venture v Attorney General*, High Court Magistracy Appeal No. 62 of 1985. For the viewpoints of unionists on the effect of subcontracting on accidents in the construction industry, see the comments by the Secretary of the Hong Kong and Kowloon Cement and Concrete Construction Trade Workers Union and by the Hong Kong Social Workers' General Union (*Ming Pao*, 12 and 29 September 1988). The Chief Factory Inspector has also blamed subcontracting for the high injury rates in the construction industry (*Oriental Daily News*, 14 November 1989).

15. The problem is not dissimilar to that of the British oil industry in which 'the plethora of subcontracting . . . generates uncertainty over the location of legitimate authority and decision-making, ignorance about work conditions, and the responsibilities of personnel, and confusion over safety procedures' (Wright 1986: 284).

16. The union density for the year 1988 was 17.5 per cent. For a discussion of the weakness of unions, see England (1989: 126–40).

17. See the comments by the Factory Inspectors Union (a trade union formed by the Factory Inspectors) in the *Oriental Daily News*, 11 December 1986. Experience elsewhere concurs with this observation. For example, Theo Nichols (1986: 290) comments as follows on the British cases: ' . . . members of strong well-organised labour forces are, all things being equal, less likely to experience industrial injury that those of poorly organised or weak labour forces.'

18. Calculated from figures in the Commissioner for Labour, *Annual Departmental Report*, various years and Census and Statistics Department (1989). Total government expenditure includes recurrent expenditures only and excludes capital expenditures.

19. The Chief Factory Inspector has remarked that improvement in the pay and entry requirements, as well as more promotion opportunities, would be the means to improve the effectiveness of the Inspectorate (*Sing Tao Jih Pao*, 8 January 1990).

20. See the interview with the Chief Factory Inspector in *Sing Tao Jih Pao*, 8 January 1990.

21. In addition, in 1987 a Safety Programme Promotion Unit was set up under the Inspectorate to promote an in-plant self-regulatory safety movement in industry. The enactment of 'general duties' provisions under the FIUO in 1989 may be viewed as yet another example of efforts to promote more self-regulation on the part of employers and employees. Apart from complying with the specific statutory requirements in the regulations, employers are obliged, from December 1990, to make their workplaces safe and without risks to health. Such obligations require employers to carry out safety audits for the workplaces and to implement safety programmes as revealed by the safety audits to be necessary. Both employers and employees are required to follow codes of practices for purposes of workplace safety and health.

22. Our account of labour's responses to the government's 'privatization' strategies is based on interviews with labour activists and the public statements of the Association for the Rights of Industrial Accident Victims, the principal pressure group concerned with industrial safety on the labour side. For the latter, see *Sing Tao Evening News*, 31 October 1989 and Hong Kong Workers, 1988, No. 156: 6–7.

13 Justice after 1997

ALBERT H. Y. CHEN

THIS CHAPTER considers the future of the criminal justice system in Hong Kong from a broad historical perspective. Given that this system is a by-product of colonization and has been transplanted from an alien political, legal, social, and cultural tradition, will it be able to survive Hong Kong's incorporation into the People's Republic of China in 1997? This question will be addressed in the third part of this essay. To prepare for this discussion, the first section of the chapter outlines some of the major characteristics of the existing system, and the second section attempts to trace their origins and evolution in English legal history. The reader might note that the issues considered here are large and general ones; in the space of one chapter it will only be possible to look at them briefly.

The Existing System

An underlying notion in the modern conception of criminal justice and in particular, the system of criminal procedure, is that it should strike a proper balance between the right to fair treatment on the part of accused persons on the one hand, and the public interest in the efficient prosecution, conviction, and punishment of members of society who have violated its criminal law. Some critics of the contemporary English system of criminal procedure have argued that the balance has been excessively and unnecessarily tilted in favour of defendants (Coutts 1966: 28, 37). Others, however, believe in the maxim 'that it is better that 10 guilty persons escape, than that one innocent man should suffer' and hold that the English model is admirable precisely because this maxim has been effectively translated into various concrete rules of criminal procedure (Holdsworth 1942: 620, 1945: 196, Radzinowicz 1948: 367–8). The following paragraphs outline some of these basic rules and principles regarding the rights of suspects and defendants in criminal proceedings.

Although the general grounds on which a person may be arrested in Hong Kong[1] are much wider than in Britain (Wesley-Smith 1988,

Morrow 1988, Rear 1971), arrested persons have the right to be informed about the reasons for the arrest, and to be brought before a court 'as soon as practicable'[2] (which is usually interpreted to mean within a maximum of 48 hours), whereupon the court can decide whether to grant bail to the suspect pending further court appearances. *Habeas corpus* is available as a remedy granted by the court for the release of persons unlawfully arrested, or lawfully arrested but detained for an excessive period without being put on trial.[3]

Judicial control on police behaviour during interrogation of detained suspects is achieved indirectly by means of legal rules concerning the admissibility of evidence. One of the most fundamental rules in this regard is that answers given and statements (such as confessions) made during the course of police inquiries are only admissible if they have been given or made voluntarily 'in the sense that they have not been obtained by fear of prejudice or hope of advantage, exercised or held out by a person in authority, or by oppression.'[4] The *voir dire*, or 'trial within a trial', is that part of the trial proceedings in which the judge determines whether a confession is admissible. In the case of a trial before a judge sitting together with a jury, the *voir dire* is conducted in the absence of the jury because it would be prejudicial to the accused for the jury to learn of the content of the confession statement (Tapper 1986: 219ff). Compared with the position in England, the *voir dire* proceeding is used much more frequently in Hong Kong—the Law Reform Commission noted that in 1983, it was used in 90 per cent of criminal trials in the High Court and 88 per cent of criminal trials in the District Court (Hong Kong Law Reform Commission 1984: para 2.08).

Various detailed rules, known as 'the Judges' Rules,' have also been formulated regarding how police inquiries should be conducted—for example, concerning when suspects should be cautioned—that is, be told that they have the right not to answer questions from the police, and be warned that any statement or answer given may be used as evidence at the trial. Breach of such rules may lead to evidence obtained as a result of the breach being held inadmissible at the trial (Brabyn 1989: 289–91, Morrow 1988: 261).

In Hong Kong, as in Britain, different trial procedures are provided for offences of different degrees of seriousness. Relatively minor offences (or 'summary offences') are dealt with in the Magistrates' Courts where there is no jury trial.[5] Jury trial for more serious offences is generally regarded as a fundamental characteristic of the English model of criminal justice and an important safeguard, because it means that it is for the jury — chosen randomly from eligible members of the community and thus reflective of public opinion and common sense — and not the judge to decide (after hearing the summing-up of the case given by the judge, including his directions on the relevant law) whether the defendant is guilty or not.[6] In Hong Kong, the jury trial is available for a much narrower range of cases than in England, and the rule that only persons who have a sufficient standard of English can serve as jurors (since High Court trials are conducted in English)[7] can be said to militate against the idea of popular participation in the administration of justice. There is in Hong Kong, strictly speaking, no right to have a jury trial even for some serious offences, because among the two courts (the District Court and the High Court) that deal with indictable offences (offences other than summary offences), only the High Court sits with a jury.[8] As in relation to most of these offences, it is for the prosecution to decide whether to seek a trial in the District Court or the High Court,[9] the decision as to whether a jury trial will take place lies with the prosecution and need not take the defendant's wishes into account. However, as the sentencing powers of the District Court are more limited than those of the High Court,[10] the principle remains valid in Hong Kong that punishment beyond a certain degree of severity — that is, more than seven years — may only be imposed on a person found guilty of a serious offence in a trial by jury.

Whether the trial takes place before a single judge or magistrate, or before a judge and jury, several general principles apply. The trial is to be held in public,[11] the adjudicators must be independent, impartial, and unbiased, and the defendant has extensive rights to defend himself, including the rights to compel attendance of witnesses for the defence, to confront and question prosecution witnesses, to be represented by a lawyer and in most serious cases, to be financially assisted by public funds for this purpose.[12]

The basic premise underlying the law of criminal procedure in Britain and Hong Kong is well-known: the defendant is presumed innocent until proven guilty, and the burden of proof is on the prosecution, which in order to be successful must satisfy the judge (in a trial without a jury) or the jury that the evidence proves 'beyond reasonable doubt' that the defendant is guilty of the offence charged (Coutts 1966: 35, Hampton 1982: 1, Tapper 1986, Chapter 2). However, the prosecution is not supposed to achieve this result by unscrupulous means. There is a tradition and principle of professional ethics of the English bar that counsel for the prosecution must conduct the case against the accused with scrupulous impartiality, and should not, for example, conceal evidence favourable to the accused (Coutts 1966: 25, 33).

The 'presumption of innocence' is not unqualified. Various statutory inroads on the principle have been made to shift the burden of proof on elements of some offences to the accused by, for example, the use of 'presumptions'. In Hong Kong, the most notable examples of such 'reverse onus' provisions can be found in the Dangerous Drugs Ordinance, the Prevention of Bribery Ordinance, and the law on loitering.[13]

Another celebrated and related principle is that concerning 'the right to silence'. An arrested suspect has the right not to answer questions from the police; a defendant in a criminal trial has the right not to go into the witness box and be questioned by either counsel or judge; and in its closing speech to the court, the prosecution is as a general rule not allowed to comment on a defendant's failure to answer questions or to give evidence.[14]

In addition to the principle regarding admissibility of confessions, other rules of evidence give further protection to the accused. For example, information on the accused's previous convictions and misconduct on occasions other than the case being tried is not admissible as evidence for the purpose of supporting an argument that the accused is the kind of person who would commit the offence charged (Coutts 1966: 32, 34, Tapper 1986, Chapter 10). There are also rules concerning the need in certain situations for a prosecution witness's evidence to be corroborated by evidence from other witnesses. In some situations, such corroboration is required as a matter of law. In others, the judge is under a duty to warn the jury in his summing-up of the danger of acting on the uncorroborated evidence of a particular witness, for example, an accomplice of the accused (Coutts 1966: 35, Tapper 1986: 71ff.). Convictions are often quashed on appeal simply because the trial judge has omitted to give such a warning in a situation when it is required by law.

Turning to the system of appeals, it should be noted that the prosecution has no general right to appeal against an acquittal in a jury trial.[15] However, the Attorney General has been given the right to apply to a higher court for a review of the sentence imposed on a convicted defendant on various grounds, including the ground that the sentence is 'manifestly inadequate'.[16] On the other hand, a defendant who has been convicted and sentenced has the right to appeal against both conviction and sentence. It has been pointed out that the English system of appeals places more emphasis on safeguarding the interests of defendants than on furtherance of the public interest in the conviction of the guilty and avoidance of unmerited acquittals (Coutts 1966: 38).

In the English and Hong Kong criminal justice systems, convictions are often quashed and defendants unconditionally released on the basis of technical irregularities in the trial, even though the error may not be directly relevant to the question of guilt or innocence (Coutts 1966: 42). Such irregularities include, for example, a defect in the indictment, a misdirection in the judge's summing-up to the jury, or admission during the trial of evidence which is by law inadmissible. The appellate court does have power to dismiss the appeal despite an irregularity if it considers that 'no miscarriage of justice has actually occurred', but in practice will do so only if it is satisfied that the conviction is not 'unsafe and unsatisfactory'.[17] In principle, the defendant may also appeal against conviction on a ground which involves a question of fact.[18] In practice, however, it is more difficult for an appellant to succeed on direct questions of fact than on procedural irregularities. This is because of the appellate court's reluctance to deal with issues of fact, which involve primarily questions of the credibility of various witnesses, which are believed to be best dealt with by the trial court (Coutts 1966: 42–8, 52).

Historical Origins

Those who are pessimistic about the prospects of survival of Hong Kong's British-style criminal justice system after 1997 will point to the sharp contrast between the Chinese and English or Western legal traditions, and, in particular, the absence of the tradition of the rule of law in China. This point should not be over-stated. Even the English or Western legal tradition has not existed from time immemorial; it is a historical phenomenon with identifiable origins and processes of growth. Changes, some quite fundamental, have occurred in the course of time. If contemporary Western systems seem to approximate the ideals of justice and protection of human rights to a greater extent than the Chinese system, there did exist many points in history where the prevailing institutions and practices would be considered uncivilized, underdeveloped, or irrational by present-day standards. For example, as a leading scholar on the English law of criminal procedure points out, until recent times the treatment of the accused under the English legal system can only be described as barbarous (Hampton 1982: 1). Similarly, two other authors observed:

> Until the nineteenth century the criminal law [in England] was barbarous in operation and antiquated in structure. The death penalty could be inflicted for over 200 offences, sometimes with gruesome incidents. Executions were in public, transportation [to overseas colonies for convict labour] was in full vigour, a person accused of felony was subject to heavy disadvantages in presenting his case, and the law of criminal evidence was unsystematic and uncertain (Keeton and Lloyd 1955: 101).

It is interesting to note in this regard the comment by an expert in Chinese history on changing Western images of Chinese justice: 'Early European observers had been well impressed with Chinese justice. It was only after the eighteenth and nineteenth century reforms of law and punishments in the modern West that China was left behind' (Fairbank 1980: 117–18).

Once the dynamic aspect of evolving legal traditions is taken into account, the distance between different legal traditions may not be as fixed, rigid, or unbridgeable as it initially appears to be. The scope for reform and progress always exists. Transplants of legal principles and institutions from one legal tradition or system to another are possible and have occurred not infrequently in history, providing stimulus for a legal system's growth and development (Watson 1974). In this sense, the legal achievements of one civilization, like its scientific and technological achievements, belong to the common heritage of, and may become available for, the common benefit of mankind.

In this part of the essay, the evolution of some basic features of the English model of criminal procedure will be briefly traced. The purpose is to provide examples of how specific ideas, institutions, and practices in criminal justice came into being, and how a complex of different forces such as historical accidents, political struggles, and conscious philosophising combined to produce ultimate results.[19] Some understanding of the historical roots of contemporary institutions will assist us in charting the courses of their future development.

Take first the institution of trial by jury. Its origin has been traced to the Frankish Inquest introduced into England by William I in the eleventh century. Potter pointed out that when it was first introduced, the jury system 'was far from being one of the bulwarks of popular rights which tradition has made it, but was in reality a royal prerogative for exacting its full dues' (Kiralfy 1958: 240–1). Originally, jurors played the role of modern witnesses; they supplied information on what they had heard about the case in the neighbourhood. It was only through a gradual process that the jury evolved into a body of persons who tried issues of fact by hearing the testimony of others.

Holdsworth (1942: 612) provided an interesting explanation of why the jury's verdict was, by the end of the thirteenth century, accepted as conclusive settlement of the case. He drew attention to the fact that the jury became the dominant mode of trial at a time when other old conceptions of the trial were still prevalent. According to these older ideas, the trial was a contest between the parties, who tried their own cases by compurgation, ordeal, or battle.[20] Just as the result of the ordeal or battle was regarded as settling the matter in a final manner, so was the result of the jury trial.

The evolution of the role of jurors from that of witnesses to triers of fact seems to be completed by the end of the sixteenth century, when witnesses — who could be compelled to appear — testified and were cross-examined at trials. In 1650, it was held that jurors might no longer use their private knowledge and must be sworn as witnesses if they wished to testify (Kiralfy 1958: 245). In 1670 it was finally and conclusively decided that jurors could not be penalized by the judge for their verdict — for example, for refusing to convict despite clear directions to do so from the judge.[21]

Although when it was first introduced, the jury system was not deliberately designed to safeguard individual liberty, in time the institution became venerated and associated with this purpose. Fortescue, writing in the fifteenth century, praised the jury and considered it superior to the criminal procedure prevailing in continental Europe (Baker 1977: 21, Holdsworth 1936: 566–71). Chapter 39 of the Magna Carta 1215, the original meaning of which was ambiguous, was subsequently regarded as a constitutional guarantee of the Englishman's right to trial by jury.[22] Writing in the eighteenth century, Blackstone hailed the jury as the glory of the English law, the palladium of English liberties, and trial by jury as the most transcendent privilege which any subject can enjoy.[23]

Let us turn to consider the presumption of innocence and the system's 'bias' in favour of the accused. The notion that it is better for the guilty to go free than for the innocent to be convicted does seem to have a long history, dating back to at least the fifteenth century (Holdsworth 1942: 620), although its earlier expression by individual writers does not mean that there was a consensus on the matter at that time. However, the presumption of innocence and clear rules of evidence in criminal cases were not yet established in the sixteenth century. Strict common law rules of evidence, such as rules regarding hearsay and written depositions, first manifested themselves in civil cases and were extended to criminal trials by analogy in the later part of the seventeenth century (Baker 1977: 38). The notions that the defendant should be regarded as innocent until proven guilty beyond reasonable doubt, that the onus of proof lies on the accuser, and that no person is required to prove his innocence, emerged over a long period and only became fully established in the accelerating changes in criminal procedure at the end of the eighteenth century and the beginning of the nineteenth (Beattie 1986: 340–1, 635).

Historical study also reveals how various rights of the accused which are taken for granted nowadays came into being. Take the privilege against self-incrimination or the right to silence. This was unknown to the common law before the seventeenth century; at that earlier stage in English legal history, accused persons were closely examined by magistrates before the trial, and by the judge and prosecuting counsel at the trial (Holdsworth 1945: 193). Toward the end of the seventeenth century, it became recognized that witnesses had the right to object to questions on the ground that they might be incriminated by the answers given. And at the beginning of the eighteenth century, this right was extended to the accused.[24] However, the right of the accused to testify on oath as a witness was not established until 1898, though for a considerable period of time before this, accused persons were allowed to speak freely at the trial without being sworn.[25]

Although the existence of the profession of lawyers in England can be traced back to the late thirteenth century, their participation in criminal, as distinguished from civil, matters has a relatively short history. From a very early period, persons accused of treason or indicted for a felony were denied the assistance of counsel (Holdsworth 1945: 192). One line of justification for this rule was that it facilitated the court's discovery of the truth; it was thought that an innocent prisoner would easily exculpate himself directly and counsel's involvement would only complicate the matter (Beattie 1986: 352–3, 356). The rule then developed that counsel's assistance to the accused would be permitted if a point of law arose upon the evidence and need to be debated (Baker 1977: 36, Manchester 1980: 168); if, however, only questions of fact were involved, the judge could in theory fulfill also the role of counsel for the accused, and such counsel was not therefore needed. Indeed, in most cases the Crown was not represented by counsel either,[26] prosecutions being undertaken mainly by individual victims of crime in the name of the Crown and not by the state machinery directly (Cornish 1989: 544, 562).

The right to counsel was made available for defendants in treason cases for both matters of fact and law soon after the Glorious

Revolution of 1688[27] as a reaction against the highly political use of treason charges by the Crown during the 1680s (Beattie 1986: 357). Beattie points out that while the emergence of prosecution counsel developed only gradually, the rule prohibiting defendants in felony cases to have counsel to assist in issues of fact gave way suddenly by the 1730s, during and after which it became normal for counsel to be permitted to conduct the accused's case or to prompt the accused.[28]

With the participation of lawyers in the criminal trial in the eighteenth century,[29] though only in a small minority of cases because few defendants could afford them, the criminal trial was transformed and its modern form emerged (Beattie 1986: 635). The changes extended to the dynamics of the courtroom, the relationship between the judge, the jury, and the accused, and the law of evidence. The notion of the accused's rights was enlarged as their lawyers made claims of rights on their behalf. The general trend over the eighteenth century was that a criminal justice system gradually emerged which provided an increasing degree of protection to the rights of the accused, and the belief became more widespread that men should be treated equally and fairly before the courts and the law, and ought to be given full opportunities to defend themselves against charges.[30] The idea of the defendant's rights in criminal law and procedure is of course a fundamental part of the more general notion of the natural rights of man or human rights which came to prevail in the intellectual climate of the Age of Enlightenment in Europe (Kamenka 1978, Robinson 1985, Chapter XV).

The Future

In the 4,000 years of traditional Chinese civilization, the concept and practice of law have never played a role as significant as in Western history. In the classical civilization of Greece and Rome, litigation in the courts, the professional work of lawyers or advocates, the compilation of codes, and the study of law as an independent and prestigious discipline occupied prominent places as civic and social phenomena.[31] Although Roman law was more highly developed in civil law than in criminal law or constitutional law (David and Brierly 1985: 48), the idea of law as an embracing system of coherent and general rules for the regulation of society and commerce was highly valued. In contrast, the Confucian culture emphasized the performance of moral obligations in voluntary compliance with ethical principles of behaviour, and deprecated the use of strict rules administered coercively by the state and the insistence on rights to the detriment of social harmony.[32] In traditional China, the ruling elite was dominated by scholars of the Confucian classics, but there were no learned professions of lawyers, scholars of law, or trial judges (Bodde and Morris 1967, van der Sprenkel 1977).

The traditional Chinese political order headed by the Emperor—the Son of Heaven—combined the exercise of spiritual, moral, and political authority.[33] Whereas tensions and conflicts generated by the dual institutions of church and state as well as plural feudal and urban social structures contributed to the development of limited government in the West, there was no corresponding phenomenon in China. Again, given the highly centralized and bureaucratic nature of the Chinese state established since the Qin Emperor united China in the third century BC (Gernet 1985: *xxvii*; 1987), there was no Chinese equivalent of the struggles in England for power among the king, the nobility, the landowners, the church, the merchants, and other social and economic groups, which interacted with the traditional idea of law to produce rights-guaranteeing constitutional documents like the Magna Carta 1215, the Petition of Right 1628, and the Bill of Rights 1689.[34] The establishment of limited government and of religious and political pluralism was associated with the protection of individual rights and also had a bearing on criminal law and procedure.[35]

It should be noted that although the idea and practice of law has a long history in the West, legal protection of the rights of the accused, as well as their humane treatment by the authorities, are relatively recent developments. The primacy of law and rights in civil, private, or property relations was established much earlier,[36] and this paved the way for their extension to the criminal and constitutional arenas when relevant political and intellectual movements came into being (David 1985: 48, 63). Similarly, it seems that a liberal criminal procedure and the emphasis on individuals' civil liberties developed in England first, partly as a result of internal political struggles against absolute monarchy, and was imitated in continental Europe in the nineteenth century when the 'natural rights' thinking of the Enlightenment came to prevail.[37]

In the nineteenth and twentieth centuries, the modernization of the legal systems—as in many other aspects of society—in the non-Western world has taken the form of Westernization. Thus today the legal systems of most Third World countries belong to either the Romano-Germanic family or the common law family (David and Brierly 1985), which are the two branches of the Western legal tradition which Berman (1983) traced back to eleventh century Europe. In the case of the People's Republic of China, it has, in the two major eras of legal system building in the 1950s and 1980s, developed its codes of law and legal institutions on the basis of Soviet or Western models.[38] In so far as the Soviet legal system shares with the Romano-Germanic family many common concepts, institutions and practices, the contemporary legal system in mainland China can be said to be basically a Westernized one and represent a radical discontinuity with the legal tradition of the Imperial and Confucian past.[39] This is particularly so as far as formal legal rules and principles are concerned. For example, the Law of Criminal Procedure of the PRC has been closely based on the corresponding Soviet law and provides for various safeguards — generally respectable by contemporary international standards — for the rights of the accused (Berman et al. 1982). The problem, however, is that the ideas in the written law have not been fully translated into practice due to factors such as the lack of trained legal personnel, the short history of legal system building, and hence lack of experience and tradition; the past habit on the part of law enforcement officials of not paying attention to the law; the dominance of the Party apparatus over the state; and the Party's unwillingness to subject itself to the supremacy and autonomy of law (Chen 1989a, Deng 1989).

These problems are not likely to be solved in the immediate future. Consider, for example, the shortage of trained legal personnel. China has more than 1.1 billion people, and yet there are only about 21,000 full-time lawyers and 10,000 part-time lawyers. The total population of law students in the 86 law schools all over the country is only 42,000. Many judges (appointed before the new era of legal system building) have not received any legal training; indeed, the plan announced in 1988 was to provide legal education for judges so that by 1991, 60 per cent of judges all over the nation would have received legal training equivalent to tertiary education level, and by 1995, 80 per cent.[40]

Cultural and ideological obstacles to the strengthening of the legal system are also not easy to overcome. The traditional Chinese approach to law has already been discussed. Marxist-Leninist ideology converges with Confucianism in a sense: they share a common distrust of, or lack of respect for, the rule of law. Most legal textbooks in China today still portray law as an instrument for class rule, and law in the socialist society (before its evolution into the classless communist society) as a tool for the dictatorship of the proletariat and for suppression of its enemies. Within such a framework, the idea of law as the enshrinement of individual rights flowing from human dignity will take a long time to mature.

If, therefore, China were to impose the Chinese law of crime and criminal procedure on Hong Kong after 1997, panic on the part of the Hong Kong population and grave concern about the deterioration in the administration of criminal justice would indeed be justified. Fortunately, this is not to be the case. The 1984 Sino-British Joint Declaration on the Question of Hong Kong provides that the laws currently in force in Hong Kong will remain basically unchanged after the establishment of the Hong Kong Special Administrative Region in 1997.[41] The basic structural features of the existing judicial system will also be maintained; judges may continue to be recruited from other common law jurisdictions, and post-1997 Hong Kong courts may still refer to precedent cases in other common law jurisdictions.[42] Rights and freedoms currently enjoyed by Hong Kong people under existing laws will be maintained, and the provisions of the International Covenant on Civil and Political Rights as applied to Hong Kong shall also remain in force.[43] These principles are now enshrined in the Basic Law of the Hong Kong Special Administrative Region — which will only come into effect in 1997 as the constitutional foundation of the Special Administrative Region — passed by China's National People's Congress in April 1990.[44] Furthermore, several articles in the Basic Law specifically provide for certain rights of the individual in relation to criminal proceedings which are not expressly mentioned in the Joint Declaration.[45]

The draft Hong Kong Bill of Rights Ordinance was proposed as a bill[46] by the Hong Kong Government as part of a series of measures aimed at alleviating the local crisis of confidence after the suppression of the pro-democracy student movement in mainland China in June 1989. Enacted into law during 1991, it must be considered a step forward in the consolidation of Hong Kong's existing system for the protection of human rights in general[47] and of its relatively liberal criminal procedure and safeguards for the accused's rights in particular. As the Hong Kong Bill of Rights largely reproduces the wording of the International Covenant on Civil and Political Rights, one of the most significant implications of the Bill is that it facilitates the introduction of standards in international human rights law[48] into the domestic law of Hong Kong. The enactment of the Bill of Rights, when complemented by appropriate amendment of Hong Kong's present constitutional instrument (the Letters Patent), enables Hong Kong courts to strike down laws which fall foul of such human rights standards (Ho 1990). In this regard, the American and Canadian experience reveals the great potential which a constitutional Bill of Rights enforced by an independent and confident judiciary may have in maintaining and further developing a liberal criminal procedure affording generous protection to the rights of suspects and accused or convicted persons.[49]

In the final analysis, however, the Joint Declaration, the Basic Law, and the Bill of Rights are merely pieces of paper. Whether the grand visions that they embody will be translated into reality depends on how much deference is paid to them, or to what extent they are really taken seriously, by the actors in the historical drama — the leaders of the Party and the government in China, the officials, politicians, judges, and lawyers in the Hong Kong Special Administrative Region, and, last but not least, the ordinary men and women who will make Hong Kong their home after 1997. In the late twentieth century world, there are still many countries and territories where human beings can be either lawfully or unlawfully detained indefinitely without trial, where prisoners are tortured, where people who dare to exercise their human rights still live in the shadow of the secret police knocking at the door in the middle of the night. It is not possible to rule out the possibility of Hong Kong becoming one of these territories, and the future of Hong Kong is not entirely in the hands of the people of Hong Kong. On the other hand, the future is not entirely out of their control either. To the extent that people understand and cherish their human rights — which may originally have been a Western notion, but are now the common heritage of mankind and internationally accepted — to the extent that people are willing to assert and defend their rights, the chances of their rights being recognized and respected are correspondingly increased. In this regard, the apparent trend of the community's growing interest in and increasing readiness to participate in discussion of human rights-related current issues in Hong Kong in the post-Joint Declaration years is a sign of hope.[50]

Notes

1. Sections 50 and 54, Police Force Ordinance (Cap. 232). See the discussions in Morrow (1988), Rear (1971), and Wesley-Smith (1988a).

2. Section 52(1), Police Force Ordinance. For arrests made by the ICAC, see Section 10A, Independent Commission Against Corruption Ordinance (Cap. 204).

3. See Denning (1949: 6–10).

4. Coutts (1966: 27, 34). The mere exhortation by a police officer that it would be better for the accused to tell the truth has been held to render the subsequent confession inadmissible. For a more detailed explanation of the

common law rules (which are applicable to Hong Kong) see Brabyn (1989), Cross (1974: 482ff). In the UK, these rules have now been superseded by the Police and Criminal Evidence Act 1984: see Tapper (1986: 219ff).

5. See part II ('Procedure in respect of summary offences') of the Magistrates' Ordinance (Cap. 227).

6. See Section 4 of the Jury Ordinance (Cap. 3) on the qualification of jurors.

7. See the Jury Ordinance (Cap. 3) Section 4; and the Official Languages Ordinance (Cap. 5).

8. According to Part V ('Summary trial of indictable offences') of the Magistrates' Ordinance, a Magistrates' Court may try certain indictable offences (those not listed in the first part of the second schedule) summarily with the consent of the prosecutor.

9. See Part IV ('Transfer of offences to the District Court') of the Magistrates' Ordinance. However, certain indictable offences (those listed in Part III of the second schedule to the Magistrates' Ordinance) are triable only in the High Court: see Section 88 of the Magistrates' Ordinance.

10. Under Section 82 of the District Court Ordinance (Cap. 336), the maximum sentence of imprisonment which the District Court may impose is seven years.

11. For the general rule and exceptions to it, see Atiyah (1983: 39–40), and Hampton (1982: 182, 340). For restrictions on reporting of committal proceedings, see Section 87A of the Magistrates' Ordinance. For the law of contempt of court and relevant restrictions on pretrial publicity, see Merry (1988: 186, 196ff).

12. See the Legal Aid in Criminal Cases Rules (Cap. 221), and especially rule 4 (on eligibility for legal aid).

13. The Dangerous Drugs Ordinance (Cap. 134) Sections 45–8 deal with presumptions in relation to possession of dangerous drugs for the purpose of trafficking, possession, and knowledge of dangerous drugs. The Prevention of Bribery Ordinance (Cap. 201) Sections 10 and 25 deal with presumptions in relation to unexplained property and bribery respectively. The Crimes Ordinance (Cap. 200) Section 160 contains presumptions on loitering. See also the Criminal Procedure Ordinance (Cap. 221) Section 94A on 'negative averments'.

14. See generally Brabyn (1989: 296–9), Hong Kong Law Reform Commission (1984), Tapper (1986: 63–4, 203–5). But see also Coutts (1966: 33): 'In the opinion of some English lawyers, this right not to be questioned constitutes an excessive protection of the accused. It is based on what is possibly an irrational English objection to compelling a person to incriminate himself out of his own mouth'. For recent discussion in the UK on the right to silence and proposals to curtail it, see the *Solicitors Journal* vol. 131, no. 37 (1987: 1195), vol. 132, no. 42 (1988: 1439), and Wolchover and Heaton-Armstrong (1990: 369).

15. See Section 81D of the Criminal Procedure Ordinance, and the comment 'The Carrian Trial: The Aftermath' (1988: 10) 18 *Hong Kong Law*

Journal. However, acquittals by a Magistrates' Court or the District Court may be overturned on errors of law in an appeal by way of case stated: see Section 105 of the Magistrates' Ordinance and Section 84 of the District Court Ordinance.

16. Section 81A of the Criminal Procedure Ordinance. In England, the Attorney General did not have a similar power until the enactment of the Criminal Justice Act 1988. Section 36 of the Act enables the Attorney General to refer an unduly lenient sentence to the Court of Appeal and empowers the Court of Appeal to substitute a different sentence. See Bell (1990).

17. Section 83(1) of the Criminal Procedure Ordinance; Hampton (1982: 306). The court may, at the same time as allowing an appeal against conviction, order a retrial if 'the interests of justice so require': Section 83E of the Criminal Procedure Ordinance.

18. Section 82 of the Criminal Procedure Ordinance. However, in such a case the leave of the Court of Appeal is needed, unless the trial court grants a certificate that the case is fit for appeal on a ground which involves a question of fact. See also Coutts (1966: 42).

19. For example, as Hayek observed, individual liberty appeared in England first 'as a by-product of a struggle for power rather than as the result of deliberate aim. But it remained long enough for its benefits to be recognised' (Hayek 1960: 162).

20. Holdsworth (1956: 299). See also Holdsworth (1936: 102), Kiralfy (1958: 353), Milsom (1981: 408), and Stein (1984: 30–1). Before the Norman Conquest in 1066, the usual methods of proof were compurgation or ordeal. Trial by battle was introduced after the Norman Conquest. Regarding trial by ordeal, Stein wrote: 'Ordeals were used to test guilt or innocence of wrongdoing. The usual form required the accused to carry a heated iron for a certain distance or to plunge his hand into boiling water to pull out a stone. Then his hand was sealed with bandages for three nights; if it was found to be clean, he was innocent; if not, he was guilty'. The development of trial by jury was related to the decline of the trial by ordeal, a direct consequence of the decision of the Church in 1215 to forbid priests from participating and assisting in trial by ordeal.

21. See Baker (1977: 23), Cornish (1989: 564), Denning (1949: 55–9), Holdsworth (1944: 229), and Stein (1984: 62).

22. See Baker (1977: 23), Creasy (1982: 207ff), and Holdsworth (1936: 214–15).

23. See Baker (1977: 21), Gavit (1941: 904–5), and Manchester (1980: 86ff).

24. Holdsworth (1944: 224). Baker (1977: 37) also notes that it was only during the eighteenth century that clear rules of evidence developed, the practice ceased of questioning the accused during the trial, and jurors no longer expected to hear a satisfactory explanation from the defendant's own lips.

25. Kiralfy (1958: 365). It should also be noted that the accused's right to

call witnesses to give evidence for the defence only came into existence by the end of the seventeenth century.

26. Baker (1977: 16). However, in some state trials during the Tudor and Stuart periods, the Crown was represented by the best advocates of the day: see ibid: 36.

27. This was brought about by a 1695 statute: Baker (1977: 37).

28. Baker (1977: 37). The right of persons accused of felonies to be defended by counsel was formally confirmed by an Act in 1837 (Holdsworth 1944: 235).

29. As regards counsel for the prosecution, they were increasingly engaged after 1714, but Beattie wrote that the reason for this development was not entirely clear: Beattie (1986: 627).

30. See Beattie (1986: 627–35), Hay (1975: 32–9). Changes in public opinion concerning the widespread use of the death penalty and corporal punishment also occurred, leading to fundamental reforms in the early nineteenth century. See generally Beattie (ibid: 619ff), Cornish (1989), Manchester (1980), Foucault (1979), Peters (1985), Phillipson (1970), and Radzinowicz (1948).

31. See Andrewes (1971), Barrow (1949), Holdsworth (1936: 5), Lindsay (1943: 52–8), and Robinson (1985).

32. See Chen (1988a), Fairbank (1980: 118–23), and Schwartz (1957).

33. See generally Gernet (1987: *xv*), Schwartz (1957: 1; 1985).

34. Holdsworth (1936, 1956: 430, 441). Holdsworth pointed out that the growth of the powers of Parliament in its struggles against the prerogative powers of the king and the political alliance between the common lawyers and Parliament strengthened the doctrine of the rule of law in English legal history.

35. Cornish (1989: 543): 'Since the country claimed at the root of its politics a rule of law in place of tyrannical discretion, the criminal law and its procedures also marked out a prime frontier of state power. The long testing, so intensely pursued during the struggles against Stuart authoritarianism, allowed the eighteenth-century Englishman his claim to be free-born'. In a similar vein Beattie (1986: 314) wrote: 'That Englishmen enjoyed fundamental liberties beyond the reach of government was a commonplace in the eighteenth century. . . . no one questioned that Englishmen had inherited liberties won by their forefathers in the struggle against despotic governments. Among the most cherished were those rights that guaranteed the rule of law and shielded the individual from arbitrary arrest and punishment, particularly trial by jury'. As early as the sixteenth century, Lord Treasurer Burghley noted: 'it was the liberty of the subject of England more than of all other nations that he cannot be molested or imprisoned without indictment . . . by the presentment of his neighbours and peers. . . . And this liberty was purchased for the subjects of England with the blood of many people, noble and ignoble' (quoted in Baker (1977: 18). See also Hay (1975) and Radzinowicz (1948: 25).

36. For a long time in English legal history, criminal law and procedure

was less well-developed than other areas of the law (see Milsom 1981: 403, 413, 417, 428). On continental Europe, the study of Roman law revived in the twelfth century also focused on private law. Since the eighteenth century, jurists in continental Europe developed a legal structure for public law parallel to that of traditional private law, but this development was not modelled on Roman law and was more inspired by the natural law thinking of the seventeenth and eighteenth centuries and by the English experience in regulating the relationship between the Crown and the subject and between governmental powers and individual liberties. See David (1985: 22, 48, 63).

37. David (1985: 48), Holdsworth (1942: 622; 1944: 235; 1945: 169), Manchester (1980: 166); Phillipson (1970); van Dijk (1986: 20ff).

38. See for example Chen (1983), Dicks (1989), and Epstein (1989).

39. See for example Liang (1989).

40. *Law Year Book of China* 1989, pp 442, 1101, 1106.

41. Para 3(3) of the Joint Declaration. For the full text of the Joint Declaration, see Hong Kong Government (1986), Chapter 1. More particularly, Section II of Annex I to the Joint Declaration provides for the maintenance of existing Hong Kong laws 'save for any that contravene the Basic Law and subject to any amendment by the Hong Kong Special Administrative Region legislature'.

42. See Section III of Annex I to the Joint Declaration. See also Chen (1985, 1986).

43. Para 3 (5) of the Joint Declaration and Section XIII of Annex I thereto. The International Covenant on Economic, Social, and Cultural Rights is also mentioned in Section XIII. See generally Jayawickrama (1988).

44. See Article 8, Chapter III (on residents' rights and duties) and Section 4 (on the judiciary) of Chapter IV of the Basic Law. The bilingual text of the Basic Law was published by the Consultative Committee for the Basic Law in Hong Kong in April 1990. See generally Wesley-Smith (1990), and Wesley-Smith and Chen (1988).

45. For example, articles 28 and 29 outlaw arbitrary arrest, detention, and (arbitrary) search of the body or premises. Article 86 provides for the maintenance of '[t]he principle of trial by jury previously practised in Hong Kong'. Article 87 provides for the maintenance of 'the principles previously applied in Hong Kong and the rights previously enjoyed by parties' in criminal and civil proceedings, and affirms that 'Anyone who is lawfully arrested shall have the right to a fair trial by the judicial organs without delay and shall be presumed innocent until convicted by the judicial organs.'

46. *Hong Kong Government Gazette, Legal Supplement No. 3* (1990) p. C776.

47. See generally Chan (1988), Jayawickrama (1989), Wesley-Smith (1988b).

48. See generally Sieghart (1983).

49. See generally Beaudoin and Ratushny (1989), Rossum (1978).

50. See generally Chen (1988b).

Collected References

Action Committee Against Narcotics, *Hong Kong Narcotics Report* (Hong Kong, Government Printer, 1978).

Adler, P., *Wheeling and Dealing: An Ethnography of an Upper-level Drug Dealing and Smuggling Community* (New York, Columbia University Press, 1985).

Andrewes, A., *Greek Society* (Harmondsworth, Penguin, 1971).

Asquith, S., *Children and Justice: Decision-making in Children's Hearings and Juvenile Courts* (Edinburgh, Edinburgh University Press, 1983).

Atiyah, P. S., *Law and Modern Society* (Oxford, Oxford University Press, 1983).

Audit Department, Hong Kong, *Report of the Director of Audit on the Accounts of the Hong Kong Government for the Year Ended 31 March 1987 and the Results of the Value for Money Audits: Report No. 10* (Hong Kong, Government Printer, 1987).

Baker, J. H., 'Criminal Courts and Procedure at Common Law 1550–1800', in Cockburn, J. S. (ed.) *Crimes in England 1550–1800* (London, Methuen, 1977).

Bankowski, Z. and Mungham, G., *Images of Law* (London, Routledge and Kegan Paul, 1976).

Barlow, H., *Introduction to Criminology* (Glenview, Ill., Scott Foresman/Little Brown, 1990).

Barrow, R. H., *The Romans* (Harmondsworth, Penguin, 1949).

Bartlett, S. and Wallace, C. D., 'Money Laundering: Who's Involved, How it Works, and Where it's Spreading', *Business Week*, 214: 18 March 1985, 74–80.

Beattie, J. M., *Crime and the Courts in England 1660–1800* (Oxford, Clarendon, 1986).

Beaudoin, G., and Ratushny, E., *Canadian Charter of Rights and Freedoms*, 2nd ed. (Toronto, Carswell, 1989).

Bell, C., 'Sentencing: An Update on Recent Developments', *Solicitors Journal*, 134: 14 (1990), 395.

Berman, H. J., Cohen, S., and Russell, M., 'A Comparison of the Chinese and Soviet Codes of Criminal Law and Procedure', *Journal of Criminal Law and Criminology*, 73 (1982), 1.

Berman, H. J., *Law and Revolution: The Formation of the Western Legal Tradition* (Cambridge, Mass., Harvard University Press, 1983).

Blumberg, A. S., 'The Practice of Law as a Confidence Game', in Aubert, V. (ed.) *Sociology of Law* (Harmondsworth, Penguin, 1971).

Blum-West, S., and Carter, T. J., 'Bringing White-Collar Crime Back In: An Examination of Crimes and Torts', *Social Problems*, 30 (1983), 545–54.

Bociurkiw, M., 'Hong Kong on Trial', *Sunday Morning Post*, 21 October 1990.

Bodde, D., and Morris, C., *Law in Imperial China* (Cambridge, Mass., Harvard University Press, 1967).

Booth, M., *The Triads* (London, Grafton, 1990).

Bottomly, A. K., and Pease, K., *Crime and Punishment: Interpreting the Data* (Milton Keynes, Open University Press, 1986).

Box, S., *Recession, Crime, and Punishment* (London, Macmillan, 1985).

Brabyn, J. M., 'The Law of Evidence', in Wacks, R. (ed.) *The Future of the Law in Hong Kong* (Hong Kong, Oxford University Press, 1989).

Bresler, F., *The Trail of the Triads* (London, Weidenfeld and Nicolson, 1980).

Brogden, M., 'The Emergence of the Police: The Colonial Dimension', *British Journal of Criminology*, 27: 1 (Winter 1987), 4–14.

Brydensholt, H. H., van der Goorbergh, B., Almeida, M. R., and Shapland, P., *Prison Management* (Strasbourg, Council of Europe, 1983).

Butters, H. R., *Report on Labour and Labouring Conditions in Hong Kong* (Hong Kong, Noronha, 1939).

Carlen, P., 'Remedial Routines for the Maintenance of Control in Magistrates' Courts', *British Journal of Law and Society* 1 (1974), 101-17.

Carson, W. G., 'Occupational Health and Safety: A Political Economy Perspective', *Labour and Industry* 2: 2 (1989), 301–16.

Census and Statistics Department, *Annual Digest of Statistics 1977* (Hong Kong, Government Printer, 1978).

—— *Crime and Its Victims in Hong Kong 1978* (Hong Kong, Government Printer, 1979).

—— *Crime and Its Victims in Hong Kong 1981* (Hong Kong, Government Printer, 1982).

—— *Crime and Its Victims in Hong Kong 1986* (Hong Kong, Government Printer, 1987).

—— *Annual Digest of Statistics 1987* (Hong Kong, Government Printer, 1988).

—— *Annual Digest of Statistics 1988* (Hong Kong, Government Printer, 1989).

—— *Crime and Its Victims in Hong Kong 1989* (Hong Kong, Government Printer, 1990a).

—— *Hong Kong Annual Digest of Statistics 1989* (Hong Kong, Government Printer, 1990b).

—— *Hong Kong Monthly Digest of Statistics, March 1990* (Hong Kong, Government Printer, 1990c).

Central Fight Crime Committee, *Report No. 5* (Hong Kong, Central Fight Crime Committee, 1985).

—— *Report No. 7* (Hong Kong, Central Fight Crime Committee, 1987).

Chan, C., 'Cheque Scheme Cost OTB $521M', *South China Morning Post,* 16 May 1987.

Chan, J., 'A Bill of Rights for Hong Kong', in Wacks, R. (ed.) *Civil Liberties in Hong Kong* (Hong Kong, Oxford University Press, 1988).

Chan, P., 'Tackling Hong Kong's Insider Trading', *Sunday Morning Post*, 2 November 1986.

Chan, S. T. J., 'The Enforcement of Labour Legislation in Hong Kong: A Study of Industrial Safety Regulation' (University of Hong Kong, M.Soc.Sci. Thesis, 1986).

Chan, T. F., Duff, P., Findlay, M., and Howarth, C., *Hong Kong Jury Project: Initial Report* (Hong Kong, City Polytechnic of Hong Kong, 1989).

—— *The Jury in Hong Kong: Working Paper No. 1* (Hong Kong, City Polytechnic of Hong Kong, 1990).

Chen, A. H. Y., 'The Developing Legal System in China', *Hong Kong Law Journal,* 13 (1983), 291.

—— 'Hong Kong's Legal System: Adaptations for 1997 and Beyond', in Jao, Y. C., Leung, C. K., Wesley-Smith, P., and Wong, S. L. (eds.), *Hong Kong and 1997: Strategies for the Future* (Hong Kong, Hong Kong University, Centre of Asian Studies, 1985).

——'The Legal System', in Cheng, J. Y. S. (ed.) *Hong Kong in Transition* (Hong Kong, Oxford University Press, 1986).

—— 'Civil Liberties in China: Some Preliminary Observations', in Wacks, R. (ed.) *Civil Liberties in Hong Kong* (Hong Kong, Oxford University Press, 1988a).

—— 'Civil Liberties in Hong Kong: Recent Controversies, Evolving Consciousness, and Future Legal Protection', *Journal of Chinese Law*, 2:1 (1988b), 137.

—— 'The Supression of China's Democracy Movement and Hong Kong's Future', *Hong Kong Law Journal* 19 (1989a), 283.

—— 'The Legal System', in Tsim, T. L., and Luk, B. H. K. (eds.), *The Other Hong Kong Report* (Hong Kong, Chinese University Press, 1989b).

—— 'The Basic Law, the Bill of Rights, and the British Citizenship Scheme', *Hong Kong Law Journal*, 20 (1990), 145.

Chen, A. H. Y., and Ng, S. H., *The Workers' Compensation System in Hong Kong: Retrospect and Prospects* (Hong Kong, University of Hong Kong, Centre of Asian Studies, 1987).

Chesneaux, J., *Secret Societies in China in the Nineteenth and Twentieth Centuries* (London, Heinemann, 1971).

Child, J., *Organization: A Guide to Problems and Practice*, 2nd ed. (London, Harper and Row, 1984).

Chin, K. L., *Chinese Subculture and Criminality* (New York, Greenwood, 1990).

Christie, N., 'Conflicts as Property', *British Journal of Criminology* 17, (1977), 1.

Clayton, A., and Killingray, D., *Khaki and Blue: Military and Police in British Colonial Africa* (Athens, Ohio, Ohio University Center for International Studies, 1989), 2nd ed. (London, Harper and Row, 1984).

Clifford, W., *Development and Crime* (Chichester, Barry Rose, 1973).

—— *An Introduction to African Criminology* (London, Oxford University Press, 1974).

Clinard, M., and Abbott, D., *Crime in Developing Countries* (New York, Wiley, 1973).

Cohen, S., *Folk Devils and Moral Panics* (St Albans, Paladin, 1973).

—— *Visions of Social Control* (Cambridge, Polity, 1985).

Cohen, S., and Young, J. (eds.), *The Manufacture of News: Social Problems, Deviance, and the Mass Media* (London, Constable, 1973).

Coleman, J. W., *The Criminal Elite: The Sociology of White Collar Crime* (New York, St. Martin's Press, 1985).

Colvin, G., 'Report on the Seventh United Nations Congress on the Prevention of Crime and the Treatment of Offenders', *Crime and Social Justice*, 25 (1988).

Commerce and Industry Department, *Annual Report 1948/49* (Hong Kong, Government Printer, 1949).

Commission of Inquiry on the Kowloon Disturbances, *The Report of the Commission* (Hong Kong, Government Printer, 1966).

Commissioner of Labour, *Annual Departmental Report 1955* (Hong Kong, Government Printer, 1956).

Commissioner for Labour, *Annual Departmental Report 1975/76* (Hong Kong, Government Printer, 1976).

—— *Annual Departmental Report 1976* (Hong Kong, Government Printer, 1977).

—— *Annual Departmental Report 1988* (Hong Kong, Government Printer, 1989).

—— *Annual Departmental Report 1989* (Hong Kong, Government Printer, 1990).

Commissioner of Police, *Annual Departmental Report 1953/54* (Hong Kong, Government Printer, 1954).

—— *Annual Departmental Report 1956/57* (Hong Kong, Government Printer, 1957).

—— *Annual Departmental Report 1961/62* (Hong Kong, Government Printer, 1962).

—— *Annual Departmental Report 1962/63* (Hong Kong, Government Printer, 1963).

—— *Annual Departmental Report 1965/66* (Hong Kong, Government Printer, 1966).

—— *Annual Departmental Report 1967/68* (Hong Kong, Government Printer, 1968).

—— *Annual Departmental Report 1968/69* (Hong Kong, Government Printer, 1969).

—— *Royal Hong Kong Police Review 1976* (Hong Kong, Government Printer, 1977).

—— *Royal Hong Kong Police Review 1983* (Hong Kong, Government Printer, 1984).

—— *Royal Hong Kong Police Review 1984* (Hong Kong, Government Printer, 1985).

—— *Royal Hong Kong Police Review 1986* (Hong Kong, Government Printer, 1987).

—— *Royal Hong Kong Police Review 1988* (Hong Kong, Government Printer, Royal Hong Kong Police, 1989).

—— *Royal Hong Kong Police Review 1989* (Hong Kong, Government Printer, 1990).

Commissioner of Prisons, *Annual Departmental Report 1973–4* (Hong Kong, Government Printer, 1974).

—— *Annual Departmental Report 1980* (Hong Kong, Government Printer, 1981).

Connor, W., *Deviance in Soviet Society* (New York, Columbia University Press, 1972).

Cooper, J., *Colony in Conflict: The Hong Kong Disturbances, May 1967–January 1968* (Hong Kong, Swindon Book Co., 1970).

Cornish, W. R., *Law and Society in England 1750–1950* (London, Sweet and Maxwell, 1989).

Correctional Services Department, *Annual Review of Correctional Services 1985* (Hong Kong, Government Printer, 1986).

—— *Annual Statistical Tables* (Hong Kong, Correctional Services Department, 1988).

—— *Annual Review of Correctional Services 1989* (Hong Kong, Government Printer, 1990).

Coutts J. A. (ed.), *The Accused* (London, Stevens, 1966).

Creasy, E., *The Rise and Progress of the English Constitution* (Littleton, Colorado, 1982). Reprint, orig. pub. London, 16th ed. 1892.

Cressey, D. R., 'Restraint of Trade, Recidivism, and Delinquent Neighborhoods', in Short, J. P. Jr. (ed.) *Delinquency, Crime, and Society* (Chicago, University of Chicago Press, 1976).

—— 'The Poverty of Theory in Corporate Crime Research' in Laufer, W. S. and Adler, F. (eds.), *Advances in Criminological Theory, Vol. I* (New Brunswick, NJ, Transaction Publishers, 1989).

Crisswell, C., and Watson, M., *The Royal Hong Hong Police 1841–1945* (Hong Kong, Macmillan, 1982).

Cross, A. R. N., *Evidence*, 4th ed. (London, Butterworths, 1974).

Cross, A. R. N., and Tapper, C., *Evidence*, 6th ed. (London, Butterworths, 1985).

David, R., and Brierley, J. E. C., *Major Legal Systems in the World Today,* 3rd ed. (London, Stevens, 1985).

Davies, J., 'Toward a Theory of Revolution', *American Sociological Review* 27 (1962), 5–18.

Deng Zhenglai, 'The Supremacy of Law: China's Rational Choice in the Twenty-first Century', in Bao Zunxin (ed.) *Pacific Review* (Hong Kong, Jinshi Press, 1989).

Denning, A., *Freedom Under the Law* (London, Stevens, 1949).

Dicks, A., 'The Chinese Legal System: Reforms in the Balance', *China Quarterly*, 119 (1989) 540–76.

Ding, L. K., Speech to the Y's Men's Club of Kowloon. Reported in the *South China Morning Post*, 24 November 1977.

Ditchfield, J. A., *Police Cautioning in England and Wales* (London, HMSO, 1976).

Downes, D., and Rock, P., *Understanding Deviance: A Guide to the Sociology of Crime and Rule Breaking*, 2nd ed. (Oxford, Clarendon, 1988).

Easey, W., 'Introduction', in Palmer, M., *Industrial Health and Safety in Hong Kong* (London, Hong Kong Research Project, 1977).

Edelman, M., *Political Language: Words that Succeed and Policies that Fail* (New York, Academic Press, 1977).

Elliot, R. K., and Willingham, J. J., *Management Fraud: Detection and Deterrence* (New York, Petrocelli, 1980).

England, J., *Industrial Relations and Law in Hong Kong*, 2nd ed. (Hong Kong, Oxford University Press, 1989).

England, J., and Rear, J., *Chinese Labour Under British Rule* (Hong Kong, Oxford University Press, 1975).

—— *Industrial Relations and Law in Hong Kong* (Hong Kong, Oxford University Press, 1981).

Epstein, E. J., 'China and Hong Kong: Law, Ideology, and the Future Interaction of the Legal Systems', in Wacks, R. (ed.) *The Future of the Law in Hong Kong* (Hong Kong, Oxford University Press, 1989).

Evans, K., *Advocacy at the Bar* (London, Financial Training, 1983).

Fairbank, J. K., *The United States and China,* 4th ed. (Cambridge, Mass., Harvard University Press, 1980).

Findlay, M., and Zvekic, U., (eds.), *Analysing (In)formal Mechanisms of Crime Control: A Cross-cultural Perspective* (Rome, United Nations Social Defence Research Institute, 1988).

Fishman, M., 'Crime Waves as Ideology', *Social Problems* 25 (1978), 531–43.

Fitzpatrick, P., *Law and the State in Papua New Guinea* (London, Academic Press, 1981).

Foucault, M., *Discipline and Punish: The Birth of the Prison,* translated by A. Sheridan (Harmondsworth, Allen Lane, 1979).

Frank, J., *Law and the Modern Mind* (New York, Peter Smith, 1970).

Frankel, M., *Partisan Justice* (New York, Hill and Wang, 1980).

Galliher, J. F., and McCartney, J. L., *Criminology: Power, Crime and Criminal Law* (Homewood, Ill., Dorsey, 1977).

Gavit, B. C. (ed.), *Blackstone's Commentaries on the Law*, abridged edition, 1892 (Washington, DC, Washington Law Book Co., 1941).

General Council of the Bar, *Quality of Justice: The Bar's Response* (London, General Council of the Bar, 1989).

Gernet, J., 'Introduction', in Schram, S. R. (ed.), *The Scope of State*

Power in China (London, School of Oriental and African Studies, 1985).

Gernet, J., 'Introduction', in Schram, S. R. (ed.), *Foundations and Limits of State Power in China* (London, School of Oriental and African Studies, 1987).

Goffman, E., *The Presentation of Self in Everyday Life* (Harmondsworth, Penguin, 1971).

Government Information Services, *Hong Hong 1974: A Review of 1973* (Hong Kong, Government Information Services, 1974).

—— *Hong Kong 1989: A Review of 1988* (Hong Kong, Government Information Services, 1989).

—— *Hong Kong 1990: A Review of 1989* (Hong Kong, Government Information Services, 1990).

Gray, P., *The Feasibility of Developing Community Alternatives to the Residential Care and Custody of Juvenile Offenders in Hong Kong* (Hong Kong, Baptist College, forthcoming).

Green, T., *The Smugglers: An Investigation into the World of the Contemporary Smuggler* (London, Arrow, 1972).

Greenwood, M,. and Wadycki, W., 'Crime Rates and Public Expenditures for Police Protection: Their Interaction', *Review of Social Economy*, 31 (1973), 138–51.

Griffith, J. A. G., *The Politics of the Judiciary,* 3rd ed. (Glasgow, Fontana, 1985).

Grindrod, B., 'On the Game', *Lawyer,* December 1989.

Gronewold, S., *Beautiful Merchandise*: *Prostitution in China 1860–1937* (New York, Harrington Park Press, 1985).

Gurr, T., 'Psychological Factors in Civil Violence', *World Politics*, 20 (1968), 245–78.

Hagan, J., *Modern Criminology*: *Crime, Criminal Behavior and Its Control* (New York, McGraw-Hill, 1987).

—— *Structural Criminology* (Rutgers, NJ, Rutgers University Press, 1989).

Hall, S., Pritcher, C., Jefferson, T., Clarke, J., and Roberts, B., *Policing the Crisis* (London, Macmillan, 1978).

Hampton, C., *Criminal Procedure*, 3rd ed. (London, Sweet and Maxwell, 1982).

Harmony House, *Annual Report 1989/90* (Hong Kong, Harmony House, 1990).

Harris, R. J., 'Towards Just Welfare: A Consideration of a Current Controversy in the Theory of Juvenile Justice', *British Journal of Criminology*, 25 (January 1985), 1.

Hay, D., 'Property, Authority and the Criminal Law', in Hay, D., Linebaugh, P., Rule, J., Thompson, E.P., and Winslow, C. (eds.), *Albion's Fatal Tree* (New York, Pantheon, 1975).

Hayek, F. A., *The Constitution of Liberty* (London, Sweet and Maxwell, 1960).

Henry, A., and Short, J. *Suicide and Homicide: Some Economic, Sociological, and Psychological Aspects of Aggression* (New York, Glencoe Free Press, 1954).

Hewett, G., 'Police Freeze $375M Alleged Drug Money', *South China Morning Post*, 8 April 1990.

Ho, A., 'Planned Letters Patent Changes to Boost Rights', *South China Morning Post*, 24 July 1990.

Holdsworth, W., *A History of English Law, Vol. II.*, 4th ed. (London, Methuen/Sweet and Maxwell, 1936).

—— *A History of English Law, Vol. III*, 5th ed. (London, Methuen/Sweet and Maxwell, 1942).

—— *A History of English Law, Vol. IX* (London, Methuen/Sweet and Maxwell, 1944).

—— *A History of English Law, Vol. V* (London, Methuen/Sweet and Maxwell, 1945).

—— *A History of English Law, Vol. I* 7th rev. ed. (London, Methuen/Sweet and Maxwell, 1956).

Home Office, *Criminal Justice: A Working Paper* (London, Home Office, 1986).

Hong Kong Council of Women, *Young Prostitutes*, (Hong Kong, Hong Kong Council of Women, 1974), unpublished monograph.

Hong Kong Government, *Report of the Hong Kong Government for the Calendar Year 1936 on the Traffic in Prepared Opium* (Hong Kong, Government Printer, 1936).

—— *Report of the Hong Kong Government for the Calendar Year 1938 on the Traffic in Prepared Opium* (Hong Kong, Government Printer, 1938).

—— *Report of the Hong Kong Government for the Calendar Year 1939 on the Traffic in Prepared Opium* (Hong Kong, Government Printer, 1939).

—— *Address by the Governor, Sir David Wilson, KCMG, at the Opening of the 1990/91 Session of the Legislative Council on 10 October 1990* (Hong Kong, Government Printer, 1990).

Hong Kong Hansard, *Reports of the Sittings of the Legislative Council of Hong Kong* (Hong Kong, Government Printer).

Hong Kong Law Reform Commission, *Report on Confession*

Statements and Their Admissibility in Criminal Proceedings (Hong Kong, Hong Kong Law Reform Commission, 1984).

Hong Kong Observers, *Pressure Points: A Social Critique* (Hong Kong, Summerson Educational Research Centre, 1981).

Hudson, B., *Justice Through Punishment: A Critique of the 'Justice' Model of Corrections* (London, Macmillan, 1987).

Huff, C., and Stahura, J., 'Police Employment and Suburban Crime', *Criminology*, 17 (1980), 461–70.

Hughes, R., *Borrowed Place, Borrowed Time* (London, Andre Deutsch, 1968).

Humphries, D., and Wallace, D., 'Capitalist Accumulation and Urban Crime', *Social Problems*, 28 (1980), 179–93.

Jayawickrama, N., 'Hong Kong and the International Protection of Human Rights', in Wacks, R. (ed.), *Civil Liberties in Hong Kong* (Hong Kong, Oxford University Press, 1988).

—— 'Protecting Civil Liberties', in Wacks, R. (ed.), *The Future of the Law in Hong Kong* (Hong Kong, Oxford University Press, 1989).

Jeffries, C., *The Colonial Police* (London, Max Parrish, 1952).

Jones, R., 'The Preventative and the Penal: A Comment on Two Models of Intermediate Treatment', *Journal of Adolescence*, 3 (1980) 307–20.

Jones, R., 'Intermediate Treatment, Research, and Social Policy', *Journal of Adolescence*, 4 (1981), 339–52.

Kamenka, E., 'The Anatomy of an Idea', in Kamenka, E. and Tay, A. E. S. (eds.), *Human Rights* (London, Arnold, 1978).

Kaplan, D. E., Goldberg, D., and Jue, L., 'Enter the Dragon', *San Francisco Focus*, December 1986, 68–79.

Karchmer, C. L., 'Money Laundering and the Organized Underworld', in Alexander, H. E. and Caiden, G. E., (eds.) *The Politics and Economics of Organized Crime* (Lexington, Mass., Lexington Books, 1985).

Keeton, G. W., and Lloyd D. (eds.), *The United Kingdom: The Development of its Laws and Constitutions* (London, Stevens, 1955).

Kidd, R. F., and Chayett, E., 'Why do Victims Fail to Report?', *Journal of Social Issues*, 40: 1 (1984) 39–50.

King, R., and McDermott, K., 'British Prisons 1970–1987: The Ever-deepening Crisis', *British Journal of Criminology*, 29: 2, (Spring 1989), 108–28.

Kiralfy, A. K. R., *Potter's Historical Introduction to English Law*, 4th ed. (London, Sweet and Maxwell, 1958).

Keung, S. C. J., 'An Assessment of Government's Role in the Creation and Evolution of Mutual Aid Committees', University of Hong Kong, M.Soc.Sci thesis, 1986.

Ko, C., 'Watchdog That Lost Its Bank', *South China Morning Post,* 15 October 1985.

Koepp, S., 'Dirty Cash and Tarnished Vaults', *Time*, 125, (25 February 1985), 65.

Kwan, M., 'Services Rendered by the Family Planning Association of Hong Kong to Sexually Assaulted Victims', in Cheung, F., Andry, R., and Tam, R. (eds.), *Research on Rape and Sexual Crime in Hong Kong* (Hong Kong, Institute of Asia-Pacific Studies, 1990).

Lal, S., 'Careful Approach to Insider Trading Bill', *South China Morning Post*, 13 November 1989.

Lau, M. P., and Yap, P. M., *An Epidemiological Study of Narcotics Addiction in Hong Kong* (Hong Kong, Government Printer, 1967).

Lau, S. K., and Kuan, H. C., *The Ethos of the Hong Kong Chinese* (Hong Kong, Chinese University Press, 1988).

Law Society of Hong Kong, *Annual Report of the Management and Administration Committee* (Hong Kong, Law Society of Hong Kong, 1989).

Lea, J., and Young, J., *What is to be Done About Law and Order?* (Harmondsworth, Penguin, 1984).

Lee, J., Course, L., and Ng, E., 'Family on Drug Charges Face US Extradition', *South China Morning Post*, 27 July 1988.

Lee, R. P. L., (ed.), *Corruption and its Control in Hong Kong: Situations up to the Late Seventies* (Hong Kong, Chinese University Press, 1981).

Lekschas, J., and Kosewhär, E., 'Criminology in the German Democratic Republic', in Kaiser, G., Kury, H., and Albrecht, H.- J. (eds.) *Criminological Research in the 80s and Beyond* (Freiburg im Breisgau, Max Planck Institute, 1988).

Leng, S. C., and Chiu, H. D., *Criminal Justice in Post-Mao China* (Albany, NY, State University of New York Press, 1985).

Lethbridge, H. J., 'The Evolution of a Chinese Voluntary Association in Hong Kong: the Po Leung Kuk', in Lethbridge, H. J. (ed.), *Hong Kong: Stability and Change* (Hong Kong, Oxford University Press, 1978a).

—— 'Prostitution in Hong Kong: A Legal and Moral Dilemma', *Hong Kong Law Journal*, 8 (1978b) 2.

——'The "Management" of Social Information During Periods of Growth: The Problem of Sexual Violence in Hong Kong', in Leung, C. K., Cushman, J. W., and Wang Gungwu (eds.), *Hong Kong: Dilemmas of Growth* (Hong Kong, University of Hong Kong, Centre of Asian Studies, 1980).

—— *Hard Graft in Hong Kong: Scandal, Corruption, and the ICAC* (Hong Kong, Oxford University Press, 1985).

Leung, J., 'OTB Head Reveals Bank's Web of Fraud', *Asian Wall Street Journal*, 14 July 1987.

Liang Zhiping, 'The Past, Present, and Future of Chinese Law: A Cultural Review', in Gan Yang (ed.), *Contemporary Chinese Cultural Consciousness* (Hong Kong, Joint Publishing, 1989). In Chinese.

Lindsay, A. D., *The Modern Democratic State, Vol. I* (London, Oxford University Press, 1943).

Lipsky, M., *Street-level Bureaucracy: The Dilemmas of the Individual in Public Services* (New York, Russell Sage, 1980).

Litton, H., 'Public Order', in Tsim, T. L. and Luk, B. H. K. (eds.), *The Other Hong Kong Report* (Hong Kong, Chinese University Press, 1989).

Liu, M., and Eads, B., 'Hong Kong's Funny Money', *Newsweek*, 106 (23 September 1985), 52.

Lopez-Rey, M., *Crime: An Analytical Appraisal* (New York, Praeger, 1970).

Maguire, M., and Pointing, J. (eds.), *Victims of Crime: A New Deal?* (Milton Keynes, Open University Press, 1988).

Manchester, A. H., *A Modern Legal History of England and Wales 1750–1950* (London, Butterworths, 1980).

Mann, J., 'US Wary of Hong Kong's Bank Secrecy', *Los Angeles Times,* 15 September 1985.

Matthews, J., 'The Future of the Legal Department', in *The Proceedings of the Conference on the Future of Legal Education and the Legal Profession in Hong Kong*, December 1989.

Mawby, R., 'Victims' Needs or Victims' Rights: Alternative Approaches to Policy-making', in Maguire, M., and Pointing, J. (eds.), *Victims of Crime: A New Deal?* (Milton Keynes, Open University Press, 1988).

McBarnett, D. J., 'Pre-trial Procedures and the Construction of Conviction', in Carlen, P. (ed.), *The Sociology of Law* (University of Keele, *Sociological Review Monograph 23,* 1976).

—— *Conviction* (London, Macmillan, 1981).

McGivering, J. and Green, S., 'The Scales of Injustice?' *South China Morning Post*, 23 March 1990.

Merry, M., 'Freedom of Expression: Defamation and Contempt', in Wacks, R., (ed.), *Civil Liberties in Hong Kong* (Hong Kong, Oxford University Press, 1988).

Milsom, S. F. C., *Historical Foundations of the Common Law*, 2nd ed. (London, Butterworths, 1981).

Miners, N., *Hong Kong Under Imperial Rule 1912–1941* (Hong Kong, Oxford University Press, 1987).

Molotch, H., and Lester, M., 'News as Purposive Behavior: The Strategic Use of Routine Events, Accidents, and Scandals', *American Sociological Review*, 39 (1974), 101–12.

Mong Kok District Board, *Working Group on Vice-associated Establishments* (Hong Kong, Mong Kok District Board Working Group on Vice-associated Establishments, 1982).

Morgan, R., and Bronstein, A., 'Prisoners and the Courts: The US Experience', in Maguire, M., Vagg, J., and Morgan, R. (eds.), *Accountability and Prisons: Opening up a Closed World* (London, Tavistock, 1985).

Morgan, W. P., *Triad Societies in Hong Kong* (Hong Kong, Government Printer, 1960).

Morris, A., and Giller, H., *Understanding Juvenile Justice* (London, Edward Arnold, 1987).

Morris, A., and McIsaac, M., *Juvenile Justice? The Practice of Social Welfare* (London, Heinemann, 1978).

Morris, N., and Hawkins, G., *The Honest Politician's Guide to Crime Control* (Chicago, University of Chicago Press, 1970).

Morrow, P., 'Police Powers and Individual Liberty', in Wacks, R. (ed.), *Civil Liberties in Hong Kong* (Hong Kong, Oxford University Press, 1988).

Mulcahy, J., 'The Chinese Laundry', *Far Eastern Economic Review*, 20 August 1987.

Netherlands Ministry of Justice, *The Price of Prisons Compared* (The Hague, Netherlands Ministry of Justice, 1984).

Ng, S. H., 'Labour Administration and "Voluntarism": The Hong Kong Case', *Journal of Industrial Relations*, 24: 2 (1982), 266–81.

Nichols, T., 'Industrial Injuries in British Manufacturing in the 1980s — A Commentary on Wright's Article', *Sociological Review*, 34: 2 (1986) 290–306.

Noble, C., *Liberalism at Work: The Rise and Fall of OSHA* (Philadelphia, Temple University Press, 1986).

Ogburn, W. F., 'Business Fluctuations as Social Forces', *Social Forces*, 1 (1923) 73–8.

Onselen, C. V., *Chiczaro* (London, Pluto Press, 1976).

Parker, H., Casburn, M., and Turnbull, D., *Receiving Juvenile Justice* (Oxford, Blackwell, 1981).

—— *Unmasking the Magistrates* (Milton Keynes, Open University Press, 1989).

Pearson, G., *Hooligan: A History of Respectable Fears* (London, Macmillan, 1983).

Pearson, V., 'Women in Hong Kong', in Leung, B. K. P. (ed.), *Social Problems* (Hong Kong, Oxford University Press, 1989).

Perkin, I. K., 'Time Ripe for Tough Insider Trading Law', *South China Morning Post*, 7 March 1990.

Peters, E., *Torture* (Oxford, Blackwell, 1985).

Phelps, H., 'Cycles of Crime', *Journal of Crime and Criminal Law,* 30 (1985) 107–21.

Phillipson, C., *Three Criminal Law Reformers: Beccaria, Bentham, Romilly* (Montclair, NJ, Patterson Smith, 1970, first published in 1923).

Pitts, J., *The Politics of Juvenile Crime* (London, Sage, 1988).

Posner, G., *Warlords of Crime* (New York, McGraw-Hill, 1988).

Public Accounts Committee, *Report of the Public Accounts Committee on the Report of the Director of Audit on the Accounts of the Hong Kong Government: Report No. 10* (Hong Kong, Government Printer, 1988).

Radzinowicz, L., *A History of English Criminal Law and its Administration from 1750, Vol. I* (London, Stevens, 1948).

Ratnapala, N., *The Beggar in Sri Lanka* (Moratuwa, Palihawadana, 1985).

Rear, J., 'The Powers of Arrest in Hong Kong', *Hong Kong Law Journal*, 1 (1971).

Richardson, G., 'Judicial Intervention in Prison Life', in Maguire, M., Vagg, J., and Morgan, R. (eds.), *Accountability and Prisons: Opening Up a Closed World* (London, Tavistock, 1985).

Robinson, O. F., Fergus, T. D., and Gordon, W. M., *An Introduction to European Legal History* (Abingdon, Professional Books, 1985).

Rodzinski, W., *The Walled Kingdom: A History of China from 2000 B.C. to the Present* (London, Fontana, 1984).

Rogers, S., 'Insider Trading Sets SFC Posers', *Hongkong Standard,* 23 March 1989.

Rossum, R. A., *The Politics of the Criminal Justice System: An Organizational Analysis* (New York, Marcel Dekker, 1978).

Rowley, A., 'Out of the Shadows', *Far Eastern Economic Review,* 11 June 1987.

Rutter H., and Giller H., *Juvenile Delinquency: Trends and Perspectives* (Harmondsworth, Penguin, 1983).

Safety Bulletin (Hong Kong, Hong Kong Occupational Safety and Health Association, March 1990), No. 7.

SARDA, *Annual Report* (Hong Kong, Society for the Aid and Rehabilitation of Drug Addicts, 1972).

Schneider, H. J. (ed.), *The Victim in International Perspective* (Berlin, de Gruyter, 1982).

Schram S. R. (ed.), *The Scope of State Power in China* (London, School of Oriental and African Studies, 1985).

—— *Foundations and Limits of State Power in China* (London, School of Oriental and African Studies, 1987).

Schwartz, B., 'On Attitudes Toward Law in China', in Katz, M. (ed.) *Government Under Law and the Individual* (Washington DC, American Council of Learned Societies, 1957).

—— *China's Cultural Values* (Arizona, Arizona State University, Centre for Asian Studies, Occasional Paper 18, 1985).

—— 'The Primacy of the Political Order in East Asian Societies: Some Preliminary General Notions', in Schram, S. R. (ed.), *Foundations and Limits of State Power in China* (London, School of Oriental and African Studies, 1987).

Scott, W. R., *Organizations* 2nd ed. (Englewood Cliffs, Prentice-Hall, 1987).

Shapland, J., 'The Victim in the Criminal Justice System', *Home Office Research Bulletin 14* (London, Home Office Research and Plannning Unit, 1982).

Shapland, J., Willmore, J., and Duff, P., *Victims in the Criminal Justice System* (Aldershot, Gower, 1985).

Shelley, L., *Crime and Modernization: The Impact of Industrialization and Urbanization on Crime* (Carbondale, Ill., Southern Illinois University Press, 1981).

Shin, K., 'Battered Spouse: A Community Responsibility?', address at the Annual General Meeting of Harmony House, 28 September 1990.

Short, J., 'A Social Aspect of the Business Cycle Re-examined: Crimes', *Research Studies of the State College of Washington,* 20 (1952), 36–41.

Sieghart, P., *The International Law of Human Rights* (Oxford, Clarendon, 1983).

Sinclair, K., *Asia's Finest: An Illustrated Account of the Royal Hong Kong Police* (Hong Kong, Unicorn, 1983).

Smale, G. J. A., 'Psychological Effects and Behavioral Changes in the Cases of Victims of Serious Crime', in Block, R. (ed.), *Victimization and the Fear of Crime: World Perspectives* (Washington DC, US Department of Justice, 1984).

Smith, R. S., 'Greasing the Squeaky Wheel: The Relative Productivity of OSHA Complaint Inspections', *Industrial and Labor Relations Review*, 40: 1 (1986), 35–47.

So, M. Y. L., 'The Assessment of Potential and Limitation for Development of District Level Associations' (Hong Kong, University of Hong Kong, MSW Thesis, 1975).

Social Welfare Department, *The Five Year Plan for Social Welfare Development in Hong Kong—Review* (Hong Kong, Social Welfare Department, 1974).

—— *Study of Closed Cases of Girls and Boys on Probation in Correctional Institutions* (Hong Kong, Social Welfare Department Research and Statistics Section, 1982).

—— *Hong Hong Annual Departmental Report by the Director of Social Welfare, 1985–6* (Hong Kong, Social Welfare Department, 1986).

—— *The Five Year Plan for Social Welfare Development in Hong Kong—Review* (Hong Kong, Social Welfare Department, 1989).

—— *Information Leaflet on Wai On House for Women* (no date).

Standing Commission on Civil Service Salaries and Conditions of Service, *Report No. 2: First Report on Civil Service Pay* (Hong Kong, Government Printer, 1979).

Stein, P., *Legal Institutions: The Development of Dispute Settlement* (London, Butterworths, 1984).

Sumner, C., 'Crime, Justice and Underdevelopment: Beyond Modernization Theory', in Sumner, C. (ed.), *Crime, Justice and Underdevelopment* (London, Heinemann, 1982).

Swimmer, G., 'The Relationship of Police to Crime', *Criminology*, 12 (1975), 293–314.

Tang, Yee-man, 'The Self-image of Young Women Involved in Prostitution' (Hong Kong, University of Hong Kong, MSW thesis, 1977).

Tapper, C., *Cross and Wilkins' Outline of the Law of Evidence*, 6th ed. (London, Butterworths, 1986).

Taylor, I., Walton, P., and Young, J., *The New Criminology: For a Social Theory of Deviance* (London, Routledge and Kegan Paul, 1973).

Thomas, D. S., *Social Aspects of the Business Cycle* (London, Routledge, 1925).

Toby, J., 'Affluence and Adolescent Crime', in Cressey, D. R. and Ward, D. (eds.), *Delinquency, Crime, and Social Process* (New York, Harper and Row, 1969).

Tombs, S., 'Industrial Injuries in British Manufacturing Industry', *Sociological Review*, 38 (1990), 352–61.

Traver, H., 'Crime and Development: The Case of Hong Kong', *International Annals of Criminology*, 22 (1984), 151–72.

Tsang, Hon-kin, 'Wan Chai's "Fish Ball Stalls": A Law Enforcement Problem', *Hong Kong Law Journal*, 12 (1982), 2.

US Department of Justice, *Operation Cashflow: The Movement and Impact of International Drug Money* (Washington, DC, US Government Printing Office, 1983).

Vagg, J., 'The Use of Custody in Hong Kong', in Dünkel, F., and van Zyl Smit, D. (eds.), *Prison Today and Tomorrow* (Freiburg im Breisgau, Max Planck Institute, 1990).

—— 'Pretrial Custody in Hong Kong', in Dünkel, F., and Vagg, J. (eds.), *Waiting for Trial: International Perspectives on the Use of Pretrial Detention and the Rights and Living Conditions of Prisoners Waiting for Trial* (Freiburg im Breisgau, Max Planck Institute, forthcoming).

van der Sprenkel, S., *Legal Institutions in Manchu China* (London, Athlone, 1977).

van Dijk, J., 'Ideological Trends Within the Victims' Movement: An International Perspective', in Maguire, M. and Pointing, J. (eds.), *Victims of Crime: A New Deal?* (Milton Keynes, Open University Press, 1988).

van Dijk, J., Haffmans, C., Ruter, F., Schutte, J., and Stolwijk, S. (eds.), *Criminal Law in Action: An Overview of Current Issues in Western Societies* (Arnhem, Gouda Quint, 1986).

Vinson, T., and Homel, R., 'Legal Representation and Outcome', *Australian Law Journal*, 47 (1973).

Vold, G., *Theoretical Criminology* (New York, Oxford University Press, 1958).

von Hirsch, A., *Doing Justice* (New York, Hill and Wang, 1976).

Wacks, R. (ed.), *Civil Liberties in Hong Kong* (Hong Kong, Oxford University Press, 1988).

—— *The Future of the Law in Hong Kong* (Hong Kong, Oxford University Press, 1989).

—— *Hong Kong's Bill of Rights: Problems and Prospects* (Hong Kong, University of Hong Kong, Faculty of Law, 1990).

Watson, A., *Legal Transplants* (Edinburgh, Scottish Academic Press, 1974).

Way, E. L., 'Control and Treatment of Drug Addiction in Hong Kong', in Milner, D. M. and Kassebaum, G. G. (eds.), *Narcotics* (New York, McGraw-Hill, 1965).

Wesley-Smith, P., *An Introduction to the Hong Kong Legal System* (Hong Kong, Oxford University Press, 1987).

—— *Constitutional and Administrative Law in Hong Kong, Vol. II* (Hong Kong, China and Hong Kong Law Studies, 1988a).

—— 'The Method of Protecting Civil Liberties in Hong Kong', in Wacks, R. (ed.), *Civil Liberties in Hong Kong* (Hong Kong, Oxford University Press, 1988b).

—— (ed.), *Hong Kong's Basic Law: Problems and Prospects* (Hong Kong, University of Hong Kong, Faculty of Law, 1990).

Wesley-Smith, P., and Chen, A. H. Y. (eds.), *The Basic Law and Hong Kong's Future* (Hong Kong, Butterworths, 1988).

Westermeyer, J., 'The Pro-heroin Effects of Anti-opium Laws in Asia', *Archives of General Psychiatry,* 33 (1976), 1135–9.

Wilson, A., *Deviance and Social Control in Chinese Society* (New York, Praeger, 1984).

Wilson, J. Q. (ed.), *The Politics of Regulation* (New York, Basic Books, 1980).

Winn, H., 'Tough Regulations Threaten to Choke Hong Kong Share Trading', *South China Morning Post*, 16 July 1989.

Wolchover, D., and Heaton-Armstrong, A., 'The Questioning Code Revised and the Flaws Which Persist', *New Law Journal*, 16 March 1990.

Wong, J., 'Rising Business Crime Taxes Hong Kong', *Asian Wall Street Journal*, 21 February 1986.

—— 'Yip Jailed in Overseas Trust Bank Case', *Asian Wall Street Journal*, 18 May 1987.

Wright, C., 'Routine Deaths: Fatal Accidents in the Oil Industry', *Sociological Review*, 34: 2 (1986), 265–89.

Yumol, D., 'Insider Bill Gets Legco Warning', *Hongkong Standard*, 28 September 1989.

Zander, M., 'Unrepresented Defendants in Magistrates' Courts', *New Law Journal*, (1972), 1041.

—— *A Matter of Justice* (London, Tauris, 1988).

Zehr, H., *Crime and the Development of Modern Society* (London, Croom Helm, Rowman and Littlefield, 1976).

Zhou, Z., 'A Summary of Scholars' Views in the Past Two Years Concerning the Causes of Crimes', in *Faxue Yanjiu*, Beijing, 23 February 1990, 28–33. Translated in US Joint Publications Research Studies report JPRS-CAR-90-045, 19 June 1990.

Index